Doctors in the Dock

The Trials of Dr Harold Shipman, Dr John Bodkin Adams and Dr Buck Ruxton

First published 2020
www.scottmartinproductions.com

The contents were first published in Great Britain in 2019 and 2020 by Scott Martin Productions
10 Chester Place,
Adlington, Chorley, PR6 9RP
lesley@scottmartinproductions.com
www.scottmartinproductions.com

Electronic version and paperback versions available for purchase on Amazon.
Copyright (c) David Holding and Scott Martin Productions.

First editions 2019 and 2020.

The right of David Holding to be identified as the author of these works has been asserted by him in accordance with the Copyright, Design and Patents Act 1988.

All rights reserved. Without limiting the rights under copyright reserved above, no part of this publication may be reproduced, stored or introduced into a retrieval system, or transmitted, in any form or by any means (electronic, mechanical, photocopying, recording or otherwise), without the prior written permission of both the copyright owner and the publisher of this book. No paragraph of this publication may be reproduced, copied or transmitted save with written permission or in accordance with the provisions of the Copyright Act 1956 (as amended).

Also by David Holding

Murder in the Heather: The Winter Hill Murder of 1838.

The Pendle Witch Trials of 1612.

The Dark Figure: Crime in Victorian Bolton.

Bleak Christmas: The Pretoria Colliery Disaster of 1910.

Contents

The Last Temptation: The Trial of Dr Harold Shipman 7

    Acknowledgements 9

    Introduction 10

    Chapter One 12

        Early Beginnings 12

    Chapter Two: The Final Reckoning 21

        The Trial 21

        Mr Richard Henriques QC, Counsel for the Prosecution: 22

        Opening Speech 22

        The Prosecution Case 24

        The Defence Case 39

    Chapter Three 54

        'Revelations' 54

        The Shipman Inquiry 54

The Trial of Dr John Bodkin Adams 123

    Acknowledgements 125

    Introduction 126

    Chapter One: Early Years 132

    Chapter Two: The Police Investigation 141

    Chapter Three: The Trial 148

        Prosecution: Opening Address to the Jury 150

        Defence: Closing Address to the Jury 163

        Prosecution: Closing Address to the Jury: The Attorney General 168

        The Judge's Summing-Up to the Jury: Mr Justice Patrick Devlin 171

        The Post-Trial Period 180

    Chapter Four: An Overview of the Case 182

The Case in Retrospect	182
The Conduct of the Case	184
The Police Investigation	186
Suggestions of External Intervention in the Case	186

Bibliographical Review on the Trial 189

The Legal Position of the 'Double Effect' Principle	192
Psychological Profile of Adams	196
The Legal Issue of 'Causation'	204

Appendices 208

Appendix A: The Current Law of Homicide	208
Appendix B: 'All I Tried To Do Was Relieve His Agony, His Distress And Suffering'	210

The Trial of Dr Buck Ruxton 213

Acknowledgements 215

Introduction 216

Chapter One: The Discovery of Human Remains ... 224

Chapter Two: The Police, Medical and Forensic Investigations 229

The Police Investigation	229
The Newspapers	232
The Blouse and Child's Rompers	233
The Ruxton Household	234
Ruxton's Personality	234
Statement of Mrs Agnes Oxley - Charwoman	241
Statement of Mrs Mary Hampshire - Patient	243
The Medical Investigation	244
Reconstructed Bodies	246
Sex	247
Body No 1	248
Body No 2	249
Stature of the Bodies	249
Cause and Time of Death	252
Identification of the Maggots	253
Final Medical Summary	254

    Ruxton's Interview and Arrest 255

    The Forensic Investigation 256

Chapter Three: The Trial 262

    Prosecution: Closing Speech to the Jury – Mr Joseph Jackson KC 270

    Defence: Closing Speech to the Jury – Mr Norman Birkett KC 271

    The Judge's Summing-Up to the Jury: Mr Justice Singleton 272

    The Appeal and Execution 278

Chapter Four: An Overview of the Case 282

Selected Bibliography 291

    Harold Shipman 291

    John Bodkin Adams 291

    Buck Ruxton 292

    Buck Ruxton Archive Sources 293

The Last Temptation: The Trial of Dr Harold Shipman

First published by
Scott Martin Productions, 2019
www.scottmartinproductions.com

Harold Frederick Shipman (1946-2004)
Common Attribution Photograph

The last temptation is the greatest treason;
To do the right deed for the wrong reason

T.S. Eliot (1888-1965)
Murder in the Cathedral

Acknowledgements

I am very grateful for the encouragement and support I have received from many quarters in the preparation of this work. I particularly wish to express my sincere thanks to members of the medical and legal professions, the magistracy, and serving and former officers of the Greater Manchester Police CID for the benefit of their expertise and opinions on the numerous matters raised.

My thanks also go to those largely anonymous, but ever helpful staff at the various university law libraries and archives I have consulted in my research for this work. My gratitude loses no sincerity in its generality.

The primary sources for this work have been the *R v Shipman (1999)*, *Shipman Trial Transcripts* on the National Archives Website, law reports and the definitive Shipman Inquiry and Reports, which have dealt in great detail with virtually every aspect of Harold Shipman's life and career. In addition, a selection of other sources including books, professional articles and media reports on the case, have been consulted, to provide the reader with as varied and comprehensive an overview of this tragic yet unique case as possible. I would, however, hasten to add, that none of the above are responsible for the contents of this work, and any errors are entirely my own.

David Holding, 2019

Introduction

This book, the first of a trilogy, takes the reader into the essentially private world of medical doctors, each coming from a different background but all with one common thread running through their respective lives. They were all living and working in England as general medical practitioners, and they all stood trial for murder.

Though there were similarities, the motives in each case were different, encompassing ultimate power over life and death, greed and revenge. Each played a prominent role in the lives of these doctors' respective lives.

The three cases have received widespread public attention and have been the subject of numerous publications and much media attention. However, this work and its companions, are unique in that they approach the subject of 'murder' in an entirely innovative way.

Each work begins by outlining the background of the respective defendant before progressing to the criminal investigation and arrest, finally culminating in the trial itself. Each work concludes with an overview of the case to stimulate discussion.

By adopting this approach, the author's intention is to totally involve the reader in each case from the outset, rather than allow them to remain merely passive observers. As each story unfolds, the reader is presented with all the relevant information relating to each case. When the trial itself is reached, all the evidence is made available to the reader as it would be in an actual criminal trial. The books conclude with a brief overview of each case to invite the reader to consider their own verdict based on all the evidence they have before them. The overall aim of these three works is to invite the reader to exercise their own judgement in a practical yet enjoyable way, and to consider and better understand the complexities inherent in criminal investigations and trials. It is also hoped that these works will provide an insight into the often misunderstood and largely unseen workings of the Criminal Justice System as administered in Britain.

This first work is concerned with the case of Dr Harold Shipman, one of the most prolific serial killers in British legal history, and it seeks to answer the most important question of all: why a well-respected, popular family GP, and prominent member of his local community, was at the same time killing over 215 of his trusting and mainly elderly patients in what have been described as 'near perfect crimes'.

His early life and medical career are examined to identify a possible 'trigger' which might possibly explain his obsession with killing: an obsession which culminated with his eventual arrest and trial. It also considers the numerous failings of those systems which were designed to safeguard patients, yet which failed them so miserably.

I also cover the findings of the definitive Shipman Inquiry, which was divided into two distinct parts.

The first part examines the individual deaths of Shipman's patients, whilst the second part examines the systems in place that failed to identify his crimes.

The Inquiry Team also carried out a separate investigation into all the deaths certified by Shipman during his time as a junior doctor at Pontefract General Infirmary, West Yorkshire. The Inquiry published a total of six reports.

1. The first concluded that Shipman killed at least 215 patients.
2. The second report found that his final three victims could have been saved if the first police investigation had been carried out more efficiently.
3. The third report found that by issuing death certificates stating 'natural causes' Shipman was able to evade investigations into deaths by the Coroner.
4. The fourth report called for more stringent controls on the use and issuing of 'controlled' drugs.
5. The fifth report on the regulation and monitoring of GPs, criticised the General Medical Council (GMC) and recommended an overhaul of the GMC's constitution to ensure it would become more focused on protecting patients rather than doctors.
6. The sixth and final report, published in 2005, concluded that Shipman had killed in the region of 250 patients.

The Last Temptation concludes with an assessment of those psychological traits which may provide a final clue to that elusive question, Why?

Chapter One

Early Beginnings

Harold Frederick Shipman, better known as 'Fred', was born on the 14th January 1946 on the Bestwood council estate in Nottingham. He was the second son of three children born to his father Harold Frederick Shipman (1914-1985) a truck driver and his mother, Vera Britton (1919-1963), who were both devout Methodists.

There were gaps between the three children. Pauline, the eldest, was born in 1938 and Clive, the youngest, in 1950. Their mother, Vera, kept her children very close to her, but Fred was the favourite who got most of her attention and encouragement during his formative years.

In 1957, Shipman passed his eleven-plus examination and entered High Pavement Grammar School in Nottingham. Harold was an accomplished rugby player and also excelled as a long-distance runner, becoming the school's athletics team vice-captain. Whilst at High Pavement, he gained seven O-levels and went on to his A-level studies.

Harold was particularly close to his mother who died of lung cancer when he was seventeen years old. Her death came in a manner which has been suggested would become Shipman's modus operandi. In the late stages of her disease, Shipman's mother had morphine administered at home by a doctor. Harold regularly witnessed his mother's pain subside despite her advanced terminal condition, and she finally died on the 21st June 1963.

In September 1965, Harold Shipman was offered a place at Leeds University Medical School at the age of nineteen. He was a student there for five years and whilst there met seventeen-year-old Primrose May Oxtoby from Wetherby who was studying at Leeds Art College. They married on the 5th November 1966, Primrose being pregnant with their first child, this causing a rift between Primrose's parents and Shipman, to the point that there was little if any further contact between them.

Similarly, Shipman's father, possibly because of his Methodist background, was displeased with this sudden arranged marriage. As a result, Shipman and his father became estranged and all contact with each other was severed. Shipman graduated MB ChB in 1970. From Leeds, Shipman moved to Pontefract

General Infirmary to fulfil his compulsory period of employment in hospital for twelve months.

At that point, he gained provisional registration with the General Medical Council (GMC). This meant that he could only work in a residential post as a doctor for his pre-registration service. To gain full registration, he had to complete a twelve-month appointment as a house officer. During the period from August 1970 to July 1971, Shipman spent six months as a house officer in surgery followed by another six months as a house officer in medicine. By August 1971, Shipman had gained full GMC registration.

This was followed by a further thirty-one months at Pontefract General Infirmary. Beginning in August 1971 until the end of January 1972, he was a senior house officer on the paediatric wards. Then from February 1972, he returned to the medical wards as a senior house officer for a further six months.

From August 1972 to the beginning of September 1973, he was back on the paediatric wards as a registrar. Finally, between September 1973 and the end of February 1974, he spent six months as a senior house officer on the obstetric and gynaecological unit.

It was while working at Pontefract that Shipman responded to an advertisement in a medical publication for a vacancy in general practice at the Abraham Ormerod Medical Centre in Todmorden West Yorkshire. His application was successful, and he left Pontefract on 28th February 1974.

After a short probationary period as an assistant general practitioner, he became a junior partner. In February 1975, the Home Office Drugs Inspectorate and the West Yorkshire Police Drugs Squad became aware that Shipman was obtaining abnormally large quantities of pethidine from local pharmacies in Todmorden. However, they were reassured that there was no drug problem with Dr Shipman.

By early June in 1975 it was noticed that a pharmaceutical company was supplying the local Boots pharmacy with excessively high quantities of pethidine specifically for injection. Shipman was subsequently interviewed again by Home Office drug inspectors and a detective constable from West Yorkshire Police.

Shipman gave convincing explanations for the amount of pethidine he had ordered and firmly denied that he was abusing the drug. At this particular time, Shipman was experiencing problems with his own health and in May 1975 he was referred to Halifax Royal Infirmary where he was diagnosed as suffering from idiopathic epilepsy.

In late September 1975, Shipman's partners discovered he was in fact abusing pethidine and had been obtaining large quantities of the drug illicitly, not for the practice use but to feed his own habit. Shipman was confronted by his partners and he admitted he was abusing the drug. After taking legal advice his partners succeeded in dismissing him from the practice. As a result, Shipman was admitted back to the Halifax Royal Infirmary and referred to a consultant psychiatrist. He arranged for Shipman to be voluntarily admitted to The Retreat – a private hospital in York which specialised in treating psychiatric disorders. As a result, the Home Office was informed that Shipman was registered as a drug addict.

During his stay in York, Shipman became withdrawn from pethidine and was later diagnosed as suffering from moderate depression. This was treated with anti-depressant medication which improved his condition. He was discharged from the clinic on 30th December 1975 but was required to continue with psychiatric supervision.

As a result of his dismissal from the practice in Todmorden, the Home Office Drugs Inspectorate, together with an officer from West Yorkshire Police, interviewed Shipman again whilst at The Retreat.

He gave the interviewers what appeared to be a satisfactory account of his criminal activities. He fully admitted using various deceptions to obtain pethidine for his own consumption which was in the region of 600 to 700 mg per day.

He then made a written statement in which he described what had occurred, adding 'I have no future intention to return to General Practice or work in a situation where I could obtain supplies of pethidine'.

On 13th February 1976, Shipman appeared at Halifax Magistrates' Court where he pleaded guilty to eight charges: three offences of obtaining ten 100 mg ampoules of pethidine by deception, three of unlawfully possessing pethidine and two of forging a prescription. He also asked for seventy-four further offences to be taken into account. Shipman was fined £75 on each charge, £600 in total, and ordered to pay compensation of £58.78 to the NHS Family Practitioners Committee.

Prior to his conviction, and following his dismissal from Todmorden, Shipman was already employed with the Durham Area Health Authority as a clinical medical officer. He did tell his new employers of his previous problem with drugs and that he was facing criminal proceedings and possible disciplinary action by the General Medical Council (GMC).

The Health Authority having discussed his case with the psychiatrists who had treated him, offered him the post on condition that he continued his follow-up care. During the course of his employment in Durham, Shipman had no access to controlled drugs.

In the meantime, Shipman's health problems appear to have been resolved, and he had ceased suffering from blackouts or seizures which, with hindsight, were obviously side-effects of his pethidine abuse.

Shipman's conviction was reported to the GMC who had to decide on whether to take disciplinary action. Shipman's case was also referred to the Penal Cases Committee. They had received reports from the consultant psychiatrists who had treated Shipman, together with a letter of support from the area medical officer in Durham, which indicated that Shipman had settled well in his new employment with no evidence suggesting any recurrence of his 'former difficulties'. In April 1976, the Committee decided that Shipman's case should not be referred to the Disciplinary Committee and could be closed.

Following Shipman's conviction for drug offences, the Home Office officials who dealt with the case also decided that no further action should be taken against Shipman. This does strongly suggest that they were influenced by the views of the police, and by the fact that there was no evidence to suggest that Shipman's patients had suffered harm as a result of his obtaining pethidine – together with the GMC's decision not to take any further action in the matter. This meant, in effect, that Shipman was able to pursue his medical career without any restrictions.

In 1977 he applied for a post with a seven-doctor practice in Hyde, Greater Manchester. The Donneybrook Practice required a new doctor to replace one that was leaving. When called for interview, Shipman informed members of the practice that he had abused pethidine and been convicted. He also referred them to one of the psychiatrists who had treated him and informed them that he could provide details of his condition. One of the partners at the practice contacted the psychiatrist, together with officials at the GMC and Home Office, and was assured by the psychiatrist that Shipman was not suffering from any mental health problems which would interfere with his duties as a general practitioner. Likewise, the

GMC and the Home Office confirmed that there were no restrictions which could affect Shipman's handling of controlled drugs. As a result of the positive information received, Shipman was invited to join the practice on 1st October 1977.

Shipman was employed at the Donneybrook practice for over fourteen years and appeared to be hard-working, dedicated and popular with his patients. He immersed himself in community activities in Hyde, serving on several committees, being a governor of one of the primary schools in the town and a Freemason member of a lodge in Rochdale.

However, in 1991, Shipman informed his colleagues at Donneybrook that he intended to leave the practice, his reason being that he disliked the computer system that had been introduced in 1989, although it is believed his arrogant and unpromising attitude to other members of the practice created antagonism.

One partner described Shipman as being 'individualistic' in his approach and said that he could become irritated if confronted by any other doctor or staff members. Accordingly, there was the assumption by the partners that these features of his personality may have led Shipman to prefer work in a single-handed practice.

From 1st January 1992, Shipman ran his own single-handed practice but remained working from the Donneybrook Practice until fresh premises became ready for him at 21, Market Street, Hyde. When he did move, he took with him several members of staff together with his own patient list.

His leaving the Donneybrook practice was acrimonious to say the least – and was followed by legal negotiations to settle financial arrangements caused by his leaving.

Shipman's practice became successful and he enjoyed a high reputation as an attentive and caring doctor, due to his willingness to visit elderly patients at home. Shipman and his staff performed regular medical audits which impressed the Health Authority Group who considered the practice as being innovative and advanced.

However, in March 1998, certain people in Hyde began to show concern about the number of Shipman's elderly patients who were dying in curious circumstances. After having discussions with her colleagues, Dr Linda Reynolds, a partner in the Brook Medical Practice situated very near to Shipman in Hyde, alerted John Pollard, the Coroner for the Greater Manchester South District, who was informed of the concerns raised by herself and others.

This resulted in Mr Pollard ordering a covert police investigation which concluded that there was no evidence to substantiate the concerns, and no further action was taken against Shipman.

However, circumstances changed in 1998 with the sudden death of one of Shipman's elderly and prominent Hyde patients.

Mrs Kathleen Grundy, a former mayoress of the town, died on 24th June 1998, the cause of death being certified as old age. Despite her eighty-one years, Mrs Grundy had enjoyed good health and her death was sudden and certainly unexpected. Mrs Grundy's daughter, Mrs Angela Woodruff, a practising solicitor living in Leamington Spa in Warwickshire, had conducted her mother's legal affairs since she qualified. In 1986, she had drafted Mrs Grundy's will in which Mrs Grundy had made her daughter the sole beneficiary to her substantial estate.

Following Mrs Grundy's death, Mrs Woodruff became aware of the existence of what appeared to be a new will dated 9th June 1998. This had been sent, together with a covering letter apparently signed by Mrs Grundy, to a firm of local solicitors in Hyde, shortly before Mrs Grundy's death. The 'new' will left Mrs Grundy's entire estate to Shipman.

Mrs Woodruff was immediately suspicious, and she reported her suspicions to the police in Warwickshire. They passed the matter to the Greater Manchester Police (GMP) to investigate. It soon became evident to the police that the doctor named as the new beneficiary to the will, had been the subject of an earlier covert police investigation.

A warrant for the exhumation of Mrs Grundy's body was obtained from the Coroner, and the exhumation took place on 1st August 1998. On the same day, the police executed a warrant to search Shipman's surgery and home. A typewriter and Mrs Grundy's medical records were seized from the surgery.

On 3rd August 1998, Detective Superintendent Bernard Postles was appointed as Senior Investigating Officer (SIO) and a major criminal investigation commenced. A post-mortem examination of Mrs Grundy's body failed to establish a cause of death and a toxicological test was carried out. On 14th August 1998, the police were informed that initial tests carried out by the Forensic Science Service at Chorley, Lancashire, had revealed the presence of an opiate, possibly morphine, in Mrs Grundy's body.

On 14th August 1998, an inspector from the Home Office Drugs Inspectorate together with a chemist inspector from Greater Manchester Police visited Shipman at his surgery. He was interviewed in connection with his use of controlled drugs. Prior to the visit, on the 10th August, the Home Office inspector informed the GMP that Shipman had previous convictions. This was the first time that GMP became aware of Shipman's criminal record. This led to further enquiries being made to establish the full nature of his previous convictions.

In the meantime, the police decided to re-examine the nineteen deaths certified by Shipman they'd become aware of during their earlier March 1998 investigation. They interviewed family members to see whether they had any concerns regarding the circumstances of their relatives' deaths. On 26th August 1998, the police were informed by Mr Michael Hall, a forensic document examiner, that the signatures on Mrs Grundy's 'new' will had been forged and that the will itself had probably been typed on the typewriter which had been seized from Shipman's surgery.

On the 28th August 1998, Mrs Julie Evans, a forensic scientist, informed the police that the levels of morphine present in Mrs Grundy's body were consistent with levels which had previously been known to have caused death by morphine overdose.

As a result of this information, Shipman was arrested on 7th September 1998 on suspicion of the murder of Mrs Grundy, and of attempting to obtain property by deception and forgery. He was interview in connection with those offences and later charged, and the following day he appeared before Tameside Magistrates' Court, when he was remanded in custody.

During September 1998, the bodies of Mrs Joan Melia, Mrs Winifred Mellor and Mrs Bianka Pomfret were exhumed.

On 5th October 1998, Shipman was arrested on suspicion of their murders and was interviewed.

On 7th October 1998 he was charged with the three murders.

In the same month, the bodies of Mrs Marie Quinn and Mrs Ivy Lomas were exhumed. Shipman was arrested and interviewed in connection with those deaths on 11th November but made 'no comment' during these interviews. On the same day, he was charged with both murders. Exhumations of the bodies of Mrs Jean Lilley and Mrs Irene Turner followed in

November 1998 and, following a further 'no comment' interview, Shipman was charged with their murders on 3rd December 1998.

On 22nd February, 1999, Shipman was charged with the murder of Mrs Muriel Grimshaw whose body had been exhumed in December 1998. He was also charged with the murders of Mrs Norah Nuttall, Mrs Kathleen Wagstaff, Miss Maureen Ward, Mrs Pamela Hillier, Mrs Maria West and Mrs Lizzie Adams – all of whom had been cremated.

The police had been attempting to prevent Shipman from continuing in practice. To this end, they had informed the GMC of the position in August 1998 but were informed that the GMC could not do anything until Shipman had been convicted of an offence.

On 18th August the West Pennine Health Authority contacted the NHS Tribunal which had the power to suspend him from practise, the Health Authority then taking control of the practice on 29th October 1998.

At Shipman's trial which opened on 5th October 1999, he pleaded not guilty to the fifteen counts of murder and one count of forging Mrs Grundy's will.

On 31st January 2000, Shipman was convicted on all counts. He was sentenced to fifteen terms of life imprisonment and, four years for the forgery, to run concurrently.

Following the trial, Shipman was suspended from practice by the GMC Preliminary Proceedings Committee and, on 11th February 2000, his name was erased from the medical register.

In the course of the police investigations, bodies had been exhumed in three cases which did not form the subject of counts on the indictment at the criminal trial. By the time of the trial, the police had investigated a large number of deaths amongst Shipman's patients, in addition to the fifteen deaths which were the subject of counts on the indictment and the additional three cases where bodies had been exhumed. Some of these investigations had been initiated by the police themselves, and others had commenced as the result of concerns from relatives.

As a result of their investigations, the police identified twenty-three further cases in which they believed that the evidence was strong enough to justify a prosecution for murder. However, on 18th February 2000, the Director of Public Prosecutions announced that no further criminal proceedings would be instituted against Shipman, because of the impossibility of his having a fair trial after the publicity surrounding his convictions in January 2000.

A further factor was that, since it had been recommended that Shipman should spend the rest of his life in prison, no additional punishment would be imposed as a result of any future conviction.

Chapter Two: The Final Reckoning

The Trial

In the Preston Crown Court before The Honourable Mr Justice Forbes

REGINA V
HAROLD FREDERICK SHIPMAN

FOR THE PROSECUTION:
MR R HENRIQUES QC

FOR THE DEFENCE:
MISS N DAVIES QC
MR P WRIGHT QC MR. I. WINTER QC
MISS BLACKWELL

Monday 11 October 1999

Mr Richard Henriques QC, Counsel for the Prosecution:

Opening Speech

'The defendant's full name is Harold Frederick Shipman. He is a General Medical Practitioner. The prosecution allege that he murdered fifteen of his patients, by administering substantial doses of morphine or diamorphine very shortly before they died, thereby causing their deaths. Nine of the fifteen patients were buried, six were cremated. The bodies of those who were buried were exhumed, tests carried out on the thigh muscle of each deceased, established a significant presence of morphine within their bodies. None of those buried, nor indeed cremated, were prescribed morphine or diamorphine. All of them died most unexpectedly, all of them had seen Doctor Shipman on the day of their death. There is no question in this case of euthanasia or what is sometimes called 'mercy-killing'. None of the deceased was terminally ill.

The defendant killed those fifteen patients because in the submission of the prosecution, he enjoyed doing so. He was exercising the ultimate power of controlling life and death, and repeated the act so often that he must have found the drama of taking life to his taste. Of these fifteen allegations, one is in 1995, one in 1996, seven in 1997 and six in the first six months of 1998. The prosecution will point to a number of similarities in each case which culminating in our submission, present a compelling case against the defendant. In a significant number of cases, he falsified the medical records in order to create a false medical history, consistent with the false cause of death attributed by him to each of the deceased patients. In a significant number of cases, he informed or persuaded relatives that a post-mortem was not necessary or desirable, when it plainly was.

Of course, from Dr Shipman's perspective, it was imperative in each case that he avoided a post-mortem. Routine testing of samples would have disclosed morphine poisoning or morphine 'toxicity' as the experts put it. In a significant number of cases, he has told relatives that the deceased requested him to visit them at home when it can be shown from telephone records and from surgery records that no such request was made. In three cases he falsely asserted that the deceased had telephoned his surgery complaining of 'chest pains'. No such phone calls were made. Examination of the telephone records demonstrated that to be true. In three cases he told relatives that at about the time of death, he had called an ambulance. Those again were lies and are exposed by examination of the telephone billing and ambulance service log records. In many cases when he arrived at the home of the deceased, he carried out no physical examination of the deceased. In the remaining cases his examination was minimal. In several cases, his manner was unsympathetic and inappropriate after death.

When each of these allegations are looked at and placed within the context of the trial as a whole, in our submission, it will be very plain that Dr Shipman killed each of these fifteen ladies, as he purported to treat them as his patients. In the final murder and count one in the indictment, he had forged the will in which the deceased, Mrs Kathleen Grundy, purported to leave all her estate, money and house to her doctor, Dr HF Shipman. Not only does a handwriting expert confirm that the will is a forgery, so too do the two purported witnesses of the forged will. They say they did not sign the document which purports to be Mrs Grundy's will. They had been asked to sign a document and did sign a document but certainly not the document in question. When it became clear that Dr Shipman was responsible for the forgery of Mrs Grundy's will, her body was exhumed and when substantial quantities of morphine were found in her thigh muscle, liver and blood, other exhumations followed, and thereafter consideration was given to cases in which the deceased was cremated. The defendant had the means to carry out these murders, namely possession of diamorphine accumulated over a period of time. Members of the Jury, it is on this evidence that we submit he is guilty on each and every count of this indictment.'

Source: National Archives Web: The Shipman Trial Transcripts.

The Trial of Harold Frederick Shipman commenced on Tuesday 5th October 1999 at Preston Crown Court, known locally as the 'Old Bailey of the North'. The Victorian building in Lancaster Road was opened in 1904, with two courtrooms and eight cells below ground. In 1965 another courtroom was added. Preston also has another modern combined court building housing both the Magistrates' and Crown courts with ten courtrooms.

The Crown Prosecution Service (CPS) felt that one charge of forgery and fifteen charges of murder would be more than enough for a jury to deal with. There was a wealth of evidence that would be presented over a lengthy period of time.

The decision to restrict it to fifteen was made between the prosecuting counsel, the CPS and the police, on the basis of practicality about what could be achieved in the time allocated for the trial.

At his first appearance, Harold Shipman faced sixteen charges, fifteen for murder and one of forging Mrs Grundy's will. The fifteen victims were Kathleen Grundy, Joan Melia, Winifred Mellor, Bianka Pomfret, Marie Quinn, Ivy Lomas, Irene Turner, Jean Lilley, Muriel Grimshaw, Marie West, Kathleen Wagstaff, Pamela Hillier, Norah Nuttall, Elizabeth Adams and Maureen Ward.

The leading prosecuting counsel was Richard Henriques QC, who was leader of the Northern Circuit. The defence team was led by Nicola Davies QC – a specialist in medical cases. The judge was Mr Justice Thayne Forbes, presiding judge of the Northern Circuit.

The Prosecution Case

Opening the trial of GP Harold Shipman, Richard Henriques QC, told Preston Crown Court, that the fifty-three-year-old doctor killed his victims with morphine injections because he was exercising the ultimate power of controlling life and death.

Dr Shipman pleaded not guilty to fifteen murders claimed to have occurred between March 1995 and June 1998. He denied forging the will of one of his victims.

In the case of Kathleen Grundy, Dr Shipman had forged a will in which she left her £400,000 estate to him. He also allegedly altered her medical records to suggest that she had been a drug abuser. When it became apparent that Dr Shipman was responsible for the forgery, the body was exhumed, and substantial amounts of morphine were found in the liver and blood. Other exhumations followed and then consideration was given to those cases in which the deceased had been cremated.

Mrs Grundy's will read, 'I leave all my estate, money and house to my doctor. My family are not in need and I want to reward him for all the care he has given to the people of Hyde'.

Mrs Grundy's daughter, solicitor Angela Woodruff, became suspicious and contacted the police. The typescript of Mrs Grundy's will was examined by experts and compared with typescript produced using a Brother typewriter recovered by police from Dr Shipman's surgery. The experts concluded the will had probably been typed out using this typewriter. A fingerprint on the will belonging to Dr Shipman was found on the will.

Dr Shipman was charged with killing:

Marie West, 81 on 6th March 1995.
Irene Turner, 67, on 11th July 1996.
Lizzie Adams, 77, on 28th February 1997.
Jean Lilley, 59, on 25th April 1997.
Ivy Lomas, 63, on 29th May 1997.
Muriel Grimshaw, 76, on 14th July 1997.
Marie Quinn, 67, on 24th November 1997.
Kathleen Wagstaff, 81, on 9th December 1997.
Bianka Pomfret, 49, on 10 December 1997.
Norah Nuttall, 65, on 26th January 1998.
Pamela Hillier, 68, on 9th February 1998.
Maureen Ward, 57, on 18th February 1998.
Winifred Mellor, 73, on 11th May 1998.
Joan Melia, 73, on 12 June 1998.
Kathleen Grundy, 81, on 24th June 1998.

May Clarke, a friend of Kathleen Grundy told the jury that the last of GP Harold Shipman's fifteen alleged murder victims was 'delighted' that he had agreed to visit her home on the day he killed her with a lethal injection of diamorphine. May Clarke said that Mrs Grundy was very pleased that Dr Shipman was calling as it would save her visiting his surgery.

Mrs Clarke confirmed that she had spent the evening of the 23rd June with Mrs Grundy and that they had been good friends for over forty-two years. She also confirmed that Mrs Grundy was in fine health.

John Green, a caretaker at the hall where Mrs Grundy organised a luncheon club, together with Ron Pickford, found Mrs Grundy's body at 11.55 am on 24th June 1998. Mr Pickford telephoned Dr Shipman who arrived within twenty minutes. He felt her pulse and said 'cardiac arrest'.

Dr John Rutherford, a Home Office pathologist who carried out an autopsy on Mrs Grundy's exhumed body on 1st August 1998 told the jury that he could not find any abnormalities to account for sudden unexpected death. He had found less coronary artery disease than he had expected and took issue with Mrs Grundy's death certificate on which Shipman registered the cause of death as 'old age'.

Dr Rutherford told the jury that old age is a condition characterised by degeneration of multiple organ systems, and that he would be very reluctant to attribute death to old age unless he had evidence that there had been considerable deterioration over a long period of time. He said that the level of morphine found in Mrs Grundy's body had killed her.

An independent GP, Dr John Grenville, stated that Shipman was not justified in certifying old age as the cause of death of Kathleen Grundy. Such a sudden, unexpected and unexplained death would almost certainly have demanded a post-mortem examination.

Mrs Joan Melia, another victim of Harold Shipman, had been certified as having died from pneumonia but had not in fact, been suffering from lung inflammation, the jury was told. A post-mortem examination revealed only minimal signs of the condition. In the opinion of pathologist Dr John Rutherford, she had died from the toxic effects of morphine.

A receptionist described to the court how Shipman continued to treat three patients while one of his alleged victims was lying dead in his treatment room. Shipman's receptionist Mrs Carol Chapman said that he looked 'red and flushed' when he emerged from the room in which he had taken Mrs Ivy Lomas. Shipman had told her that he tried to put Mrs Lomas on the ECG machine, but he thought it was not working because he couldn't obtain a reading. It was then that he realised she was dead. He told police that she died of natural causes, but a post-mortem examination of her body proved that it was an injection of morphine that had killed her.

In the case of Mrs Marie West, the prosecution maintained that Dr Shipman killed her at home on 6th March 1995, unaware that a friend was in the next room. Shipman said that Mrs West had died of a massive stroke. Her medical records were found at his home rather than his surgery.

Another patient, Mrs Irene Turner, had a complicated medical history and had recently returned from holiday suffering from a cold. The prosecution maintained that Dr Shipman injected her with morphine at her home on 11th July 1996. Dr Shipman is said to have made conflicting statements regarding her admission to hospital and maintained that she died from diabetes. After exhumation, Mrs Turner's body was found to contain morphine.

In the case of Lizzie Adams, the prosecution alleged that Dr Shipman killed the former teacher at her home on 28th

February, 1997. Dr Shipman is said to have stated that she died of pneumonia and pretended to call for an ambulance when a friend arrived – but no call was ever made. Her medical records were found in a carrier bag in Shipman's garage.

In the case of Jean Lilley, Dr Shipman called at her home on 25th April 1997, and was seen to leave by a neighbour who went to see her friend and found her dead. Dr Shipman maintained that she died of heart failure. However, a pathologist found no evidence of severe heart problems and the cause of death was found to be morphine poisoning.

In the case of Ivy Lomas, according to the prosecution, Dr Shipman killed Mrs Lomas at his surgery on 29th May, 1997. He then continued to see other patients before altering her medical records two days later. He stated that she had died of a medical condition which should have required his attention. Dr Shipman is said to have told police that Mrs Lomas was a 'nuisance' patient.

Muriel Grimshaw was found dead in her home on 14th July 1997 by her daughter. Dr Shipman is said not to have examined the body, but declared her death to be from a stroke and hypertension. He is also alleged to have changed her medical records. Mrs Grimshaw's body was exhumed and a pathologist found death to be from morphine poisoning.

Marie Quinn is alleged to have injected herself with morphine at her home on 24th November 1997. Dr Shipman told her son that Mrs Quinn had phoned him saying she had had a stroke and that she was dead by the time he arrived. The prosecution maintained that no such call was made and there was no evidence of the medical problems that Dr Shipman claimed she had.

In the case of Kathleen Wagstaff, the prosecution maintained that Dr Shipman confused Mrs Wagstaff with another patient and called at the wrong address. After injecting her with morphine on 9th December 1997, he stated that death was due to heart disease. Dr Shipman also claimed that he had received a call to attend Mrs Wagstaff, but no such call was made, and no evidence of heart disease was found.

Mrs Bianka Pomfret phoned Dr Shipman requesting a home visit on 10th December 1997, and she was later found dead in her chair. Dr Shipman stated that she had heart trouble and had died of coronary thrombosis and ischaemic heart disease. The prosecution maintains that Shipman altered Mrs Pomfret's records the hour before her body was discovered in order to generate a backdated history of heart disease. Pathologists found excessive morphine levels in her exhumed body.

In the case of Mrs Norah Nuttall, the prosecution claimed that Dr Shipman visited Mrs Nuttall at her home on 26th January 1998. Her son returned to find his mother slumped in a chair. Dr Shipman maintains that he called an ambulance but when Mrs Nuttall died, he phoned to cancel it. The prosecution says neither call was made.

Mrs Pamela Hillier was an active sixty-eight-year-old who was preparing her home for decorating before she died. She was found dead on 9th February 1998, by paramedics who said that the police should be informed. Dr Shipman said that she had died of a massive stroke and there was no need for a post-mortem. The prosecution maintained that, in the two hours before her body was discovered, he had made ten changes to her medical records to support his diagnosis.

Miss Maureen Ward had been suffering from cancer but was not in ill-health at the time of her death on 18th February 1998. Dr Shipman reported her death to the warden at the flats where she lived, stating that the cause was a brain tumour. The prosecution says Dr Shipman gave two different explanations for why he had gone to see Miss Ward and had falsified records to make it look as though she had complained of brain tumour symptoms.

Mrs Winifred Mellor was found dead in her chair on 11th May 1998 having been complaining of a sinus problem. Dr Shipman was reported to have visited her earlier in the day. He is alleged to have made only the most cursory examination of Mrs Mellor. The prosecution alleges that morphine was later found in the body and that Dr Shipman had altered her records.

Mrs Joan Melia had visited Dr Shipman at his surgery on 12th June 1998, suffering from a chest infection. He made a house call to her the same day and she was later found dead in her chair. The prosecution says that Dr Shipman did not examine her, merely issuing a death certificate for pneumonia aggravated by emphysema. A pathologist later found evidence of morphine but not of serious lung problems.

The prosecution stated that Mrs Kathleen Grundy was in good health and very active the day before her death on 24th June 1998. She was visited by Dr Shipman early that morning for a blood sample and was later found dead on her sofa. When her body was exhumed one month later, high amounts of morphine were found. There was no record of any blood sample having been taken, and Dr Shipman falsified written and computer records to make it look as if Mrs Grundy was a 'drug abuser'.

Angela Woodruff, a fifty-four-year-old solicitor, told Preston Crown Court she was concerned when she found her mother Kathleen Grundy had changed her will, leaving her entire estate to Dr Shipman. Mrs Woodruff, who worked in Leamington Spa, Warwickshire, told the jury she was notified of her mother's death on 24 July 1998. The following day she went to her mother's home in Hyde to arrange the funeral and sort out her affairs. She also visited Dr Shipman's surgery. He told her that he had seen her mother at his surgery the day before her death. He did not say what the appointment was regarding. He said that she had conveyed to him that she was feeling unwell with chest pains. The doctor told Mrs Woodruff that he had visited her mother on the morning of her death to take a blood sample. He wasn't specific but did say that sometimes old people complain about feeling unwell before they die and then simply die. He implied it was old age.

Mrs Woodruff told the jury that approximately two weeks later she became aware of a new will that her mother had allegedly made, and it was then that she began to worry. She told the court how her mother had never mentioned the second will which was lodged with the Hyde solicitors Hamilton Ward.

'I became very concerned; it was badly typed and my mother was meticulously tidy. The whole thing was just unbelievable, leaving everything to her doctor,' she said.

'It was inconceivable the thought of her signing a document which was badly typed.'

Mrs Woodruff also said that her mother's signature looked strange and was too big. After speaking to the people who had 'witnessed' the new will, she handed it over to police, together with diaries, a repeat prescription and her mother's driving licence, to enable the police to check for forgery.

Under cross-examination by defence counsel, Nicola Davies QC, Mrs Woodruff stated that she had suspicions about the will and also about her mother's death. She told Miss Davies that she had handed six blue capsules found in her mother's handbag to the police. Miss Davies told the court that the Woodruff family was not in financial need as her husband had recently inherited his father's £1.3m estate. The final witness, Detective Sergeant Bob Hampson of Greater Manchester Police, told the court that when he visited Dr Shipman's surgery, the GP handed over a Brother typewriter which the prosecution alleged was used to produce the false will. The GP said that Mrs Grundy had often borrowed it.

Mrs Grundy's close friend, ninety-one-year-old, May Clarke, told the court that Mrs Grundy had thought very highly of Dr Shipman and had known him for a long time. The month before her death she had suggested a donation to Dr Shipman's patient fund by the Mayoress's Appeal Committee. She later rejected the idea because the fund was not a public charity. Mrs Clarke said that Mrs Grundy thought he was a good doctor and admired his work.

Mrs Clarke told the court that the day before she died, Mrs Grundy said that Dr Shipman was coming to visit her to take a blood sample. She thought it was very good of him to go along to her home to save her the trouble of going to the surgery. Dr John Rutherford, the Home Office pathologist who examined Mrs Grundy's exhumed body, stated that he found the cause of death to be an overdose of morphine.

Brian Burgess told the jury that no one at his legal firm, Hamilton Ward, of Hyde, Greater Manchester, had ever heard of Mrs Grundy. The will dated only two days earlier, arrived in Mr Burgess's office about two hours before the eighty-one-year-old's body was found. Mr Burgess stated that he thought it was 'very strange' that an actual will, rather than a copy, had arrived in his office without any prior knowledge.

Earlier, John Green, the caretaker of the day centre where Mrs Grundy helped run a luncheon club, told the court how he found her lying dead at her home. Mr Green said that he and luncheon helper Ron Pickford, drove to Mrs Grundy's home after she failed to arrive. He opened the unlocked door, went into the living room and found Mrs Grundy lying fully-clothed on the sofa. Dr Shipman was telephoned and arrived between fifteen and twenty minutes later. Mr Green stated that he found Kathleen lying on the sofa and felt her hand for a pulse. When asked, he replied that he believed she had suffered a cardiac arrest. Mr Green then asked Dr Shipman whether he had seen Mrs Grundy earlier that morning, and Dr Shipman admitted this, but said it was just for a talk. The doctor told the men to contact Hamilton Ward solicitors.

The Preston Crown Court jury were told that the document arriving unexpectedly at a solicitor's office on the day eighty-one-year-old Mrs Grundy died, also carried the fingerprint of Dr Shipman in the bottom left-hand corner. Handwriting expert, Michael Allen, told the fifth day of the GP's trial that he had compared the signatures on what was supposed to be Kathleen Grundy's will and an accompanying letter, with other genuine specimens of her signature. His opinion was that the two queried signatures were not written by Kathleen Grundy. They were, 'in effect, poor, crude simulations, forgeries of her signature, written by some other person'.

Another fingerprint expert, Andrew Watson, stated that a print matching that of the little finger of Shipman's left hand was found on Mrs Grundy's will. There were no prints matching those of Mrs Grundy on the will, but Andrew Watson was positive that the fingerprint on the bottom left-hand corner was that of Dr Shipman.

Earlier, two of the doctor's patients told how they were summoned from the waiting room and asked to witness a document in his surgery. Mrs Grundy was sitting in the surgery when Paul Spencer and Claire Hutchinson signed a document with the signature 'K. Grundy' already on it. Mr Spencer said he assumed he was signing a medical form, but Mrs Hutchinson said she saw the words 'Last Will and Testament' on a document. When he was shown the will, Mr Spencer told the jury that the signature was not his.

The murder jury heard that the youngest alleged victim of Dr Harold Shipman could only have died from morphine poisoning. They were told that Shipman certified the death of manic depressive forty-nine-year-old, Bianka Pomfret, was due to coronary thrombosis and ischaemic heart disease. He also cited smoking and chronic manic depression as contributory factors, but these were all rejected by a Home Office pathologist.

Dr John Rutherford told the court that Mrs Pomfret, a divorcee, had died from the toxic effects of morphine. There was no other pathological evidence of cause of death than that of morphine poisoning. Mrs Pomfret's ex-husband, Adrian, told the jury that he had seen her three days before her death. She had long-standing psychiatric problems and was visited regularly by care workers.

At the time she was recovering from flu. She had been to see Dr Shipman and was due to see him again that week. He had been her GP since the early 1980s. Care worker, Susan Adshead, said in a statement that she called at Mrs Pomfret's home on the afternoon of 10th December and got no reply, though she could see Mrs Pomfret through the living room window sitting on the settee. She then called on Mrs Pomfret's son, William who lived nearby and followed him into the house through the unlocked door. She noticed that she was wearing her day clothing and was leaning against the settee, sitting up with her hands on her lap. Her head was on one side and she almost seemed relaxed.

Dr Shipman came to the house and said he had seen Mrs Pomfret earlier that day because she had been unwell. William Pomfret told the jury that he asked Dr Shipman what had happened and was told his mother had died of a heart attack. He said that she was suffering from angina, but William had not been aware of this.

Dr Harold Shipman paid one of his alleged victims a surprise visit less than an hour before she was found dead in her home. According to her neighbour, Margaret Walker, Kathleen Wagstaff, eighty-one, had seemed pleased to see the doctor when he arrived at her flat in Hyde. Mrs Walker said she had a brief conversation with a man standing at Mrs Wagstaff's door before Mrs Wagstaff answered. She later learned that this man was Dr Shipman.

After the brief conversation, Mrs Walker then went out on an errand, and returned about three quarters of an hour later to the news that Mrs Wagstaff was dead.

The Crown stated that on the day of Mrs Wagstaff's death, there was no record of any visit in Dr Shipman's visiting book, and the surgery diary showed no record of any appointment for Mrs Wagstaff.

Mrs Wagstaff's daughter-in-law, Angela Wagstaff, told the court of her shock at being informed of her mother's death by Dr Shipman at Dowson County Primary School in Hyde where she was a teacher. He said that he had been called to her mother's home and claimed she had died while he was there. Mrs Wagstaff told the court she ran to her mother's home and found her alive and well. It was only after calling Dr Shipman's surgery that she discovered it was in fact her mother-in-law who had died. The following day she and her husband saw Dr Shipman in his surgery where he apologised for the 'mix-up'. She said that Dr Shipman had asked her husband if he had known that his mother, Mrs Wagstaff, had suffered from heart problems, to which her husband replied that he had 'no idea'.

Independent GP, Dr John Grenville, was called as an expert witness by the prosecution. He said the medical records showed no evidence that Mrs Wagstaff had been suffering from heart disease, which was linked to the coronary thrombosis certified by Dr Shipman as the cause of death.

The son of another of Dr Shipman's alleged victims, sixty-five-year-old Norah Nuttall, told the court how after leaving his mother in her home for less than an hour he had returned to find Dr Shipman on the doorstep and his mother lying dead in a chair. Mrs Nuttall died in her home on 26th January 1998. John Nuttall said he knew his mother had seen Dr Shipman earlier that day at his surgery because she had been troubled with a cough and Dr Shipman had prescribed her some medicine.

John Nuttall said when he arrived back at the home, Dr Shipman was there and told him his mother was 'not so well' and that he had called an ambulance. After they both went back inside the house, Dr Shipman told him his mother was dead.

Dr Shipman then allegedly went on to cancel the ambulance. Earlier, Peter Wright QC prosecuting, produced telephone records showing that no calls were made to the ambulance service from Mrs Nuttall's home on that day.

In a statement to the court, a close friend of Mrs Nuttall, Ann Robinson, told how she had seen the alleged victim just a few hours before her death in Hyde shopping centre. She said that she looked well and appeared very smart.

The court was told that Dr Shipman made the children of one of his alleged victims feel guilty for not knowing their mother was 'ill'. Pamela Hillier, age sixty-eight, was found dead in her bedroom on an afternoon in February 1998 when Dr Shipman was due to visit. Mrs Hillier's daughter, Jacqueline Gee, told the court that her mother had mildly high blood pressure. When she and her brother visited Dr Shipman the day after Mrs Hillier's death, he told them her mother had died from a stroke.

Mrs Gee told the court that they were totally confused. She could remember coming out of the surgery and feeling guilty. Dr Shipman had been trying to intimate that her mother was unwell and that she should have expected that she might die at any time. Mrs Gee also stated that Dr Shipman said he could tell the cause of death from the way she was lying.

He explained that if she had suffered a heart attack, then she would have been holding her chest or reaching for something. Her brother, Keith Hillier, said they asked for a post-mortem examination but accepted Dr Shipman's reply. He felt that it was unnecessary, and he pointed out it was an unpleasant thing to happen and to put mum through.

The court then heard a statement from a police computer expert detailing computer entries for Mrs Hillier, which were allegedly altered by Dr Shipman on the afternoon of her death, two hours before her body was found. One entry dated three days before her death indicated that Mrs Hillier had raised blood pressure and that Dr Shipman had spoken to her about diet and exercise. However, Mrs Gee said she had no recollection of her mother, who was exceptionally active, having seen the doctor on that day. She said that Mrs Hillier had been in good health apart from the knee problem, for which she had been due to see the doctor on the day of her death. Mrs Gee's husband, Martin, told the court how he arrived at Mrs Hillier's home shortly after her death to find his wife with Dr Shipman. He told the jury that his wife was asking very sensible questions and that Dr Shipman was extremely unhelpful and uncaring towards a daughter who had just lost a mother. He would always remember Dr Shipman saying, 'Put it down to a stroke'.

Mrs Hillier's next-door neighbour Peter Elwood found her body. He had been asked to investigate by Mrs Gee, who could not contact her mother. Paramedics arrived shortly after the body's discovery, followed by Dr Shipman. Mr Elwood told the court that he heard one of the ambulance men say, 'I shall have to notify the police, this is a sudden death at home'. Then Mr Elwood heard Dr Shipman say, 'I don't think there is any need to do that'.

Dr John Grenville, a GP called by the prosecution as an expert witness, said that Mrs Hillier had been diagnosed with slightly high blood pressure in 1995 but that this had been extremely well-controlled with a low dosage of medication. He said that Mrs Hillier was at no greater risk of suffering a stroke or heart attack than any other member of the population. Asked if Dr Shipman's diagnosis of a stroke was justified, Dr Grenville replied 'No'.

The jury was told that Dr Shipman wrote on Maureen Ward's medical record that she was unwell before her death in February 1998. Her computer records stated that she had suffered headaches and nausea through December 1997 and early 1998.

Richard Henriques QC prosecuting, said a computer entry dated 17th December 1997 described how Miss Ward, age fifty-seven, had complained of headaches, and that she was to notify the local hospital. However, this entry had been made on the day of her death the 18th February 1998. Dr Shipman gave the cause of death as cancer.

The jury was told that on the day of her death Miss Ward was in good spirits and had been looking forward to a Caribbean cruise with her friend, Mary France. Miss Ward was taking medication for breast cancer and had received treatment for skin cancer but was currently clear.

Mr Andrew King, a consultant neurosurgeon at Hope Hospital, Salford, Greater Manchester, told the court it would not have been possible for the GP to diagnose the cancer without a post-mortem or scan. After examining Miss Ward's medical records, he said he would have expected her to have suffered a variety of symptoms including loss of concentration, lethargy and drowsiness before her death. To be entirely well, having booked a holiday and being in good spirits, is not something one would expect from someone with cancer throughout their body, stated Mr King.

The court heard how Miss Ward, a higher education teacher, was found dead in her sheltered home by Dr Shipman. Warden, Christine Simpson, told the court that despite having to pass through two secure doors, the GP claimed he walked in and found Maureen 'dead on the bed'.

Mrs Simpson told the court on the morning of 18th February 1998 she had seen Miss Ward briefly. Around 3.30 pm she answered a knock at the door from Dr Shipman who said he had found Miss Ward dead. Mrs Simpson stated that she had been very surprised and shocked. Dr Shipman said she did have a brain tumour and had been suffering with it for a long time. As she walked over to Miss Ward's flat, she asked Dr Shipman how he had got in. He said that the door had been left open on the latch by Miss Ward, but this was something that Miss Ward had not done before. Dr Shipman had an envelope in his hand and told Mrs Simpson he was expected as he was delivering a hospital appointment letter to her. Mrs Simpson found Miss Ward, lying on her bed fully clothed.

The jury heard that Shipman had recorded Mrs Simpson as being present at the time of death, but Mrs Simpson said this was untrue as she had been alerted to Miss Ward's death by Shipman. In his medical records, some of which were backdated, Shipman described how Miss Ward had had a fit in an ambulance, but the court was told that no call to the ambulance service had been made from Miss Ward's flat.

The bodies of several of Shipman's alleged victims

were found to contain 'excessive morphine' level, a scientist told the court. Toxicologist, Julie Evans, stated that tests revealed levels of the drug consistent with samples from people who died of a morphine overdose. Healthy people die within five minutes if thirty milligrams of morphine is injected into their veins. Pain relief expert Professor Henry McQuay said that an injection of the drug dissolved in water would make a person not suffering from pain sleepy. Describing the symptoms, he said that within minutes their breathing would slow down until it stopped. Their lips would go blue and, as no oxygen could reach the brain, they would die.

Mrs Evans told the court that varying amounts of the drug were found in samples taken from the thigh and liver of Mrs Kathleen Grundy.

Tests performed at the forensic science laboratory in Chorley, Lancashire, showed Mrs Grundy had one microgram of morphine per gram of thigh muscle and that two areas of the liver showed no presence of the drug. Mrs Evans said the samples were relatively well preserved, although Mrs Grundy had died on 24th June 1998.

When asked by prosecuting QC Peter Wright, whether 'Kathleen Grundy had taken or been given a substantial amount of morphine or morphine', Mrs Evans stated that she would agree with that assertion. She also stated that her findings were 'entirely consistent' with levels that are seen in other deaths attributed to excessive doses of morphine. The scientist also added that death, decomposition and the process of embalming, would not increase the levels of morphine found in the body.

The jury heard that samples taken from the other alleged victims Bianka Pomfret, Winifred Mellor, Joan Melia, Ivy Lomas, Marie Quinn, Irene Turner, Jean Lilley and Muriel Grimshaw also revealed morphine.

There was no scientific evidence for the other six alleged victims as they had been cremated.

The court was told that morphine in the body of one of Dr Shipman's alleged victims could have come from drugs she was prescribed in the month before her death. Cross-examined by the defence, toxicologist, Julie Evans, told the court that tablets prescribed to Ivy Lomas in May 1997 could have broken down into morphine. Earlier, Mrs Evans said she had found excessive levels of morphine in the body of Kathleen Grundy, Mrs Pomfret and Winifred Mellor.

Counsel for the prosecution asked Dr Shipman 'You

had both the means and opportunity to kill Kathleen Grundy, didn't you?' Shipman replied: 'I don't think I did, and I didn't'. Dr Shipman said he was unable to explain the disappearance of six ampoules of diamorphine missing from a box of ten, originally prescribed for a patient who had died. The box containing the drug was found at his home.

Dr Shipman was asked about another alleged victim, forty-nine-year-old Bianka Pomfret, who was found dead at her home shortly after he visited. He said Mrs Pomfret had only told him she had been suffering from chest pains on the day she died. Mr Henriques asked Shipman why, after her death, he had not told her family of her problems. Dr Shipman replied 'because I asked them if they knew she had chest pains. If they had known I would then have asked why she had not told me about it'.

Shipman made ten entries on his computer relating to Mrs Pomfret between the time of him visiting her at home and of her body being found. He admitted that one of the entries which gave the patient's blood pressure reading back dated to April, was a mistake. Challenged by Mr Henriques who replied: 'You didn't make a mistake. You made it up'.

He also stated that it was not the only mistake on the medical records, adding that Shipman had recorded Mrs Pomfret as smoking forty cigarettes a day, four times what her son William said she smoked. He also denied telling Mrs Pomfret's psychiatrist, Dr Alan Tate, on the day after her death that he detected a 'thready pulse' when he examined her.

Mr Henriques believed that Dr Tate was anxious about Mrs Pomfret's death because she had talked several times about taking her own life. He put it to Dr Shipman that this was a very dangerous situation for him. Shipman admitted that if Dr Tate had suspected suicide there would have been a post-mortem examination. Mr Henriques commented that 'You had to put on your best persuasive boots didn't you, and make sure that he didn't inform the coroner, because you knew what the consequences would have been?' Shipman replied 'No'.

Mr Henriques described Dr Shipman's attitude towards the family of Winifred Mellor, as 'uncaring and insensitive' when he visited a few hours after her death. He said the whole reason for the visit was 'to make sure there was no post-mortem examination'.

Shipman denied evidence from Father Denis Maher that he had told him Mrs Mellor had telephoned his surgery earlier that day. Shipman stated that the priest had not heard properly what he was saying. In response, Shipman stated that he did not think he was unkind and that he was reasonably compassionate and answered his questions as best he could. Mr Henriques concluded by saying that Shipman was trying to bludgeon this family into accepting your cause of death and making sure there was no post-mortem examination. To this assertion Shipman replied 'No'.

The prosecution and defence finished giving evidence on the 13th December 1999, with more than a hundred witnesses, including Dr Shipman, having given evidence since the trial began on 5th October 1999.

The trial resumed on Wednesday 5th January 2000, with the closing speech of prosecuting counsel Mr Richard Henriques QC. He began by telling the jury that the doctor told 'bare-faced lies' to his alleged victims' families to convince them they had died naturally. The defendant not only had the opportunity to kill but also had the means to kill because of the availability of diamorphine. He possessed the doctor-patient relationship which enabled him to administer diamorphine. Mr Henriques continued to say that Dr Shipman had told lies to grief-stricken relatives to dupe them into believing that their loved ones had suffered natural deaths and that he had called an ambulance.

Four times Dr Shipman lied about the alleged victims telephoning his surgery before they died, to give him a pretext for visiting them at home.

There had been a failure to resuscitate any of the patients because there was no point – Dr Shipman knew that they were dead. He was too arrogant and self-confident to even go through the motions. Earlier in the day, the prosecuting counsel told the court that it could not be coincidence that fifteen women patients died on the same day as Dr Shipman saw them. They trusted him to care for them, their relatives trusted him to tell the truth about the circumstances of their death, and the community trusted him to keep records and documentation with insight and knowledge.

The prosecution submitted that he had breached that trust, that he did not care at all for these fifteen patients he killed. If relatives of some of the victims had been able to meet and compare notes, Dr Shipman's 'trail of murder' could have been halted. Mr Henriques continued: 'While of course sudden deaths do occur, Dr Shipman faced the problem, he saw each and every one of those deceased patients on the day that she died. Is that a coincidence as he would contend, or are the prosecution accurate when they contend he saw each patient and killed each of them?'

Dr Shipman, as their GP, had been in a position to administer diamorphine. There could hardly be some other killer on the loose in Hyde, seeking out Dr Shipman's patients and following the same route as Dr Shipman himself. Mr Henriques continued to say that the reason Dr Shipman had been determined to avoid post-mortem examinations needed no elaboration. The accused fears pathologists, fears ambulances and fears hospitals. In all of the fifteen cases, there had not been a single post-mortem, a single ambulance called, a single proper examination of the patient, or a single attempt at resuscitation.

The Defence Case

The case against Dr Harold Shipman was based on unreliable scientific evidence, the jury was told. Mrs Davies, Defence Counsel, said Dr Shipman, who denied murdering fifteen patients and forging the will of one of his alleged victims, had been a caring general medical practitioner since the 1970s. She said that before his arrest in 1998, he had a patient list of 3,100.

'No patient had to register with Dr Shipman, but the fact that so many did must mean some inferences can be drawn,' she said. 'With a list of 3,100, well-above the national average, Dr Shipman must have been doing something right'.

Miss Davies said the fact that the doctor was so caring he cold-called on his patients and visited them at home, so they did not have to come to the surgery had been 'turned on its head and that caring evidence used against him'. The fact that Dr Shipman avoided the need to put relatives through the distress of a post-mortem examination was just another example of his caring ways. She said, 'You may have formed the view that keeping records was not his forte. Within the scale of things, what is really more important, that patients are seen and cared for, or that immaculate records are kept?'

Miss Davies said that during the weeks and months of evidence one thing the prosecution had failed to raise was a motive. 'Why should this doctor murder fifteen of his patients?' she asked.

In the opening of his case for the Crown, Mr Henriques suggested there was a power motive behind the actions of Dr Shipman. 'Where is the evidence? No psychiatrist has been called. We are not here to consider psychological theories. What we are here to consider is proof'.

Miss Davies added: 'The prosecution case is built on one foundation stone and that is toxicology. Without it there would be no case. Toxicology is a new science and untested by proven scientific methods'. Miss Davies continued: 'We contend that it is inherently unreliable and therefore unsafe, and without that toxicological evidence, all that flows from it, that you are asked to draw inferences, fail'.

She said there needed to be clear, unequivocal proof that the doctor administered 'a specific and identifiable substance to each of the fifteen women which wholly or substantially caused their death' and not novel, unreliable scientific evidence. The jury was told by defence counsel that Mrs Evan's analysis may have been ground-breaking but it was based on anecdotal evidence and was not definitive.

Mrs Evans told the court she could not say what levels of drugs were in the bodies of the alleged victims when they died, due to various factors such as decomposition.

Defending QC Nicola Davies said: 'You don't know as a matter of fact where and at what level any drug was in the body at the time of death'. Mrs Evans replied, 'That's correct'.

Miss Davies also suggested to the court that the morphine found in the stomach of alleged victim Joan Melia, could have come from slow-releasing morphine tablets.

In the case of the youngest alleged victim, Bianka Pomfret, Miss Davies told the court that after her death her psychiatrist suspected she could have taken her own life.

The court was told that family GP Dr Harold Shipman had no motive for the fifteen murders he was accused of. In her closing speech to the jury, Miss Davies told the court that the case against the doctor was based on unreliable scientific evidence. Miss Davies said the entire case against Dr Shipman foundered on the unreliability of tests for poison carried out on the bodies of Dr Shipman's alleged victims. She reminded the jury that forensic scientist, Julie Evans, had told the court that she was embarking on 'novel scientific territory' and that she was 'breaking new ground' when she began working on the case.

The court was told that neither the evidence relating to Shipman's behaviour nor the toxicological evidence could stand alone. Miss Davies said the prosecution was using examples of Shipman's actions to 'shore up the unreliability of the scientific evidence'. It was the defence's contention that the behaviour only became sinister if you were satisfied as to the toxicology. The actions of Dr Shipman were not sinister, as they were part of his everyday practice.

The court heard from prosecuting counsel that Dr Shipman told 'many lies' in documents and in interviews to the police.

If it wasn't for the forging of Mrs Grundy's will, he would have avoided detection.

It was claimed that a woman who GP Harold Shipman is alleged to have killed with a lethal dose of morphine, could already have had the drug in her body. The prosecution alleged that Dr Shipman injected Ivy Lomas, age sixty-three, with morphine at his surgery. However, there was a more likely explanation for Mrs Lomas' death. Before her death, and at the surgery, Mrs Lomas had been prescribed a painkiller which breaks down into morphine. Miss Davies explained how the drug pholocodine exacerbated Mrs Lomas' pre-existing heart condition, and that there was no case against Dr Shipman.

She also explained how it was impossible for the doctor to have murdered Marie Quinn, another of his patients, because there wasn't enough time. Dr Shipman's computerised medical notes and Mrs Quinn's itemised telephone bill showed a very tight window of time for the alleged murder to be carried out.

Turning to the evidence given by some of the prosecution witnesses, Miss Davies questioned their reliability. For example, one policeman made a statement more than a year after the event referring only to his brief notes, while the memories of close friends and relatives of the deceased may have been affected by the distress that they suffered following the deaths of their loved ones.

Miss Davies said that forensic evidence may also not have provided all the required information because of the state of decomposition of the exhumed bodies. She suggested that the youngest alleged victim, Bianka Pomfret, aged just forty-nine, had suicidal thoughts two days before her death.

Miss Davies believed that, in relation to the fifteen counts of murder, the prosecution wholly relied on the base findings of toxicology. In the context of these cases based on scientific evidence, she said: 'It is our submission to you that because of the inherently unreliable nature of scientific evidence, that is the very basis upon which the Crown's case rests. In the absence of such evidence, the inferences to be drawn from it relating to the behaviour of the doctor by the Crown also fail, and with it so does the entirety of it'. The case against Dr Harold Shipman was based on unreliable scientific evidence and lacked a motive for murder. Dr Shipman cared so much for his patients that he called on them unannounced and visited them at home, sparing them trips to the surgery. The fact that he spared relatives the distress of post-mortem examinations also proved how much he cared.

The prosecution contended that Dr Shipman avoided post-mortem examinations to hide the fact he had injected them with lethal amount of diamorphine. However, during months of evidence, Ms Davies believe that the prosecution had failed to raise a motive. She reminded the jury that a forensic scientist, Julie Evans, had told them the she was embarking on 'novel scientific territory' when working on the case, therefore her results were unreliable, especially as there was no comparable data available. Ms Evans also did not know whether the levels of diamorphine found were an accurate reflection of the levels at the time of death, a 'damning' fact for the prosecution since decomposition would affect the results.

The dose of diamorphine administered needed to be at a fatal level, yet the level had not been scientifically proven. Ms Davies said that the morphine found in Mrs Joan Melia's body raised questions and that the cause of death was uncertain, due to decomposition. In the case of Winifred Mellor, there was no evidence that she was at home at the time she was allegedly visited by Dr Shipman on the afternoon of her death. The case relating to Ivy Lomas was probably the most damning. She had died while visiting Dr Shipman's surgery and her body was found to contain morphine. Ms Davies suggested that Mrs Lomas had died because the prescribed morphine already in her body had exacerbated her heart condition.

Ms Davies stressed how easy it was for Dr Shipman's actions to appear suspicious when the underlying basis for them is not known. She also argued that it was virtually impossible that Dr Shipman murdered Marie Quinn. Shipman's computerised medical notes and Mrs Quinn's itemised telephone bill indicated that there wasn't enough time. Family GP, Dr Harold Shipman, had no motive for the fifteen murders he was accused of.

In her closing speech to the jury, defence counsel, Nicola Davies QC, told the court that the case against the doctor was based on unreliable scientific evidence.

Wednesday 5th January 2000

Mr Richard Henriques QC

– Counsel for the Prosecution

– Closing Speech to the Jury

'Ladies and gentlemen, the fifteen ladies whose names appear as victims in this indictment, they had all chosen or at least accepted Dr Shipman as their doctor. In doing so, they entrusted their health, indeed they entrusted their lives to him. They trusted him to care for them. Their relatives trusted him to tell the truth about the circumstances in which his patients died. The community trusted him to keep records and to complete documentation with honesty and integrity. We submit that he breached that trust. He did not care at all for those fifteen patients, he killed them. He did not, with truth, relate the circumstances of their death to their grieving relatives. He duped them in order to save his own skin. His medical records were falsified in order to cover his tracks. In misleading relatives, he took advantage of their grief and their lesser knowledge of medicine and procedures. As they grieved, this determined man deployed any and every device to ensure that no post-mortem examination took place. It is on this evidence that we submit he is guilty on each and every count on this indictment.'

Source: National Archives Web: Shipman Trial Transcripts.

Ms Nicola Davies QC

– Counsel for the Defence

– Closing Speech to the Jury

'Members of the Jury, the man before the court charged with fifteen counts of murder and one of forgery is Harold Shipman, a doctor, specifically a General Medical Practitioner. A doctor's primary objective is to care for his patients. A doctor's training, the knowledge he acquires, is directed to that one aim. Doctors are there to care for their patients, not kill them. This particular doctor, Dr Shipman, has been in general medical practice since the 1970s. If this doctor, as the prosecution alleges, deliberately administered a toxic substance to each of these fifteen women, what was the substance? In what quantity? In what way was it administered? Was it oral? Was it intramuscular? Was it intravenous? Was it morphine? Was it diamorphine? Was it one dose or more than one dose? How proximate to the defendant was each woman? These questions are critical to any analysis of the evidence and they are difficult, if not impossible to answer, because there is no direct evidence of any action on the part of Dr Shipman, which actually caused the death of any one of these women. Before the court is a doctor, faced with fifteen counts of murder and one of forgery. In respect of those fifteen counts of murder, they are wholly reliant on the base findings of toxicology.

In the context of this case, that toxicology is based on the scientific evidence as it presently exists, and that evidence is unsafe and unreliable. It is our submission to you, because of the inherently unreliable nature of that scientific evidence, the very basis of the Crown's case has to go. In the absence of such evidence, that is the scientific evidence, the inferences to be drawn from it relating to the behaviour of the doctor as relied on by the Crown, also fail. With them fails the entirety of the prosecution case.'

Source: National Archives Web: Shipman Trial Transcripts.

Mr Justice Forbes, summing up on day forty-one of the trial, told the jury the case was 'tragic and deeply disturbing' and that the allegations could not be more serious than a doctor accused of murdering fifteen of his patients. The judge told the jury that when considering the evidence of witnesses, they should make allowances for the strain of giving evidence in court. They must also apply the same fair standards to the evidence given by Dr Shipman.

Dr Shipman accepted pathological evidence which showed that doses of morphine had killed Mrs Grundy, Ivy Lomas and Marie Quinn. Dr Shipman had also told the court that he did not know how the fatal dose was administered.

At the time of completing death certificates, Dr Shipman believed the victims had died from the causes he had certified. He did not accept that the other deaths were caused by morphine. The jury had heard about Dr Shipman's possession of diamorphine since 1993 which suggested he had committed offences under the 1971 Misuse of Drugs Act. This was relevant to whether he had the means to kill.

'You must not therefore assume that Dr Shipman is guilty of the offence with which he is charged. Neither did the various alleged lies Dr Shipman is accused of telling necessarily make him a murderer.'

The judge listed the lies, including those to bereaved relatives about why he was at attendance during the deaths, those allegedly designed to hinder and deceive police, and false entries made on patients' medical records. In making any judgements, the judge advised the jury to: 'Draw upon your common sense, your experience of life, your human nature. Each of the sixteen charges must be considered on their own. They do not stand or fall together'.

On Monday 24th January, the jury retired to consider their verdicts and on Monday 31st January, they returned with their verdicts:

GUILTY ON ALL CHARGES.

Addressing Shipman, Mr Justice Forbes said:

'You have finally been brought to justice by the verdict of this jury. I have no doubt whatsoever that these are the true verdicts. The time has now come for me to pass sentence upon you for these wicked crimes.

Each of your victims was your patient. You murdered each and every one of your victims by a calculated and cold-blooded perversion of your medical skills for you own evil and wicked purposes. You took advantage of and grossly abused their trust. You were, after all, each victim's doctor. None realised yours was not a healing touch, none knew in truth you had brought their death disguised as the caring attention of a good doctor. The sheer wickedness of what you have done defies description. It is shocking and beyond belief. You have not shown the slightest remorse or contrition for your evil deeds and you have subjected the families and friends of your victims to having to re-live the tragedy and grief you visited on them'.

The judge then passed fifteen life sentences and a four-year sentence for forgery.

He concluded by saying:

'I am satisfied justice demands that I make my views known at the conclusion of this trial. I have formed the conclusion that the crimes you stand convicted of are so heinous that in you case life must mean life. My recommendation will be that you spend the remainder of your days in prison.'
Mr Justice Forbes.

This ended the fifty-seven day momentous trial of Britain's most prolific serial killer.

Overview of the Case

The conviction of Dr Harold Frederick Shipman on fifteen counts of murder ended the trial of Britain's most notorious serial killer. However, it would seem that this did not signal the end of the investigation into Shipman's activities. Those investigating the case believe that Shipman went on to commit many more murders than those for which he was found guilty. The police in fact, investigated the deaths of one hundred and thirty-six of his patients. South-Manchester Coroner John Pollard believes that a figure of one hundred and fifty would be a more realistic estimate. The Crown Prosecution Service stated in January 2000 that it was prepared to prosecute in twenty-three of those cases if families of the deceased gave permission.

Once the trial ended, information withheld from the jury was made public for the first time. There had been an earlier police inquiry into Shipman six months before he was eventually arrested. However, the investigation had been closed because of insufficient evidence. The fact that Shipman had a previous conviction (dating back to his time in Todmorden) was also withheld from the jury. Although at the time (the mid-1970s), the matter was referred to the General Medical Council, Shipman had been allowed to continue in practice as a GP.

Harold Shipman had been a respected and trusted local doctor with more than three thousand patients. They all thought him to be caring, conscientious and hard-working. Behind this 'smokescreen' of respectability, there was a more sinister individual.

His life became dominated by the desire to kill, which he did over a considerable period of time. He was only finally caught following the death of Mrs Kathleen Grundy in June 1988.

When the police confronted him with proof that Mrs Grundy had not died from 'old age' but as the result of diamorphine poisoning, Shipman attempted to brand the widow as a drug addict. In fact, Shipman had drawn the police's attention even before Mrs Grundy's death. Three months earlier, doctors at the Brooke Surgery (also in Hyde) had raised concerns about the number of cremation certificates Shipman had been asking them to countersign. However, the 'covert' investigation was closed down because of lack of evidence.

It was the evidence of a suspicious will which renewed police action and the decision to exhume the body of Mrs Grundy.

In parallel with this, the police decided to investigate the deaths of more than one hundred and thirty of Shipman's other patients. Part of their investigation involved examining old medical records and questioning the surviving relatives of the deceased.

When the post-mortem results on the body of Mrs Grundy revealed traces of morphine, Shipman was arrested. The police discovered in his surgery the typewriter on which Mrs Grundy's will had been written. Evidence of other murders began to emerge together with a pattern of his type of victim.

The most consistent pattern was that all were women who were middle aged or elderly and lived alone. In all but one of the murders, Shipman visited them at home usually by appointment but sometimes unannounced. He then injected them with morphine under the pretext of taking a blood sample. This was supported by evidence that there were no signs of struggle. After every death, Shipman ensured that there would not be any need for a post-mortem which could implicate him.

It is not known with any certainty when Shipman began killing his patients. However, the means by which he obtained diamorphine (heroin) to commit his murders was the same as the method he'd used to obtain his earlier pethidine – through false prescriptions and stock-piling.

Once the trial had ended, the police had to decide what further action needed to be taken over the allegations of further killings. The case raised many questions which still required answers, but the most fascinating one was – why did he kill? This question and possible answers form the substance of the final chapter.

At Shipman's trial, the jury found he had administered a large injection of opiate to each victim – this constituted an unlawful act because the opiate was not intended for therapeutic purposes. Given his profession, the jury must have been satisfied that he was fully aware of all the consequences of the drug. Since the dose killed the patient, then the jury must have inferred that this was precisely what Shipman intended.

In nine of the fifteen conviction cases, the bodies were exhumed, and morphine was later found in the remains. In each of those cases, the medical evidence for the true cause of death was morphine poisoning.

In the case of Kathleen Grundy, Shipman tried to suggest that the presence of the drug in her body tissues was because she was a drug-addict. The jury quite rightly rejected this explanation.

In all of the other cases, Shipman offered no explanations for the presence of morphine in the bodies. In eight of the nine cases, the discovery of morphine together with evidence that Shipman was present at the death or shortly before the body was discovered, provided devastating evidence that he had administered an injection.

In the one remaining case, that of Joan Melia, the prosecution could not demonstrate that Shipman had been present at the death or at her home shortly before death. However, the jury must have inferred it.

In the other six cases, the bodies had been cremated ensuring that no remains were available for examination. Consequently, this lack of physical evidence of morphine poisoning meant that there was less evidence of Shipman's guilt. However, the particular circumstances of each case and subsequent conduct of Shipman in both the cremation and burial cases, were so similar, that when considered together, the evidence in the cremation cases became very compelling.

As a result, the jury drew the inference that Shipman had injected all fifteen victims with morphine or diamorphine. It is highly likely that the fifteen cases for which Shipman was prosecuted, represented the strongest evidence.

The most striking feature in fourteen of the conviction cases was the association between Shipman's contact with the victim and their subsequent deaths. Only in the case of Joan Melia was the Crown unable to demonstrate the close temporal association between the two parties. Of the victims with morphine in the body, Shipman admitted that he had been with two of them at the moment of death. These were Mrs Ivy Lomas who died in the surgery, and Mrs Marie Quinn.

Mrs Irene Turner and Mrs Jean Lilley were found dead minutes after Shipman had been in their homes. Mrs Kathleen Grundy and Mrs Bianka Pomfret were found dead not long after Shipman had left. In fact, Shipman was seen outside Mrs Winifred Mellor's house shortly before her death was discovered, though he later denied even visiting her on that day. Mrs Muriel Grimshaw's death was discovered at home the day after Shipman's last visit. In each of those eight cases, Shipman had been alone with the patient.

Of the six cremation cases where there was no physical evidence of the presence of morphine, Shipman did admit that he had been present at the death of four: Mrs Kathleen Wagstaff, Mrs Lizzie Adams, Mrs Nora Nuttall and Mrs Maria West. The death of Mrs Pamela Hillier was discovered only about half an hour after Shipman had visited her, and in the case of Miss Maureen Ward, Shipman claimed that he had found Miss Ward dead when he arrived at her flat.

The jury plainly disbelieved him.

A second feature common to many of the conviction cases was that the patient was found sitting peacefully in a chair or on a sofa, as if asleep. Mrs West, Mrs Adams, Mrs Lilley, Mrs Wagstaff, Mrs Pomfret, Mrs Nuttall, Mrs Miller and Mrs Melia were all found sitting in their chairs or sofas. Mrs Turner, Mrs Grimshaw and Miss Ward were lying on their beds, and Mrs Grundy was lying on the sofa.

A third feature of the conviction cases was the fact that none of the patients was terminally ill and in no case did it appear that Shipman had been sent for on account of a sudden or serious deterioration in the health of the patient. The deaths were sudden and unexpected by both family and friends.

Source: The Shipman Inquiry: First Report (2002), pp 109-122, (Crown Copyright)

Timeline: Harold Shipmman

1946	Harold Shipman is born in Nottingham.
1970	Graduates from Leeds University and begins work at Pontefract General Infirmary.
1974	Starts work as a GP in Todmorden, Lancashire but colleagues discover he is addicted to the painkiller Pethidine. He had been using patient prescriptions to feed his habit. As a result, he was convicted and fined then dismissed by his practice.
1977	Shipman obtains another GP post in Hyde,

	Greater Manchester.
1993	He sets up his own single-handed practice in Market Street, Hyde with approximately 3,000 patients on his list.
1998	Shipman is arrested for the murder of Kathleen Grundy, on 7th September. The trial begins at Preston Crown Court on 5th October. Shipman accused of killing 15 elderly patients.
2000	On 31st January, the Jury convicts Shipman on all 15 counts of murder. He is sentenced to life in prison.
	On the 1st February, Health Secretary Alan Milburn announces an Inquiry into the circumstances surrounding the murders and the investigation.
	Police reveal that they are investigating Dr Shipman's role in 175 further deaths. However, the DPP decides that no further prosecutions will take place. Shipman is moved from prison in Manchester to Frankland Prison in Durham.
	In April, South Manchester Coroner John Pollard announces he will hold inquests into 23 deaths not originally covered by the police investigation.
	In July, relatives of the suspected victims win a court battle to force the government to hold a Public Inquiry.
2001	In January a government report suggests that as many as 236 of Shipman's patients may have been murdered.
	In June the Shipman Inquiry opens in Manchester, chaired by High Court Judge Dame Janet Smith. Its first phase is devoted in part to an examination of more than 466 cases in which foul play is suspected.

2002	In July, the Report of the first phase of the Inquiry is published. It concludes that Shipman killed at least 215 of his patients, possibly more. Of these 215 victims, 171 were women and 44 men, the oldest being a 93-year-old woman, the youngest a 47-year-old man.
2003	In June, Shipman is moved from Frankland Prison to Wakefield Prison.
	In July, the second and third Reports are published. In the Reports, Dame Janet Smith criticises the police investigation into the murders. She also called for 'radical reform' of the way coroners work in England and Wales, after Shipman managed to evade their scrutiny by stating that his victims had died of natural causes.
2004	13th January, Shipman is found hanging in his cell in Wakefield Prison. Staff attempted to revive him, but he was pronounced dead at 0810 GMT.

Shipman's 'Modus Operandi'

As more suspicious deaths were investigated by the police, it emerged that Shipman's killings followed a consistent and routine form. This would begin with a routine visit by Shipman to an elderly patient usually living alone, for the purpose of obtaining a blood sample. Other times, the patient would request the doctor to pay a call because of some health issue. In addition, Shipman would quite often deliver repeat prescriptions to the patient. Finally, he quite often made unsolicited calls on his elderly patients disguised as 'keeping a watchful eye on them'. These visits concluded with Shipman killing his patients. He would go to great lengths to cover up his tracks by having ready-made explanations for what had occurred. He would on numerous occasions claim that he had found the patient dead when he arrived at their home. If challenged by how he gained entrance to their property, the usual explanation would be that 'they left the door off the latch for me to enter, expecting me to visit'.

On other occasions, he would remain at the premises and make telephone calls to the patient's relatives or would call on neighbours and inform them of the death. He would also say that the patient suddenly died whilst he was present. After each killing, Shipman would lock the door to the premises and then seek out a neighbour who held a key or, if in sheltered accommodation, he would go to the warden. Together, they would then return to the premises and 'discover' the body. He would even on occasions, leave the body unattended waiting for a neighbour or relative to discover the death and to then call him at the surgery. Shipman's usual method of killing his patients was by intravenous injection with a lethal dose of diamorphine or another opiate drug. On occasions, if the patient was ill in bed, he would kill by an intramuscular injection. There is no reliable evidence that he killed other than by the administration of a drug. Shipman must have committed drug offences virtually every day he was in general practice, because he was always in possession of controlled drugs without lawful authority. He obtained large quantities of pethidine and diamorphine by illegal, dishonest means, using deception and forgery.

Source: The Shipman Inquiry: First Report, pp 197-8 (Crown Copyright).

The Scale of Shipman's Killings

YEAR	LOCATION	NUMBER
1975	Todmorden, West Yorkshire	1
1977-92	Donneybrook Practice, Hyde	71
1992-98	Market Street Practice, Hyde	143
	Estimated Total:	215

Breakdown of Killings 1992-98

1992 - 1
1993 - 16
1994 - 11
1995 - 30
1996 - 30 *
1997 - 37 *
1998 - 18

Victims by Age Group
Age Range Total

40s	3
50s	8
60s	22
70s	85*
80s	80*
90s	7

The * indicates the predominant age range of the victims.

Chapter Three

'Revelations'

The Shipman Inquiry

On the 31st January 2000, Harold Frederick Shipman was convicted by a jury at Preston Crown Court of the murder of 15 of his former patients, and of forging the will of one of them. He had killed them by administering lethal doses of diamorphine. He was sentenced to fifteen concurrent terms of life imprisonment, which in effect, meant that he would remain in prison until his death. Shipman had been a well-respected general practitioner until his eventual arrest for the murder of Mrs Kathleen Grundy in September 1998.

There was a general concern that a doctor had been able to amass large quantities of diamorphine and to kill so many of his patients without detection. Why had the regulations which require a record to be made of the acquisition and supply of all controlled drugs failed to prevent Shipman from obtaining diamorphine illicitly? Why had this not been noticed, particularly in view of his previous convictions for drug abuse in 1976? Why had our system of death certification with the availability of post-mortem examination and a coroner's inquest failed to detect and arrest the progress of this killer?

In response to these concerns, the Secretary of State for Health set up an Inquiry in February 2000 under the National Health Service Act 1977. Although its report was to be made public, the panel chaired by Lord Laming, was to sit in private. Many people, particularly those in Hyde, were dissatisfied with this aspect of the Inquiry. A group of relatives of both known and suspected victims of Shipman applied to the High Court for a judicial review of the then Secretary of State's decision. In July 2000, those applications succeeded, and in September, the Secretary of State announced that the Laming Inquiry would be disbanded. In place of this, he invited Parliament to set up a Public Inquiry under the Tribunals Inquiry (Evidence) Act of 1921. On the 31st of January 2001, Parliament confirmed the Inquiry's terms of reference. Dame Janet (now Lady Justice Smith) a High Court judge was invited to chair the Inquiry. In addition to the Inquiry's legal investigation team, it also had access to expert medical and statistical advice.

Source: The Shipman Inquiry, First Report, Opening Statement, 2002 (Crown Copyright)

Terms of Reference

- To consider the extent of Harold Shipman's unlawful activities.
- To enquire into the actions of the statutory bodies, authorities, and other organisations and individuals concerned in the procedures and investigations which followed the deaths of those of Harold Shipman's patients who died in unlawful suspicious circumstances.
- To enquire into the performance of the functions of those statutory bodies, authorities and individuals with responsibility for monitoring primary care provision, and the use of controlled drugs.
- Following these enquiries, to recommend what, if any, steps should be taken to protect patients in future, and to report to the Secretary of State for Home Affairs and the Secretary of State for Health.

The Inquiry was conducted in three phases. The first phase investigated how many patients Shipman killed, the means employed and the period over which these killings occurred. Professor Richard Baker, Professor of Quality in Health Care at the University of Leicester, conducted a statistical analysis of data drawn from Shipman's practice and compared it with other general practitioners in the same area. He also examined the medical records of a large number of Shipman's former patients. From his review of the medical records and the cremation forms available, he formed the view that the most likely number of deaths about which there should be concerns was two hundred and thirty six. The second phase covered the second and third paragraphs of the terms of reference. This particular phase was further broken down into four stages. The first dealt with post-death procedures, including death and cremation certification, the role of the police and ambulance services in the investigation of sudden and unexpected deaths, the functions of the coroner and the roles of the Office of National Statistics. The second stage covered the 1998 police investigation into the concerns raised about Shipman. The third dealt with controlled drugs, including the procedures for prescribing, dispensing, storage and disposal of drugs, and the monitoring of these procedures by the police and Home Office. The final stage dealt with the systems

for dealing with complaints against general practitioners, whistle-blowing, the disciplinary control of general practitioners, and the monitoring of their work. Phrase three considered proposals for changes to the existing systems.
Source: The Shipman Inquiry (2002): First Report - Opening Statement (Crown Copyright)

Chronology

2000 – In September, the Secretary of State for Health announced that a Public Inquiry would be held under the Tribunals of Inquiry (Evidence) Act 1921. In December, Dame (now Lady) Janet Smith DBE, a High Court judge, was invited to become Chairman of the Inquiry.

2001 – On the 23rd of January, the House of Commons debated the proposed Inquiry, which was ratified by both Houses of Parliament. On the 10th of May, a Public Meeting was held at Manchester Town Hall and on the 20th June, the Public Hearings began into Phase 1 of Stage 1.

2002 – On the 7th of May, the Public Hearings began into Phase 2 – Stage 1 and were completed on the 17th of July. On the 19th of July, the First Report of the Inquiry was published. Public Hearings into Stage 2 of Phase 2 began on the 7th October.

2003 – On the 27th of January, the Public Hearings into Phase 2, Stage 2 ended. On the 19th of May, the Public Hearings began into Phase 3 of Stage 3, and on the 14th of July, the Second and Third Reports of the Inquiry were published. Public Hearings into Stage 3 of Phase 2 were completed on the 18th of July. The Public Hearings into Stage 4 of Phase 2 began on the 14th of July and were completed on the 18th of December.

2004 – In January, a series of seminars relating to topics discussed in Stages 3 and 4 of Phase 2 were held. On the 13th of January, Harold Frederick Shipman committed suicide in Wakefield Prison. On the 15th of July, the Fourth Report of the Inquiry was published and one the 9th of December, the Fifth Report was published.

2005 – On the 27th of January, the Sixth and Final Report of the Inquiry was published, and the Inquiry officially closed on the 24th March.
Source: The Shipman Inquiry First Report (2002) – Chronology (Crown

Copyright).

It became very clear from the outset that there would be very few cases in which physical evidence would be available to the Inquiry to show whether Shipman killed the patient in question. The Chairman's decisions were largely based on inferences drawn from circumstantial evidence.

'In a criminal trial, the jury is not usually permitted to draw inference that the defendant is guilty of the crime with which he is charged from evidence that he has done something of a similar nature in the past (Similar-Fact Evidence). The jury is allowed to take past conduct into consideration only if the similarity between past conduct and the present allegation is so similar, that it would be against common sense not to do so. In a civil action, a judge is allowed to take a person's propensities to act in certain ways into account. A public inquiry is neither a criminal trial nor a civil action. The purpose of this Inquiry is to find out what Shipman has done. It is therefore necessary to consider all Shipman's conduct throughout his professional career in order to assemble as complete a picture as possible of the ways in which he conducted himself.'

Source: *The Shipman Inquiry: First Report (2002), pp109-110 (Crown Copyright)*

The Inquiry found that Shipman killed 215 of his patients, the first being Mrs Eva Lyons who was killed in March 1975 when Shipman was practising in Todmorden, the last being Mrs Kathleen Grundy who died in June 1998. During Shipman's time at the Donneybrook Practice in Hyde, it was estimated that he killed 70 patients, and the remaining 143 during the six years at his Market Street practice. While at his surgery, he killed one patient in 1992, 16 in 1993 and 11 in 1994. In each of the year 1995 and 1996 he killed 30 patients, which increased to 37 in 1997. During the first three months of 1998, he killed another 15 patients. There was an interval of about seven weeks before he went on to kill another three patients before his final arrest on the 7th September 1998. While the majority of the deaths for which Shipman was responsible, occurred while he was working from Market Street, Hyde, it is now clear that even when working from the Donneybrook Practice, he was able to kill undetected over a considerable number of years. In total, the Inquiry examined 888 cases of which 494 were given written decisions. Of the remaining 394, there was compelling evidence that Shipman was not responsible for these deaths. Professor

Richard Baker, Professor of Quality in Health Care at the University of Leicester, conducted a review of Shipman's clinical practice which was published in 2001. He carried out a number of analyses of the estimated excess of deaths among Shipman's patients during his career as a general practitioner.

He estimated that the true number of excess deaths to be between 198 and 277 and concluded that an excess of 236 deaths reflected the true number about which there should be concerns. Professor Baker's figures support the conclusion that excess deaths were in the region of 220-240. This striking compatibility between Professor Baker's findings and those of the Inquiry clearly suggest that the conclusions reached by the Review and the Inquiry were very likely to be correct. All but three of the deaths for which the Inquiry found that Shipman was responsible were entered in the register of deaths relying upon the Medical Certificates of Cause of Death completed by Shipman. The majority of these deaths were followed by cremation. Before a cremation can be authorised, a second doctor must confirm the cause of death and the cremation documentation must be checked by a third doctor employed by the crematorium. These procedures are intended to provide a safeguard for the public against concealment of the fact that a person has been unlawfully killed. Yet, even with these procedures in place, Shipman was able to kill 215 people without detection. It is clear that, in reality, those procedures provided no safeguard at all.

Shipman's patients frequently died suddenly at home, without any previous history of terminal or life-threatening illness. In these cases, such deaths should be reported to the coroner. Yet Shipman managed to avoid a referral to the coroner in all but a few cases of those who he had killed. He did this by claiming to be able to diagnose, and therefore, to certify the cause of death, and by persuading relatives that there was no need for a post-mortem examination. In Phase Two of the Inquiry, consideration was given to measures which can be taken to ensure that all unexpected or unexplained deaths are reported, and their cause properly investigated. After Shipman's convictions for drug offences in 1976, he declared his intention not to carry controlled drugs again and as a result, he was not obliged to hold a controlled drugs register. Despite this, he was able, by a number of methods, to obtain large quantities of controlled drugs. As late as 1996, he prescribed and obtained over 12,000 mgs of diamorphine on one single occasion, purporting to be for a dying patient. This was enough to kill about 300 people. Despite the fact that the possession and supply of such drugs is said to be controlled, those controls did not prevent Shipman from acquiring large amounts of diamorphine without detection. How could that happen, and what measures should be taken to strengthen the system of controlling access to such drugs? Professor Baker observed in his Review, that one implication of the high number of patients killed by Shipman, is that an effective system of monitoring the death rates of patients of general practitioners would have detected the excess number of deaths. Regrettably, no such system was in place during Shipman's time in general practice.

Total Deaths Attributed to Shipman

Shipman was found guilty at his trial of the murder of 15 patients. The Inquiry considered a total of 888 deaths. Of these, there were 394 cases where there was compelling evidence that the patient had died of natural causes. This was confirmed by considering the evidence of every patient who died while Shipman was in practice. The remaining 494 cases were investigated. It was found that Shipman committed serious criminal offences throughout his professional career. From as early as 1974, he regularly obtained controlled drugs by illicit means. He first killed a patient, Mrs Eva Lyons in March 1975 who had terminal cancer, by giving her a lethal overdose to hasten her death. In the 24 years during which Shipman practised, it was found that, in addition to the 15 patients of whose murders he was convicted, he killed another 200 patients. In another 45 cases, there was suspicions that he might have killed the patient.

System Failures

It was deeply disturbing that Shipman's killing of his patients did not arouse suspicion for so many years. The systems that should have safeguarded his patients or at the very least detected misconduct when it occurred, failed to operate efficiently. However, the esteem in which Shipman was held ensured that very few relatives felt any real sense of disquiet about the circumstances surrounding their relatives' deaths. It was not until March 1998 that another fellow professional felt sufficiently concerned to make a report to the coroner. Unfortunately, Dr Linda Reynold's report of the 24th March 1998 came to nothing. In effect, if it had not been for Shipman's incompetent forgery of Mrs Grundy's will, it is unlikely that his crimes would ever have been detected. It is of great significance that the majority of the deaths for which Shipman was responsible, were followed by cremation., resulting in Shipman being able to kill 215 people without arousing any suspicion.

Shipman's Time at Pontefract General Infirmary

Shipman was at Pontefract General Infirmary from the 1st August 1970 until the 28th February 1974. commencing as a junior doctor then progressing through to a Senior House Officer (SHO). It was the practice for junior doctors to rotate between posts in different specialities within the hospital. Usually, each placement was for a period of six months. Professor Baker in his Review of Shipman's career examined the number of Medical Certificates of Cause of Death (MCCDs) completed by Shipman and by other doctors on the two adult medical wards at Pontefract Infirmary.

Shipman issued a total of 99 MCCDs in respect of deaths occurring at PGI, 23 for the period from February to July 1971 when he was a House Officer (HO) and 76 between February and July 1972 when he was a Senior House Officer (SHO). During his other placements which covered a period of 31 months in total, he certified the cause of death in 28 cases at PGI.

At this point, the proportions of male and female deaths were not significantly different from that certified by other doctors. For the period from August 1970 to January 1971 whilst Shipman was a Pre-Registration House Officer on the surgical wards at PGI he gave no cause for concern. He signed 14 MCCDs, where most of the patients had undergone surgery and were seriously ill immediately before their deaths. Shipman was not fully qualified and would therefore have been under close supervision by the more senior medical staff, and to a lesser extent, by the nursing staff. Professor Baker's analysis did not detect any abnormalities during this period, so it is very unlikely that Shipman did anything unlawful during this period of time. During the following six month period from February to July 1971, Shipman signed 24 MCCDs all except one relating to deaths of patients at PGI. Incidentally, he was working on those wards in which most deaths in the hospital occurred. This was usual and inevitable because the patients on the medical wards were often old and very ill.

It is of significance that Shipman did not sign any MCCDs during July of that year when it was very likely he was on holiday. However, what is of more significance is that during this period, there is some evidence of imbalance in the times at which the deaths occurred. In general, one would expect about three or four natural deaths to occur in each six-hour period of the day. However, the fact that 6 of the 11 deaths for which Shipman completed the MCCDs, occurred in the period between 6 pm and midnight, with none of these 11 occurring between midnight and 6 am, appears strange. This fact does suggest a possibility that, during the evening, Shipman might have hastened the deaths of one or two patients who would otherwise have been expected to die during the early hours of the morning. During the period from August 1971 to January 1972, Shipman was Senior House Officer (SHO) on the Paediatric Wards at PGI. During this six-month period, he signed 5 MCCDs of which four related to the deaths of young babies. There was reason to believe that these deaths were unnatural and no reason to suspect otherwise. From February to July 1972, Shipman was SHO back on the medical wards and this is the period of time which gave rise to the greatest concern regarding Shipman's activities. Consideration was given to 81 deaths that occurred during this period, of which 79 of those deaths were certified by Shipman. A total of 76 deaths certified by Shipman occurred on the medical wards and 3 elsewhere at PGI. Of those 76 deaths that took place on the medical wards, only 24 cases were considered to be natural.

In 12 cases there was suspicion that Shipman may have been involved in the death. In another 3 cases there was a strong suspicion about Shipman's actions, and in another 3 cases, it was concluded that Shipman probably did kill the patient. Concerns arose in respect of this six-month period because of the unusual distribution of the times at which the deaths took place. The time of death can be reliably established only from the cremation certificates and medical records. There is no reason to suppose that Shipman would lie about the time of death, and where medical records exist, they confirm the time of death given by Shipman on Cremation Form B. Shipman completed 40 Form Bs during this period. One of the 40 related to a death at a residential home which Shipman certified while working as a locum for the patient's GP. Of the remaining 39 deaths, 17 took place between the hours of 6 pm and midnight. Only three took place in the early hours of the morning, between midnight and 6 am. This imbalance suggest that Shipman might have been hastening the deaths of patients who would otherwise have died within a few hours.

Particular suspicion arose in respect of deaths occurring between 8 pm and midnight. Visiting time at PGI was from 7 pm until 8 pm. From 8 pm until around 9 pm, the nurses would be very busy settling the patients down for the night. There would be a period of changeover to the night staff. Following this, there would be fewer nursing staff on duty. After 8 pm it would be fairly unusual for a doctor to be on the ward unless he or she had been sent for, although some doctors would check on their patients in the evening and others would spend time with the nursing staff. There is some evidence that Shipman was sometimes seen on the ward after this time, although his presence was attributed to his hard-working and caring nature. However, it has now become clear that, in later life, Shipman cultivated a reputation for being hard-working and caring as a guise for his unlawful activities. It cannot be ignored that it is possible that he was already doing just that during this time at PGI. Another relevant factor to consider is that during this period, Shipman was in effect, running the wards, even though he was still only a SHO. However, his presence on the wards in the evening would not arouse surprise. Since he was trusted and highly regarded as a doctor, it would not be surprising that the nurses would be prepared to leave him alone with a patient if he suggested that. With being in charge of the ward this enabled Shipman to decide which patients should be accommodated in cubicles and which on main wards. This suggests that his position and habits made it easy for him to be alone at the bedside of a patient during the late evening. This provided him with the opportunity to give a patient something to hasten his or her death if he chose to do so.

Three Unlawful Killings

All three deaths for which Shipman was responsible took place in the late evening. Mr Thomas Cullumbine who died on the 12th April 1972, was suffering from chronic bronchitis and emphysema. Despite him being only 54-years-old, his state of health was such that he did not have long to live. It was concluded that Shipman was alone with this patient in the late evening and that he probably administered 10 mg of morphine which Shipman would have known to be dangerous for a patient with severely impaired lung function. The second death was that of Mr John Brewster who died at about 8.55 pm on the 28th April 1972. he had suffered a heart attack on the day he died and was at considerable risk of another attack which could prove fatal. It was concluded that Shipman probably killed him from the evidence of the medical records and cremation forms which were available. Members of Mr Brewster's family were with him until about 6 pm on the day of his death, and they left him conscious and comfortable. The medical notes do not record any deterioration in his condition, only his death. However, cremation Form B which was completed by Shipman stated that Mr Brewster was in a coma for 40 to 50 minutes prior to his death, and that Shipman was with him for at least part of that time, which were not recorded in the medical notes. Cremation Form B also recorded that Shipman was present, apparently alone, with Mr Brewster at the moment of death. This is very unlikely if, in fact, Mr Brewster had been in a coma for 40 to 50 minutes. It is far more likely that a nurse would have stayed close by to keep an eye on him, and that Shipman would have left the bedside. Consequently, Cremation Form B presents an unlikely account of events, and certainly gives rise to suspicion that Shipman gave Mr Brewster something that caused his death and staying at his bedside while it happened.

It is not clear what the drug would have been, but it may possible have been potassium which, if injected in sufficient concentration, will cause cardiac arrest and death very rapidly. Suspicion in the case of Mr Brewster arose because Shipman had recorded in the medical notes that there was no requirement to report this death to the coroner, whilst in reality, there was indeed such a need. Mr Brewster had been in hospital for only about eight or nine hours prior to his death, yet Shipman avoided referring this case to the coroner. Suspicions were further raised because Shipman's letter to Mr Brewster's GP written after Mr Brewster's death contained a lie. Mr Brewster's GP had seen him at midday on the day of his death and had in fact arranged for his admission to hospital. Shipman also informed the GP that Mr Brewster's condition had deteriorated on the way to hospital, yet there is no evidence that this had, in fact, occurred. It is more likely that Shipman told the GP that the patient had deteriorated in order to explain what might otherwise have been an unexpected death.

The third death which it was concluded was caused by Shipman, was that of Mr James Rhodes, who died during the evening of the 22nd of May 1972. Mr Rhodes had almost certainly had a heart attack shortly before his admission in the early hours of the morning on the day of his death. It is quite possible that he may have had another attack shortly after his admission, and was, consequently, at risk of having another attack which might prove fatal. It was quite possible that this was in fact, a natural death but because of the prevailing circumstances around the time of death, it was concluded to be highly suspicious. Mr Rhodes was seen by members of his family about three hours before his death, and he was conscious and comfortable. It appears from the Cremation Form B that Mr Rhodes fell into a coma about 20 to 30 minutes before his death, and that Shipman was aware of this fact from his own observations. This certainly implies that Shipman was with Mr Rhodes during the time, yet no entry was made in the medical notes. It also appears that he did not call a nurse which was the normal practice. Consequently, the nursing records contain no note of this vital change is Mr Rhodes's condition. Shipman claimed on Cremation Form B that Mr Rhodes was found dead by the nurses at 9.25 pm. It is far more likely that Shipman was with Mr Rhodes at about 9 pm but chose not to make an entry in the records or to summon a nurse because he was, in effect, administering to Mr Rhodes, something which caused his death. He might then have left Mr Rhodes' body to be discovered by a nurse.

Further Suspicions

In addition to the three cases in which it was found that Shipman probably killed the patient, there are in this same period, three other deaths which remain suspicious and thirteen that gave rise to some suspicion. All these deaths occurred in the three month period between the 29th February and the 1st of June 1972. After Shipman's return to the medical wards, his conduct appeared to change considerably. The death of Mrs Macfarlane on the 29th February 1972 was the first in this period which raised concerns. Shipman prescribed an excessive dose of Valium for Mrs Macfarlane. She was given this dose (either by Shipman himself or possible a nurse on his instructions) some hours before her death. Shipman's intentions cannot be ascertained, but there must have been the real possibility that he at least, was reckless as to the consequences of his actions.

During the following three months, there were a number of cases in which it was suspected that Shipman had deliberately killed the patient or administered a drug with reckless regard as to the outcome. It appeared that Shipman's best opportunities for killing arose during the evening when the wards were quiet with a reduced level of nursing staff on duty. There were some specific periods which caused particular concerns during the period from the 12th to the 14th of April 1972. Shipman certified the cause of three deaths. On the 14th April these three deaths occurred all on Ward 1, the female ward. Two of them occurred late at night around 10.30 pm Within three days, there were five more worrying deaths. Another smaller but nonetheless worrying cluster of deaths occurred on the 22nd May. Shipman certified four deaths on that day. The fact that attention was drawn to particular clusters of deaths did not imply that there was no suspicion about Shipman at other times during the three-month period, there were indeed suspicions. There were strong grounds to believe that Shipman embarked upon a course of conduct during this time which resulted in a significant number of premature deaths. There are common threads which ran through these suspicious cases that allowed general conclusions to be drawn. His most likely victims were patients who were very ill and whose death were imminent. It is thought that he killed patients in the late evening in order to avoid being called out in the middle of the night. The greatest suspicion occurred during a period of only three months. After the 1st June 1972, there were no suspicious deaths during Shipman's period on the medical wards. Between 9th June and the 26th, he was probably away from the wards for two weeks.

Mrs Sandra Whitehead, one of the nurses working on the medical wards in the Spring of 1972, raised concerns with the Inquiry in respect of happenings during the spring. Another two nurses gave evidence and recalled clusters of deaths on particular days during that period. From August 1972 to September 1973, Shipman was a Registrar in Paediatrics. During this time, Shipman certified the causes of death of seven babies and young children. Only one of these deaths gave cause for concern. This was the death of Susan (Susie) Garfitt. There were no medical records or cremation certificates available, and the decision about the death of this child was based entirely on the account given by Susie's mother. Susie suffered from cerebral palsy; she was quadriplegic and suffered from severe epilepsy. At the time of her last admission to hospital, she was suffering from a severe chest infection. Mrs Ann Garfitt described how a doctor (who was almost certainly Shipman) explained to her, in a gently and kindly way, how ill her daughter was and how poor her prognosis. He told Mrs Garfitt that it might be possible to keep Susie alive by the administration of strong medication.

Mrs Garfitt realised that Susie was dying and did not insist that she should be given the medication to prolong her life. She told Shipman to 'be kind' to Susie. She certainly did not give permission for Shipman to do anything to hasten Susie's death and did not understand Shipman to be telling her that death was imminent. She went away for a cup of tea and when she returned about ten minutes later, Susie was dead. That her death should have occurred so soon after the conversation between Shipman and Mrs Garfitt gave rise to a strong suspicion that Shipman did not simply withhold medication, but actively administered something that precipitated the death. During the period between September 1973 and February 1974, Shipman was a Senior House Officer (SHO) in Obstetrics and Gynaecology. This was the period immediately prior to his entry into general practice at the Abraham Ormerod Medical Centre in Todmorden. Some witnesses suggested that Pethidine was in general use as an analgesic on all wards at the Pontefract General Infirmary, whilst others insisted that and other drugs, particularly morphine and diamorphine were in more regular use on the medical and surgical wards.

Evidence suggests that the use of controlled drugs was very strictly regulated at PGI and it would not be easy for Shipman to obtain this drug for his own use. However, further evidence does suggest that, because pethidine was so frequently used during childbirth, it would have been much easier and quite practicable for Shipman to obtain supplies for himself during this final period in 1973 and 1974. In view of the rapidity with which Shipman began to obtain supplied illicitly on arrival in Todmorden, it can be concluded that in all probability, he commenced his abuse of pethidine during his last twelve months at Pontefract. It is quite likely that Shipman killed one or two patients while working on the medical wards in 1971 but exactly how many presents difficulty. However, the three patients, Mr Cullombine, Mr Brewster and Mr Rhodes have been correctly identified as victims of Shipman whilst working at Pontefract General Infirmary. Again, it is difficult to state categorically how Shipman killed patients at PGI. Controlled drugs were well-regulated and it would not have been easy for Shipman to obtain such drugs unless they were officially prescribed. It is believed that he used morphine to kill Mr Cullombine because he had prescribed morphine for him to be given if necessary. He claimed that he had not administered it, but the Inquiry was satisfied that he did, and he knew that the dose given (10 mgs) would be dangerous for a man with severely compromised respiratory function. The general impression that was formed while he was working at Pontefract, was that Shipman's most likely victims were patients who were very ill and were likely to die in the very near future in any event.

It is thought that in the early days, one of Shipman's motivations may well have been a desire to experiment with drugs. There is some evidence that he liked to 'test the boundaries' of certain forms of treatment. The Inquiry estimated that, while at Pontefract, Shipman probably caused the deaths of between ten and fifteen patients. In the light of reaching the conclusion that Shipman did begin killing patients while working at PGI, then it is necessary to reconsider those deaths that occurred at Todmorden about which suspicions were aroused. The fact that when he arrived in Todmorden, Shipman was an already established killer, this inevitably raises the level of suspicion about his activities there. Since the publication of the First Report, in which 215 deaths were identified for which Shipman was responsible, there have been speculations in the media about the total number for which he was responsible. It is very likely that some of the deaths which were suspicious may well have been unlawful killings. Professor Baker's statistical analysis suggested that the total number of unlawful killings was in the order of 236. Assuming then that 50% of the deaths regarded as 'suspicious' were in fact, unlawful killings, then the estimate for the Todmorden and Hyde years would come to about 237 or 238 as the most reliable estimate. If the estimated unlawful killings at Pontefract are added to this total, this would produce a figure of about 250 deaths. The Inquiry reached the overall conclusion that Shipman killed about 250 patients between 1971 and 1998, of whom 218 were positively identified.

Source: The Shipman Inquiry, Sixth Report (2005) (Crown Copyright)

The Police Investigation, March 1998

On the 31st January 2000, Harold Frederick Shipman was convicted of the murder of 15 patients and of the forging of the will of one of them. The trial was the culmination of an investigation which started in July 1998 into the death of his patient Mrs Kathleen Grundy. In fact, Shipman had been the subject of an earlier police investigation following concerns raised by the senior partner of the Brooke Practice in Hyde, Mrs Linda Reynolds. On the 24th March 1998, she reported to Mr John Pollard, HM Coroner for Greater Manchester South District, her concerns and those of her partners regarding the number of Shipman's patients who were dying, and the circumstances of their deaths. John Pollard requested a confidential investigation by the Greater Manchester Police (GMP). That investigation was conducted by Detective Inspector David Smith under the supervision of Chief Superintendent David Sykes. DI Smith concluded that there was no substance in Dr Reynold's concerns and his investigation concluded on 17th April 1998. After that time, Shipman killed three more patients before his final arrest. They were Mrs Winifred Mellor, Mrs Joan Melia and Mrs Grundy. Following Shipman's trial, there were concerns raised regarding the thoroughness of the first police investigation and, if it had been conducted differently, Shipman's course of killing could have been stopped and the deaths of his three victims prevented. During the course of hearings conducted between May and July 2002, the Inquiry conducted a detailed examination of the evidence relating to the March 1998 police investigation. What follows is a summarised account of this examination.

When Dr Reynolds made her report to the Coroner, she highlighted two particular grounds for her concerns. She informed him that she knew that Shipman had signed 16 cremation Forms B in the previous three months, whilst her own practice with a patient list of 9,500, had only 14 deaths during the same period. Shipman's patient list was only a third of that of the Brooke Practice. The significance of these factors was that, if Shipman's practice followed the usual pattern, those cremations which members of the Brooke Practice were aware of were likely to represent no more than approximately 21% at most of Shipman's total deaths during the relevant period. Given the fact that Shipman had a patient list approximately a third the size of that of the Brooke Practice, it is apparent that the disparity between the number of deaths of patients in Shipman's practice and that of the Brooke Practice was significantly large. It was this disparity which concerned Dr Reynolds and her partners.

The second cause for concern was the presence of certain features concerning the deaths, in that the deceased persons were elderly women who had been discovered dead at home, apparently alone and fully dressed. More surprisingly, they had not been ill, and it was Shipman himself who often found them. These features were unusual because it is more common for deaths to be more or less equally distributed between men and women. Also, most deaths at home occur after a period of illness where the patient is confined to bed and relatives and friends are in attendance. It is uncommon for a GP to be present at the death of a patient or to discover a patient dead. It appears that it was not only Dr Reynolds who had raised concerns, Mrs Deborah Bambroffe, a partner in the firm of Frank Massey and Son, Funeral Directors in Hyde, had also expressed concern to Dr Reynolds about the very same features regarding Shipman's deaths.

On receiving Dr Reynold's concerns, the Coroner communicated with Chief Superintendent Sykes (CS) and DI Smith (DI). He informed them that Dr Reynolds had expressed her concerns. The first was that Shipman was a caring doctor, who looked after his elderly and sick patients at home, rather than having them admitted to hospital and who visited them regularly when he knew them to be ill. The second was that he was in fact, killing his patients. DI Smith commenced his investigation by interviewing Dr Reynolds and during the four years which elapsed since the investigation and the Inquiry, he gave several accounts of that interview. In his earlier accounts, the Inquiry found that DI Smith sought to diminish the seriousness and even credibility of Dr Reynolds' concerns as she explained them to him. It was concluded that he did so in the hope of avoiding criticism in respect of his own conduct of the investigation. However, in his oral evidence to the Inquiry, DI Smith abandoned his previous attempts to diminish Dr Reynolds' concerns. Instead, he admitted for the first time Dr Reynolds had informed him early in their meeting that she thought Shipman was killing his patients, either through lack of care or by murdering them and, that if he was murdering them, he was doing it by giving them some type of drug. However, DI Smith denied that Dr Reynolds had told him that there were two bodies lying at the premises of the funeral directors, which would be available for autopsy. As a result of notes made in his own day-book and other contemporaneous evidence, it was concluded that Dr Reynolds did indeed give DI Smith that information. The bodies were those of Mrs Lilly Higgins and Miss Ada Warburton, both killed by Shipman. However, DI Smith failed to pursue with the Coroner, the possibility of autopsies on either or both of their bodies. It is very likely, if asked, that the Coroner would have agreed to that course of action.

Had the Coroner been made aware, either by DI Smith or Dr Reynolds of Dr Reynolds' belief that, if Shipman was killing his patients, he was doing it by administering a drug, the Coroner would have ordered an autopsy with toxicological examination, in which event the presence of morphine in either or both of the bodies would have been detected. Mrs Higgins was cremated on 25th March 1998, but Mrs Warburton's body was available for autopsy until her cremation on 30th March 1998. In the course of his interview with Dr Reynolds, DI Smith failed to ask many important questions. He did not discover the basis of her concerns about the disparity between the death rates of Shipman's practice and her own, nor did he ask to see the records from which the rates had been derived. He did not ask why the features of the deaths which Dr Reynolds had identified gave rise to concern. He did not seek to find out more about the circumstances of the individual deaths for which she had completed Forms C. He did not seek an explanation of the procedures for death and cremation certification, and he did not ask to meet Dr Reynolds' partners. As a consequence of these failures, DI Smith left the interview, uncertain about the basis for Dr Reynolds' concerns and, in particular, with no understanding of the potential of the comparative death rates about which Dr Reynolds and her partners were so concerned.

DI Smith then visited the Tameside register office and requested the Superintendent Registrar to provide him with copies of all the entries in the registers of deaths relating to deaths certified by Shipman over the previous six months. During that period, Shipman had certified 31 deaths. On 26th March, the Registrar handed to DI Smith a bundle of copy death certificates confirming that those were the number requested. However, DI Smith maintained that he was given significantly fewer certificates about 20 copies in all. If DI Smith was correct, the register office staff were at fault. If they were correct and DI Smith was given 31 certificates, he must then have lost 11 or 12 of them almost immediately and failed to locate them during the investigation. Because DI Smith did not understand the significance of the number of deaths or the comparative death rates reported by Dr Reynolds, he did not recognise that the number of copy certificates which he received from the register office (19 or 20, covering a period of six months) was incompatible with the number of cremation forms signed for Shipman's patients by members of the Brooke Practice (16 in three months). It is because of that lack of understanding and the fact that DI Smith attached no importance to the numbers or death rates, that it was concluded that the error made by the register office staff had no significant effect on DI Smith's conduct of the investigation.

DI Smith visited the Hyde office of the West Pennine Health Authority to seek access to the medical records of 17 of the 19 or 20 deceased persons for whom he had copy death certificates. Not having obtained the consent of the next of kin or personal representatives of the deceased, he was informed that he could not have access to the records. Instead, it was arranged that Dr Alan Banks, Assistant Director of Primary Care and Medical Adviser to the Health Authority, would examine the records for him, seeing that 14 of the 17 sets of records were available for examination. A 15th set became available at a later stage. The Inquiry concluded that the main task which Dr Banks believed he had to undertake was to ascertain whether the medical records confirmed or denied the presence in all the deaths of the pattern of 'common features' reported by DI Smith to the Authority. These common features were that the deaths were of elderly females, all had been found at their homes by Shipman who had apparently called on them unannounced, all had been found during the day and in their day clothes and all had been certified as having died from stroke or heart disease. Dr Banks also looked to see if the causes of death, as disclosed by the records, were generally compatible with the medical histories. Dr Banks claimed that he did not realise that the concern being investigated by the police was that Shipman might be killing his patients. The Inquiry did not accept that claim. It found that he must have known that the underlying concern was that Shipman was killing patients, either deliberately or by gross negligence. Dr Banks found this suggestion so incredible that it is doubted that he ever contemplated it as a real possibility.

Dr Banks examined the medical records on 26th-27th March 1998 and compiled a chart on which he sought to display the presence or absence of the common features which had been identified to him. On 1st April 1998, he met DI Smith to discuss the results of the examination. At that meeting Dr Banks told DI Smith that there were two or 'a few' deaths in which he considered there was insufficient information in the medical records to enable a proper diagnosis of the cause of death to be established. He told DI Smith that he himself would have referred those deaths to the Coroner. It was the view of the Inquiry that Dr Banks failed when examining the medical records, to recognise features within them which tended to support those concerns that had been identified to him. He did not recognise as unusual the fact that 13 out of 14 deaths for which he initially examined records were of female patients. Not withstanding the fact that he noted on his chart that Shipman had been present around the time of death in ten out of the 14 cases, he did not draw that to DI Smith's attention. It also does not appear that he noticed that Shipman had visited seven of the patients not long before the death was discovered.

The medical records did not disclose any serious concern about the patients' condition, yet within a short time, the patient had been found dead. Dr Banks did not seem to have noticed that 12 out of the 14 deaths occurred at the patients' homes, with only two in residential or nursing homes. It was concluded that Dr Bank's prior knowledge of, and respect for, Shipman 'clouded his judgement' and as such made him an unsuitable person to carry out the task of examining the medical records 'impartially'. He obviously approached the records on the basis that all would be normal, therefore his search for 'common features' was superficial. When he realised that not every feature of concern was present in the circumstances of all the deaths, Dr Banks erroneously concluded that there was no 'pattern' to be found. He failed to recognise the unusual features which characterised many of the deaths. If he did notice anything which struck him as odd, he immediately found an innocent explanation for it. He approached his examination of the records with a pre-conceived belief that there would be no cause for concern and was influenced by 'confirmation bias'. He failed to appreciate the potential significance of the fact that Shipman was not referring deaths to the Coroner which he himself believed should have been referred.

The Inquiry accepted that Dr Banks was not given all the information he could and should have been given. He was not told about the comparative death rates of the Brooke Practice and Shipman's practice. If he had been in possession of these important facts, his approach might have been more objective. If DI Smith had received all 31 copies of the death certificates from the register office and Dr Banks had been aware of most or all of them, the chance that he would have realised that the death rate among Shipman's patients was abnormal would have been certainly increased. The additional records which would have been available for Dr Banks to examine contained a number of unusual features which tended to support the concerns raised. DI Smith was reassured by what Dr Banks told him and this effectively marked the end of the investigation. On 1st April 1998, DI Smith visited the Duckinfield crematorium but failed to ask any questions about the system of cremation certification. He failed to discover the fact that the crematorium held a bundle of certificates for each cremation which contained information supplied by the certifying (Form B) doctor about the circumstances of death. He also failed to look at the cremation register. Had he done so; he would have found that the name of the certifying doctor appeared in the record of each death. If he had looked back over the previous six months, he would have found entries for the 11 deaths of which he was at that time unaware. Because he asked no questions about cremation procedures, he also remained unaware of the existence and role of the crematorium medical referee. He lost the opportunity to inter view Dr Betty Hinchcliffe, the Medical Referee at the crematorium.

DI Smith discussed the investigation with Chief Superintendent Sykes, and it was agreed that it should be closed. There was no detailed discussion of the evidence collected by DI Smith and he submitted no written report. In effect, CS Sykes delegated the decision to close the investigation to DI Smith. During the course of the investigation, DI Smith had made no check on the Police National Computer (PNC) to ascertain whether or not Shipman had any previous convictions. He said that he had forgotten to do so. The Inquiry doubted that he forgot and thought it more likely that he thought his search of the Greater Manchester Police Integrated Computer System would suffice, because a person like Shipman would not have any criminal convictions. Had he enquired, he would have discovered that Shipman had previous convictions for drug offences involving dishonesty, committed in the early 1970s. DI Smith claimed that, even had he known about Shipman's criminal record, it would not have affected his view of Shipman.

The Inquiry did not accept that assertion. The knowledge that Shipman had past drug convictions would not immediately have led to the conclusion that he was killing his patients. However, when considered together with Dr Reynolds' suggestion that Shipman might be killing his patients by giving them some sort of drug, knowledge of his conviction would have raised the index of suspicion of any reasonable police officer. On 16th April 1998, DI Smith visited Dr Reynolds and told her that he had found no evidence to confirm her suspicions and had stressed to her the apparent lack of motive. Dr Reynolds was disappointed at DI Smiths emphasis on this aspect of the enquiry because she was concerned, not about motive, but about the obvious disparity in death rates between the two practices. DI Smith could not give any explanation for that disparity because he was not in any position to do so.

On 17th April 1998, DI Smith spoke to Mr Pollard and mentioned the fact that he had had medical records examined, two sets of which had been 'questioned' but there had been nothing that 'gave any indication of any criminal acts'. He had also 'inspected' the 'cremation records' of 20 people and spoken to the female undertaker. He informed Mr Pollard that Shipman tried to get all his patients out of hospital and visit them without prior appointment. Mr Pollard accepted what was said and did not question whether the explanation given by DI Smith could satisfactorily account for the obvious disparity between the death rates. Furthermore, he did not take any further steps to discover whether Dr Reynolds was satisfied with the result of the investigation. He totally accepted that the police enquiry had revealed nothing of concern and consequently, put the whole matter out of his mind. This effectively ended the March 1998 police investigation.

Conclusions of the First Police Investigation

Chief Superintendent David Sykes

The Inquiry was told that DI Smith, although an experienced detective, was not accustomed to working without direction and supervision. CS Sykes should have known this or, if he did not, he should have discovered it. He should have instructed a suitably experienced detective to undertake this unusual and potentially serious investigation. He should have realised also that he himself did not have the necessary experience to direct and supervise the investigation. He should have consulted Detective Superintendent Bernard Postles (now Detective Chief Superintendent Postles) who would have advised as to the appropriate level of seniority to which the concerns should be reported. If that had been done, a properly directed investigation would have taken place. Once the investigation was under way, CS Sykes failed to recognise that DI Smith was out of his depth. He failed to discuss the issues with DI Smith in any detail. If he had done so, he would have realised the extent of DI Smith's lack of understanding. He should not have left it to DI Smith to decide whether and when the investigation was to close. If, even at that stage, he had asked a senior detective to scrutinise the information that DI Smith had gathered, the outcome would have been different.

Detective Inspector Smith

DI Smith himself made many mistakes in the course of the investigation. Some of those were the result of his lack of experience of criminal investigations of a non-routine nature. Consequently, he was wrong to continue with his investigation, pretending that he knew what he was doing when, as he admitted in evidence, he did not know 'where to go'. He should have sought the advice of a senior detective. As a result of his failure to seek advice, he never understood the issues, did not have a plan of action, had no one to assist him analyse the information he received, had no one to make suggestions as to the information he should seek from the available witnesses and was allowed to close the investigation before it was complete. He should have had, without needing to ask for it, the benefit of supervision by a senior detective. In addition, he was not assisted by the poor advice which he received from Dr Banks, nor by the failure on the part of Tameside register office to provide him with a complete bundle of copy death certificates.

Although the Inquiry did not consider that DI Smith was primarily responsible for the failure of the investigation, his inaction contributed directly to the adverse result. There was a failure to collect detailed information from Dr Reynolds and his failure to report to the Coroner the fact that the bodies of Mrs Lily Higgins and Miss Ada Warburton were available for autopsy if the Coroner thought them fit. In addition, DI Smith's lack of frankness about his part in the investigation merits strong criticism. In the various accounts of his investigation given to the police, he consistently sought to attribute its failure to the fault of others. He told lies in those accounts and repeated some of those lies in statements made to the Inquiry. In oral evidence, he told the truth about some matters for which he deserves credit. However, he has continued to lie about the circumstances in which he learned of the death of Miss Warburton. He did so in an attempt to evade responsibility for his failure to arrange an autopsy on her body.

Dr Alan Banks

It was the view of the Inquiry, that Dr Banks should bear some responsibility for the failure of the investigation although his contribution was substantially less than that of CS Sykes and DI Smith. His examination of the medical records was inadequate and also his inability to open his mind to even the remote possibility that Shipman might have killed his patients or even given them substandard care. His mindset would have been excusable if he had been unaware of the reason why the police were making enquiries because a concern had arisen that Shipman might be killing his patients. It was accepted that Dr Bank's knowledge of, and respect for Shipman made it more difficult for him to have an open mind. The 'credibility gap' does amount to mitigation for Dr Bank's failures, but it cannot provide an excuse in the case of a professional man asked for his professional opinion.

Had CS Sykes put the investigation in the hands of a more senior detective, one with experience of devising and supervising a criminal investigation, and if that person had acted with reasonable expedition, the whole course of the investigation would, in the opinion of the Inquiry, have been very different. It is likely that the opportunity would have been taken to conduct an autopsy, with toxicological tests, on the body of Miss Warburton or of Mrs Martha Marley, of whose death on 24th March 1998 DI Smith remained ignorant throughout the investigation Had that been undertaken, morphine would have been found, an inquest ordered and Shipman would have realised that he was under suspicion. It is very unlikely that he would have killed any more patients after that.

Even if the opportunity for an autopsy had been lost, in due course suspicions would have been such that the police would have applied for an exhumation and autopsy, with toxicological tests. It is also possible that by that time, concerns would have been raised about the death of Mrs Bianka Pomfret, and that her body would have been exhumed, and morphine found. If the police and the Coroner had moved with reasonable expedition, the lives of Shipman's last three victims would probably have been saved. If CS Sykes had initially instructed DI Smith to carry out the investigation but had subsequently discovered that he was 'out of his depth', then it is more difficult to say what the probable outcome would have been. This would depend to a large extent on how much time had elapsed before the discover was made and the investigation was put into the hands of a more senior detective. Plainly, the later the change of officer in charge of the investigation, the poorer the chance that Shipman would have been stopped before killing again.

The Role of the Greater Manchester Police (GMP)

At an early stage in the later police investigation into the death of Mrs Kathleen Grundy, it was discovered that there was no written report regarding the March 1998 investigation. DI Smith submitted two written reports, setting out details of the investigation. Following an examination of these reports, the Inquiry found that he sought to diminish the seriousness of Dr Reynolds' original concerns and to suggest that Dr Banks had raised no concerns regarding his examination of the medical records. It was quite clear that DI Smith was seeking to deflect possible criticism of his own conduct of the investigation. By the end of 1998, the GMP had good reason to suspect Shipman of being a serial killer, which the first police investigation had failed to detect. The potential for criticism of the Force was recognised. However, on the basis of DI Smith's report alone, senior officers in the GMP concluded that the March 1998 investigation had been 'appropriate at the time'. Immediately following Shipman's conviction, it was announced that there would be an Inquiry into the Shipman case, to include the first failed police investigation. In preparation for the Inquiry, Detective Superintendent (Det Supt) Peter Ellis was instructed to prepare a 'comprehensive document' recording as accurately as possible, a detailed account of the March 1998 investigation. The document was prepared following interviews with CS Sykes and DI Smith. The subsequent account given by DI Smith to Det Supt Ellis was different in a number of respects from his oral evidence given to the Shipman Inquiry.

Most significantly, he told Det Supt Ellis that Dr Reynolds had at no time said that she suspected that Shipman was killing his patients, which was in direct contrast to the oral evidence he gave to the Inquiry. The account given to Det Supt Ellis, was similar in context to DI Smith's previous reports tending to minimise the seriousness of the concerns raised and, in effect, excusing DI Smith's failure to find evidence which would substantiate the concerns raised. Having recorded DI Smith's account of the investigation, Det Supt Ellis proceeded to compile a series of 'observations' which had the overall effect of exculpating DI Smith. He excused DI Smith's failure to ascertain whether Shipman had previous convictions, he criticised Dr Reynolds and Mrs Bambroffe in a number of respects, he emphasised the limitations placed on the investigation by the constraints of confidentiality. In essence, his conclusions totally supported those views previously expressed by the senior command in GMP, namely that the investigation was 'appropriate at the time' His only hint of criticism was of DI Smith's failure to keep records of his enquiries, but mitigated this suggesting that written records might have been kept if any evidence supporting the suspicions came to light.

Det Supt Ellis should have not been given the task of preparing the report, this should have been undertaken by a more senior officer. He was not in a position to investigate the actions of CS Sykes nor form a judgement regarding his supervision of the investigation. He was certainly influenced by the well-known views of the senior officer in the Force. Notwithstanding, Det Supt Ellis's report was accepted by senior officers, who still maintained the view that DI Smith's investigation had been 'as thorough as possible'. It is hardly surprising that after the report had been submitted to the Shipman Inquiry, subsequent witness statements by officers of the GMP reflected the same view. On the first day of the Inquiry hearings of evidence relating to the March 1998 police investigation, GMP conceded that the investigation had been seriously 'flawed' in a number of respects. This conclusion was prompted by a review of the investigation being undertaken by Detective Chief Superintendent (DCS) Peter Stelfox. This review constituted a careful, detailed and objective analysis of the evidence relating to this first investigation. It is highly relevant to note that DCS Stelfox was deeply critical of DI Smith in regard to his conduct of the investigation, and equally of CS Sykes for his failure to properly direct and supervise it. It was the view of the Inquiry Chairman, Dame Janet Smith, that GMP should not have waited until 2002 to undertake a searching enquiry into the failure of the first investigation, but it should have been carried out in late 1998 or early 1999.

Instead, over a period of three years and more, they

accepted DI Smith's own account and subjected it to no critical analysis whatsoever. On discovering that DI Smith had not made any proper record of an investigation that was, in effect, known to have failed, then continued unquestioning confidence in his veracity should not have been maintained. Had it not been for the Shipman Inquiry, it is very doubtful that GMP would have made any more thorough enquiry into the matter than that carried out by Det Supt Ellis. However, full credit should be given to DCS Stelfox for his 'balanced' and 'objective' conclusions based on a through re-investigation of all the factors involved.

Source: *The Shipman Inquiry: Second Report (2003), pp. 1-11 (Crown Copyright)*

What Did Primrose Shipman Know?

On Friday 16 November 2001, Primrose Shipman, wife of Harold Shipman was subpoenaed to appear before the Shipman Inquiry. Up to that point, Mrs Shipman had refused any interviews with the police over three years since Shipman's arrest. She had hoped to be able to give her evidence over a video link. Her lawyers told the Inquiry that she was 'uniquely terrified of appearance before the public and the press'. Her counsel, Mr Jim Sturman submitted that 'ever since her husband's arrest, Mrs Shipman has been intimidated by the media. She feels the pressure she is under will be reflected in her evidence and the quality of her evidence. Within the context of this case, she is by far the most vulnerable witness'. However, Caroline Swift QC, Counsel for the Inquiry argued that allowing Mrs Shipman to testify in private would be unfair on other vulnerable nervous witnesses. Dame Janet Smith who is chairing the Inquiry, said, 'She will be treated with courtesy and consideration. She is not suspected of any criminal activities or any conduct for which she might be criticised. This Inquiry is looking at the activities of her husband and not her'.

Questioned by Mr Andrew Spink, Counsel for the families of Shipman's patients, confirmed that she remains convinced of his innocence. She was being questioned on three cases which evidence suggested that she should have knowledge about. She was allegedly present in a room when 52-year-old Mrs Elaine Oswald was resuscitated by Shipman 27 years ago, when he was practising in Todmorden, West Yorkshire. Mrs Oswald may be the only patient to have survived an attempted murder by Shipman. She had visited the Abraham Ormerod

Medical Centre in Todmorden after several days of pain down her left side which she feared was appendicitis.

Shipman diagnosed kidney stones and prescribed her the painkiller Diconal, telling her to take two tablets before going to bed and he would visit her later that day. However, Mrs Oswald first went shopping and to the library and by the time Shipman arrived at her home it was about 11.30 am. She had only just taken the tablets and gone to bed. She said that she was vaguely aware of Shipman preparing a needle for her right arm before she fell unconscious. She awoke on the bedroom floor at the foot of her bed to find Shipman, his wife, their young son and two ambulance men in her room. She could remember people slapping my face and telling me not to go to sleep. After a few days in hospital, Mrs Oswald returned to her house to find Shipman tentative to her in the extreme. Within days, she and her husband were even being entertained to supper by the Shipmans. The supper conversation about her illness was dominated by Shipman insisting she was acutely allergic to an opiate-based painkiller he had prescribed, and that he subsequently saved her with the 'kiss of life'. Tests taken during her confinement in hospital revealed no trace of kidney stones. Caroline Swift QC stated that Shipman was a pethidine addict and may have used Mrs Oswald to test the consequences of opiate abuse, rather than kill her. The death of a previously healthy 25-year-old would have attracted considerable publicity and been subject to a post-mortem. When questioned about the particular incident, Mrs Shipman was unable to provide any information or knowledge of the event.

She was also called by her husband into the houses of Mrs Joyce Woodhead and Mrs Irene Chapman to comfort relatives around the time of their deaths in 1997 and 1998. The death of Mrs Chapman, a 74-year-old widow on 7 March 1998, provided more evidence than the other two cases but Mrs Shipman could account for none of it. During the morning of Mrs Chapman's death, Mrs Shipman had been receptionist at Shipman's Market Street surgery, and the log she made of Mrs Chapman's telephone call with complaints of 'chest pains' was put at 8.45 am. Shipman visited Mrs Chapman during the morning before returning with his wife following the morning surgery. Mrs Shipman recalled waiting in the car until Shipman asked her inside to deal with Mrs Chapman's relatives, while he returned to the surgery to 'pick up medical records'. This was an exceptionally unusual request because Shipman hardly ever invited his wife into patient's homes, and she had not been present after the death of a patient. However, she could not remember anything of her time at Mrs Chapman's home. Shipman had left her to greet Mrs Chapman's bereaved relative Roy Saxton, but she was given no explanation of the death as far as she could remember. However, Mr Saxton's evidence contradicted her. He insisted that Mrs Shipman had told him 'coronary thrombosis' was the cause of death and that they had, in fact, spent about half an hour near the body before Shipman eventually returned.

However, Mrs Shipman insisted that Mrs Chapman was dead before she had gone into the house. She was confronted with the only tangible evidence that her story was contradicting her husband who had refused to speak to the Inquiry about it and the other 400 cases. In addition, the cremation certificate Shipman signed stated that Mrs Shipman was present at the time of Mrs Chapman's death. However, Mrs Shipman reiterated that as far as she could remember, Mrs Chapman was dead when she went into the house. The Inquiry heard how two wedding rings being kept by Mrs Chapman for her daughter, Dorina, and prospective son-in-law vanished on the same day as her death. Mrs Shipman had refused to answer questions about Mrs Chapman's death put to her by the Inquiry's solicitors, contending that she had valid legal objections. She was also present at the death of another Hyde patient Mrs Joyce Woodhead and also present when Elaine Oswald was resuscitated by Shipman.

Though Greater Manchester Police were unlikely to arrest Mrs Shipman, the force did indicate that such a move remained a possibility if she incriminated herself. Despite Dame Janet's insistence that 'she is not suspected of any criminal activities or any conduct for which she might be criticised' this is not how the British public regarded Primrose Shipman. There was something 'intangible' that attached to her, for the wives of serial killers have pariah status, and this was how she was described in the press. 'She must have known' was the unspoken accusation circulating at the time. Primrose always played the subordinate role, putting her husband before her own parents. She stayed loyal through his arrest, trial for murder, and she visited him in jail every day whilst on remand and turned up at the trial. According to Paul Vallely, 'She had never sought to challenge the intellectual superiority on which Shipman prided himself'. By comparison with his medical peers, his was a pretty mediocre ability. There was also an emotional domination too. Shipman was also something of a bully with irrational mood swings which he took out on staff at work and on Primrose and the children. Surgery staff remember Shipman being very hard on his youngest sons. His eldest daughter, Sarah, could not tolerate his bullying and left home as soon as she could. Primrose's instincts fed Shipman's fantasies of control by doing exactly what she was told, and yet she went on to mask some of Shipman's traits. From the first time that detectives called at Shipman's surgery in 1998 as they began to investigate the scarcely credible allegations against her husband, Primrose Shipman had refused to say a word. She stayed silent in the face of police's inquiries and refused to speak to the press. In two years, she had uttered only two words publicly, 'No Comment'.

Source: 'What Primrose Knew' by Paul Vallely – The Independent Friday Review, 16 November, 2001

Media Coverage of the Shipman Case and Inquiry

'Shipman Unlikely to Face More Charges'

'It appeared increasingly unlikely yesterday that convicted serial murderer Harold Shipman will be charged with killing a further 23 of his patients. Greater Manchester Police have consulted the families of 23 women, aged between 54 and 82 and all cremated, before reaching a decision on whether to charge Shipman with their murders. Police said 'the considerable majority' of families did not expect it to be possible for Harold Shipman to face a further trial. The families' views have been passed to the Crown Prosecution Service which is now expected to reveal within days whether charges will be brought. The CPS said it had not yet reached that decision ('We appreciate the concerns and anxieties among relatives, and we hope to reach a decision soon'). But considerable legal difficulties are understood to be hindering any chance of a prosecution. Publicity relating to Shipman's four-month trial and subsequent conviction earlier this month, is understood to be the biggest impediment, making the chances of establishing a fair trial for the 54-year-old former GP extremely remote'.

The Independent: 17th February 2000 – Ian Herbert, Northern Correspondent

'No More Charges for Shipman Says DPP'

'The relatives of 23 women whom Harold Shipman is suspected of murdering voiced dismay yesterday as the Director of Public Prosecutions (DPP) announced that the GP would not face further charges. David Calvert-Smith QC said that Shipman, 54, could not be fairly tried again because of the 'enormous publicity' surrounding his trial and conviction on 15 counts of murder.

'There is sufficient evidence, but I have reluctantly concluded that it would be wrong to proceed to a second, and possibly a third trial, in respect of 23 further alleged murders. This is a quite exceptional course I have taken.'

Police investigated 175 suspicious deaths among the Hyde GP's patients. The 23, all women aged between 54 and 82, comprised a 'B' list of patients whom police suspected the doctor of killing. All were cremated. Although many relatives had anticipated the decision, they were dismayed. The decision overruled recommendations from Greater Manchester Police detectives who investigated the case.

The force was 'of the firm opinion' that there was sufficient evidence to charge Shipman. Police hoped Shipman would be committed to the Crown Court, where a judge would either have ruled that the charges be allowed to stay on file or that they be dismissed because of the impossibility of a fair trial. The police have now been formally advised by the DPP not to bring the further charges. Mr Calvert-Smith said he had taken into account that the first trial had to be limited to 15 charges of murder so that the jury was not overburdened. There was nothing the law could do to increase Shipman's sentence. He added that consideration of other deaths would now be a matter for the coroner. A man who survived a potentially lethal overdose administered by Harold Shipman will seek £200,000 compensation next week.'

The Independent: 19th February 2000 – Ian Herbert, Northern Correspondent

A Mass-Murderer is Unmasked in Meticulous Detail

'The opening page of Professor Richard Baker's 145-page report on the Shipman killings carries a quotation from the Hippocratic Oath: 'I will use my power to help the sick to the best of my ability and judgement; I will abstain from harming or wrongdoing anyone by it. I will not give a fatal draught to anyone if I am asked, nor will I suggest any such thing'. No doctor in history has so comprehensively breached those moral principles and been found out. But found out Shipman has been, by meticulous academic detective work. Professor Baker's report is rigorous, painstaking and a model of the statistician's craft. It identifies as accurately as is likely to be possible, the full scale of Shipman's crimes. The total is 297 'excess' deaths over 24 years compared with the death rate at other general practices in the area.

Based on his examination of Shipman's clinical records, Professor Baker believes that the true excess is likely to be closer to 236. More than half of all those patients, whose deaths Shipman certified may have died by his own hand. Professor Baker said at yesterday's packed press conference to launch his report: 'I have a quite dreadful story to tell you. I am conscious that these findings are going to be distressing to the families of Shipman's victims, but I hope presenting the facts will be helpful in coming to terms with what happened'. He added: 'You won't find much about the shocking nature of the findings in the report. One of the most difficult things has been finding words to express what all this means and how to react to it'.

His report is based on death and cremation certificates, medical records, and controlled drug registers. Professor Baker compared Shipman's practice with that of four other GPs in Todmorden, West Yorkshire, and six in Hyde, Greater Manchester, where Shipman practised. The result is a jigsaw of pieces of evidence, some missing but from which a clear picture emerges of a cunning, devious killer. Professor Baker focussed on six aspects of Shipman's practice. These were the excess of observed deaths over those expected, when compared with other local GPs. Shipman issued 521 death certificates during his 24 years as a GP, 499 of them while he worked in Hyde. The highest number issues by a Hyde GP over the same period was 210. The excess was greatest among elderly women of 75 or older, but a number of men died in suspicious circumstances too.

Deaths clustered at particular times: death came to most of Shipman's victims in the afternoon, when GPs go out on their home visits. Fifty-five per cent of the patients whose deaths he certified died between 1 pm and 6 pm, with a peak between 2 pm and 4 pm. Other local GPs recorded deaths at all hours of the day or night, with no peaks. Deaths were clustered in particular places: Shipman's patients were more likely to die at home, or in his practice. Six died in his practice compared with two among the patients of other local doctors. The relationship between the patient's medical history and the cause of death given on the death certificate: often Shipman's patients appear to have died of conditions of which there was no sign in their medical history. Of 288 patients, who died between 1985 and 1998 and for whom clinical records existed, 166 were classified as highly suspicious and 43 as moderately suspicious.

The integrity of the medical records: Shipman's records were poor, badly written, brief and sometimes perfunctory, raising considerable concern about their veracity. It is known some were fabricated. The prescribing of restricted drugs: The instrument of murder was the syringe filled with a lethal dose of diamorphine, the medical term for heroin. However, no convincing evidence of the need to prescribe excess diamorphine, used by doctors to control extreme pain especially in terminal cases, was found. Shipman is thought to have amassed his supplies from terminal patients who died in their own homes. Professor Baker said his findings could not be accounted for by the number of patients on Shipman's list, their age, sex, or socio-economic status; all of which had been considered.

He stressed that the evidence was circumstantial and that it was not possible to say any individual or group of individuals was murdered. He allowed himself only one comment yesterday on the nature of the man whose evil practice he had laid bare. 'I feel essentially rage, that someone betrayed the trust of people who were completely dependent on him,' he said.

Source: The Independent, Saturday 6 January, 2001 – Jeremy Laurance, Health Editor

'Shipman Questioned Over 1975 Killings'

'Harold Shipman, the GP and serial killer serving a life sentence for murder, was interviewed yesterday by detectives investigating claims that he may have killed three patients in one day. West Yorkshire Police said they were looking into nine suspicious deaths among Shipman's patients in Todmorden, where he worked between 1974 and 1976 at the start of his career as a family doctor. The three patients who died on 21st January 1975 – Lily Crossley, Robert Lingard and Elizabeth Pearce, were each visited by Shipman shortly before their bodies were discovered. Relatives of the deceased say there were all in reasonable health at the time.

Shipman, who later moved to Hyde, Greater Manchester, was convicted in January last year of murdering 15 patients by giving them lethal injections of diamorphine – medically pure heroin and forging the will of one of them. In January this year, detectives said that there were to investigate all 22 deaths certified by Shipman when he worked as a GP in Todmorden. A review of his practice published the same month found that he issued 521 medical certificates of cause of death, 300 more than any of the six practices he was compared with. The review concluded that Shipman may have murdered up to 297 patients during his career. It found that Shipman was 25 times more likely to be present when a patient died than other GPs.'

The Independent: 1st May 2001 – Jeremy Laurance: Health Editor

'Shipman's Method Claimed Patients Within Minutes'

'The final moments of serial killer Harold Shipman's victims were outlined in detail yesterday as a hospital drugs expert explained the effect of the doctor's favourite method of murder. Harold Shipman convicted in January last year of murdering 15 elderly women, always killed by lethal injection of diamorphine. Yesterday, the public inquiry chaired by Dame Janet Smith into the deaths of the former Hyde GP's known victims and a possible 444 others heard that they would all have been dead within minutes. Dr Henry McQuay, Professor of Pain Relief at Churchill Hospital, Oxford, said the diamorphine would take effect swiftly, causing the person to stop breathing. 'If you do not breathe for three minutes then your brain will be starved of oxygen and you will die' the professor explained. 'Breathing would become very slow and then stop within two minutes of the end of the injection. Lips would then go blue and then fingers and toes would go blue. Skin colour would become pallid, and death would follow' he added in a report prepared for the second day of the Inquiry in Manchester.

A small dose administered intravenously would prove lethal to a fit person who had not previously used the drug, he explained. A patient injected with 30 mg or more over a period of five minutes would be dead in less than double that time. The effects of the diamorphine would be worse on the elderly, the very patients Shipman targeted, as kidney function is reduced. The professor told lead counsel to the Inquiry, Caroline Swift QC, that the standard dose used to deal with acute pain relief in an adult would be 10 mg of morphine or 5 mg of diamorphine repeated every four hours.

'The greatest amount I have ever administered is 15 mg of diamorphine over about five minutes to a large Swedish man who had been out cross-country skiing and had broken his femur (thigh bone),' he said. 'When there is pain it is relatively safe to administer morphine. But if the person is not in pain, there is no opposition to the potential for morphine to stop the breathing. It comes up against no barriers. Morphine travels in the blood stream after injection until it reaches special receptors in the nervous system in both the brain and the spinal cord. When morphine reaches the pain receptors it binds to them causing any pain messages to be dampened down. It also depresses the rate at which we breathe. This action is more apparent if the morphine is given to someone who is not in pain.'
The Independent: 22nd June 2001 – Terri Judd Correspondent

'Shipman Suspected of Three Murders in a Night'

'The serial killer Harold Shipman may have murdered three patients in the space of five hours at the beginning of his medical career, the public Inquiry into the former GP's activities was told yesterday. The two women and a man died in 1975 in disturbingly similar circumstances to those of the 15 female patients Shipman was convicted of killing in January last year. Each patient is believed to have received a visit from the doctor on the day they died, the Inquiry at Manchester Town Hall was told. The three dead were registered at the Abraham Ormerod Medical Centre in Todmorden, West Yorkshire, where Shipman worked between March 1974 and September 1975. The cases are among 31 deaths being linked to Shipman, who was the on-call doctor at the Todmorden practice on 21st January 1975.

At 4.10 pm that day he filled out the death certificate of Elizabeth Pearce, 84, who suffered from osteoarthritis but had been in good spirits when visited by her grand-daughter, Anne Price, a few hours earlier. Christopher Melton QC, senior counsel to the Inquiry, said he had repeated the process a few hundred yards away at 7.30 pm at the home of Robert Lingard, 62, having been at his bedside when he died. Shipman certified the cause of death as bronchitis and emphysema. His last visit was less than an hour later. It is believed he was called out to 73-year-old Lily Crossley's house by family members who were concerned for her health. She was agitated and seemed distressed. As he left, he told Mrs Crossley's sister-in-law, Margaret Gilyeat, that he had given her an injection to calm her down. An hour later she was dead.'

The Independent: 7th November 2001: Jason Bennetto – Crime Correspondent

'Police Admit Flawed Shipman Inquiry'

'Greater Manchester Police have admitted their first investigation into the actions of the convicted serial killer Harold Shipman was flawed. The second phase of the Shipman Inquiry has heard how police dropped the case after four weeks because of lack of evidence. At least three more patients died before the doctor was finally arrested. The police have offered their 'regrets' to the families of the GP's victims. The investigation was launched in March 1998 in response to concerns raised by local doctors over the high death rates among his patients. The Inquiry found no evidence on which to arrest Shipman and it was ended. Finally, the solicitor daughter of one of his victims, Kathleen Grundy, raised the alarm. Shipman was eventually arrested in August 1998.

As a family doctor in Hyde, Greater Manchester, he murdered 15 of his women patients and is now serving a life sentence in prison. Caroline Swift QC, leading counsel to the Inquiry, told the hearing the police investigation was hampered by a catalogue of errors. Michael Shorrock QC, counsel for Greater Manchester Police, said confusion over whether the case was 'owned' by the Coroner or the police, and what it hoped to achieve had hampered the investigation. He said following a recent review of the inquiry, Greater Manchester Police had concluded that it was 'flawed'. The collection of available information was incomplete, not fully recorded and the interpretation was flawed, he told the public Inquiry.

He also suggested there had been 'a failure to recognise' that various pieces of information tended towards supporting the suspicion. He said for these reasons, the investigation was 'terminated prematurely', even though it was by no means certain that, had it continued, it could have saved lives. Mr Shorrock said, 'It is important that the families and friends are not forgotten, and we offer our deepest regrets for what has happened'. The Inquiry into the convicted serial killer has entered its second phase and is investigating why this preliminary police inquiry found insufficient evidence to proceed against the GP.'

Source: BBC NEWS: Tuesday, 7 May, 2002

'Police Made Basic Errors in Shipman Case, Inquiry Told'

'An abortive police investigation that failed to uncover anything suspicious about the serial killer GP Harold Shipman was riddled with basic errors, a public inquiry was told yesterday. The Greater Manchester Police inspector alerted to concerns about Shipman kept no written record of his work and did not inquire about death rates at the surgery, which were startlingly high. The investigation was dropped after four weeks, leaving Shipman free to kill at least three elderly women before he was finally arrested. The Inquiry was told Detective Inspector David Smith of Greater Manchester Police was asked to lead the investigation after a GP Dr Linda Reynolds, warned the local coroner that an unusually high number of Shipman's patients were being cremated. She was also concerned that Shipman often seemed to be present when his patients died.

An undertaker shared her concerns but what happened next was 'extremely difficult' to put into a 'coherent' order, Caroline Swift QC counsel to the public Inquiry, said. Det Insp Smith had clearly met Dr Reynolds but had made no notes of what he said. There was no discussion of the number of deaths being registered by Shipman, the detail that led to Dr Reynolds calling the coroner in the first place. Ms Swift said Det Insp Smith failed to interview Dr Reynolds' medical partners and emerged with nothing of 'evidential value'. Either Dr Reynolds did not tell him what had caused her concerns or Det Insp Smith failed to ask the right questions, Ms Swift said. Det Insp Smith's mistakes were compounded by the register office, which when asked to provide details of deceased Shipman patients, gave little more than half the required cases. Michael Shorrock QC, counsel for Greater Manchester Police said confusion over whether the case was the responsibility of the coroner or the police had hampered the inquiry.'

Source: The Independent: 8 May 2002 – Ian Herbert, North of England Correspondent

'Shipman Inquiry Hears From Coroner'

'The coroner who held inquests for the elderly patients of serial killer GP Harold Shipman has been giving evidence to the Inquiry into the deaths. South Manchester Coroner John Pollard appeared before the hearing in Manchester on Friday. He said that if concerns had been raised with him over the suspicious death of one of Dr Shipman's patients, then he would have ordered a post-mortem examination several months before

the doctor's arrest in September 1998. But he claimed he was not alerted, and another three elderly patients died before Shipman was arrested. Earlier this week the Inquiry heard that one of Dr Shipman's colleagues, Dr Linda Reynolds, registered concerns with the coroner six months before the doctor was arrested. Dr Reynolds is now dead but her husband, Nigel, told the Inquiry that she believed Dr Shipman was killing his patients. There was one death she was particularly concerned about, and her family said she contacted Mr Pollard to express her fears. However, the coroner has told the Inquiry that he was never told about this patient. Dr Reynolds, 48, worked at the Brooke Surgery in Hyde, Greater Manchester, close to Shipman's surgery. Doctors at the Brooke Surgery would sign death and cremation certificates for Shipman. Dr Reynolds, who died from cancer in March 2000, grew concerned about Shipman soon after moving to the area. She reported her suspicions, but the police decided there was insufficient evidence to proceed with an investigation at that time. As a family doctor in Hyde, Greater Manchester, Shipman murdered 15 of his women patients, and is now serving a life sentence in prison. The Inquiry into the convicted killer has entered its second phase and is investigating why the preliminary inquiry found insufficient evidence to proceed against the GP.'
Source: BBC NEWS: Friday, 10 May, 2002

'Death Count May Have Found Shipman'

'A system for analysing the numbers of deaths at each GP practice might have helped reveal Dr Harold Shipman's killing spree say researchers. An Inquiry is currently underway looking at how the GP was able to murder so many of his elderly patients and go undetected. The method was developed with funding from the Inquiry and could be introduced widely in future. It could also help pick out other problems in particular areas and monitor GP's general performance. Researchers from Imperial College London are keen to point out that a high death rate may not mean that anything as extreme as the Shipman case is occurring. They collected data from more than 1,000 GPs, including Shipman, between 1993 and 1999, using information from death certificates and patient lists. From this they could work out how many patients died per practice. These were compared with average deaths for patients of various age groups held at local health authority level. A further statistical analysis allowed researchers to highlight any unusual trends year on year.

This gave clear warnings of anything out of the ordinary.

In retrospect, the system first issued a warning about Shipman back in 1997 but also would have highlighted the performance of more than 30 other doctors. This can be narrowed down to 12 doctors including Shipman by using an adjusted model. By 1997, Shipman had already killed many of his victims. 'From this chart, we expect to detect more than 99.9% of truly out-of-control family physicians within seven years of monitoring,' the researchers write. 'We suggest that local health organisations such as primary care trusts in the UK would be ideally placed to monitor and act on any surveillance information provided to them.' Dr Paul Aylin, one of the team said, 'Excess mortality will not necessarily mean bad practice or even criminal behaviour. It could result from many different situations, for example, practices involved in terminal care for cancer patients or treating patients in nursing homes'. Any GPs or practices that are seen as having unusual mortality patterns could be investigated further through audit. Having extra information on the death certificates of patients, such as the name of the doctor who usually treated the patient, rather than just the one who certified death, would aid this process.'
Source: BBC NEWS: Monday 28 July, 2003

'Suicide Inquiry Will Start in Days, Says Ombudsman.'

'The Inquiry into Harold Shipman's apparent suicide, an embarrassing blow to continuing efforts by the Prison Service to cut the death toll behind bars, will begin within days. It will be conducted by Stephen Shaw, the Prisons and Probation Ombudsman, who promised yesterday to make his conclusions public. He echoed the feeling within the Prison Service that little could have been done to prevent Shipman, 57, an accomplished liar who had fooled medical colleagues for decades, from taking his life. Wakefield Prison's most notorious inmate had developed a reputation for arrogance and aloofness, and had lost some privileges as a result, but there was no inkling that he could be suicidal. As with most Category A prisoners, his single cell was checked hourly by officers, who confirmed that he was alive and well at 5 am. Sixty minutes later, he was found hanging from bedsheets tied around bars.

Mr Shaw said yesterday; 'You have 70,000 people in prison. You do not have a situation, nor would you seek a situation, where they are all under 24-hour surveillance. That isn't possible, it isn't desirable, it isn't humane. What I will need to investigate is whether there were any warning signs at Wakefield in the case of Shipman'. His remit will include making recommendations on the balance between watching potentially vulnerable prisoners and affording them some privacy. With a prisoner committing suicide every four days in England and Wales, Mr Shaw faces a momentous challenge. Ninety-four inmates, including 14 women, committed suicide last year, one below the all-time high of 2002. In acute cases, inmates can be placed under permanent surveillance. But Shipman did not fit into that category. He was on a standard security watch and even appeared to be preparing a fresh appeal against conviction.'

Source: *The Independent*: Wednesday 14 January 2004 – Nigel Morris, Home Affairs Correspondent

'Case Was Not Unique But Highlighted Need For Tighter Controls On GPs, To Regain Trust'

'It takes a great man or an evil one to leave a legacy to the world. Harold Shipman, who transmuted his vocation as a doctor from healer to killer, has changed the way people think about, investigate and record deaths. Doctors have presented Shipman as a uniquely evil man, whose 30-year murder spree was a one off. But the record shows he was merely the latest in a series of doctors convicted or suspected of murdering their patients. One of the most famous suspects to escape conviction was John Bodkin-Adams, the Eastbourne GP who may have provided the model for Shipman. Adams forged prescriptions and also admitted at his trial in 1957 that he had 'eased the passing' of some of the elderly women in his care, thought to number up to 400. He was mentioned in 132 of their wills but the jury acquitted him.

The public inquiry into Shipman's case, chaired by Dame Janet Smith, called last July for an overhaul of the coroner's system, with a team of investigators ready to examine any death. The index of suspicion should be raised, she said, and all deaths where medical error or neglect was a concern should be examined. She also called for tighter controls over death certification and an end to the present system which relied solely on the honesty and competence of a doctor attending at death. It provided few safeguards against dishonest or homicidal doctors and Dame Janet was pointedly critical of those who said there would 'never be another Shipman'. Critics, however, fear that

Dame Janet has over-reacted, creating unnecessary bureaucracy which will detract from the proper business of doctors caring for their patients. They also maintain that a man as cunning and determined as Shipman would have been able to evade any system designed to stop him.

The biggest mystery which Shipman has taken to his grave, is why he did it. One of the greatest difficulties for doctors in the modern world is that, having started their careers with hopes of healing the sick, they find there are severe limits to what they can do. Most conditions they encounter in their surgeries are long-term chronic illnesses for which modern medicine has little to offer. Shipman was a man who liked to control those around him and, if he found the limitations of medicine frustrating, he always knew that the syringe or morphine that he carried in his bag gave him the power over life and death that he otherwise lacked.

There may be few ways of stopping a determined killer. But in the final part of her Inquiry, due to report this year, Dame Janet has raised doubts about the robustness of mechanism introduced by the General Medical Council to check on the performance of doctors. Her intervention has dismayed members of the GMC, which has spent three years winning acceptance for the mechanisms. But her concern reflects the extent to which the Shipman case has undermined public trust in doctors.'

Source: *The Independent: Wednesday 14 January 2004*, Jeremy Laurance, Health Editor

'Shipman Suicide Not Preventable'

'The death of serial killer Harold Shipman at Wakefield Prison in January 2004, could not have been predicted or prevented, a report has found. But Prisons and Probation Ombudsman Stephen Shaw said the death raised 'procedural issues relating to the management of the incident'. His report examined how the former GP was able to kill himself in his cell. Mr Shaw criticised decisions which had curbed Shipman's prison privileges, meaning he could not ring his wife. The serial killer had served just four years after being given 15 life sentences for murdering 15 patients. However, he is thought to have killed a further 235 patients. Mr Shaw said procedures dealing with at-risk prisoners such as Shipman needed to be re-examined. Shipman had been on suicide watch when he came to the prison, but was subsequently taken off it, an Inquest heard in April. Mr Shaw dismissed allegations that Shipman had been taunted into killing himself by prison officers. He said that staff should have been given more information about his state of mind. He said, 'I am critical of the fact that staff at Wakefield do not appear to have been alerted to the man's long-term risk of suicide or what might finally trigger it'. Shipman's privileges had been dropped from standard to basic because he had refused to take part in courses in which inmates are encouraged to discuss their crimes and admit their guilt. This meant he could no longer afford to ring his wife Primrose and he was described as 'very emotional' and 'close to tears' by prison doctor Sunil Spirvastava.

Mr Shaw's Report made 17 recommendations and was critical of Wakefield's record keeping, which meant the exact timings of events leading to Shipman's death could not be established. The report found prison staff tried to resuscitate Shipman for around half an hour, but Mr Shaw said he was 'critical' of the failure to call paramedics and the delay in calling a doctor. The doctor arrived two hours after the body was discovered, but Mr Shaw added he had 'no reason to believe' he could have got there faster as he lived on the other side of Leeds. Peter Atherton, director of High Security Prisons, said the service was pleased the report found the death could not have been prevented. 'The report has been with the Prison Service for some time, during which we have drawn up an action plan,' he said. 'The report makes 17 recommendations, every one of which we have accepted and have either implemented or are in the process of doing so'.

However, some of the friends and families of Shipman's victims say they feel cheated by his death and have been critical of the Prison Service and the report. Gloria Ellis, who found her close friend Winifred Mellor, 73, dead after one of Shipman's home visits in 1998, said prison authorities should have 'kept a closer eye on him' and that 'They left him unattended when he should have been watched.'
Source: BBC NEWS: Thursday 25 August 2005

Recommendations Of The Shipman Inquiry

The Shipman Inquiry published a total of six reports, the first of July 2002 and the sixth of January 2005, were factual and sought to establish which of Shipman's patients died of natural causes and those as the result of Shipman's criminal activities. The Sixth Report also examined the time when Shipman was a medical student at Pontefract General Infirmary. The Second, Third and Fourth Reports were concerned with how it was possible for Shipman to continue with his killings without arousing suspicion? The Second Report of July 2003 examined the shortcomings of the police investigation undertaken during March and April 1998. The Third Report also published in July 2003, examined in detail, the processes of death certification and the coronal system, and questioned whether clues could have been discovered through a greater scrutiny of individual deaths or the pattern of deaths among Shipman's patients. The Fourth Report of July 2004, examined the safeguards on the access to controlled drugs, and how it was possible for Shipman to evade controls in order to stockpile large quantities of lethal drugs. The Fifth Report published in December 2004 examined the systems for monitoring the performance of doctors in general practice, and for dealing with complaints from patients or the general public or concerns of fellow professionals.

The main conclusion of the Second Report was that the Greater Manchester Police investigation was delegated to an officer who lacked experience to work without direction and supervision. Consequently, the officer failed to understand the nature of the concerns he was required to investigate and failed to follow up vital leads. The Inquiry suggested that guidelines should be issued to detectives who are required to investigate allegations of unprofessional conduct by health professionals. The Third Report concluded that the systems of death certification and that of the coroner provided inadequate safeguards against the possibility that the doctor completing Medical Certificates of Cause of Death (MCCD) was responsible for the patient's death. It proposed an overhaul of both the coroner's system and that for death certification. One single system for the over-seeing of Death Certificates should be established, irrespective of whether the deceased is to be buried or cremated. The doctor certifying the death would be required to provide a summary of the chain of events leading to the ultimate death, together with an opinion on the cause of death, and would refer all deaths to the coroner's service.

A new national coroner's service would be established under a Chief Coroner to replace the existing system of local coroners appointed and funded by local authorities. This service would be responsible for the final certification of death and the decisions whether further investigations were necessary into specific deaths. This system would contain both 'medical coroners' with responsibility for establishing the medical cause of death, and 'judicial coroners' to pursue further investigations in cases of suspicious deaths. The Fifth Report examined the use of routine monitoring of data on the performance of health professionals. At the time of Shipman's criminal activities, there was little systematic data collected on performance, in particular in general practice. However, from the early 1980s, data on prescribing patterns was collected but mainly as a cost-cutting exercise. Any information on complaints or concerns arising in relation to individual GPs was kept in informal files in the offices of Primary Care Trusts. The most crucial aspect was the lack of any systematic arrangements for the sharing of information between health care organisations. Research undertaken for the Shipman Inquiry revealed that, if data on the number and pattern of deaths of Shipman's patients had been analysed, unusual patterns would have been highlighted, particularly the excess number of patients who died in the afternoon following Shipman's visits. The Inquiry concluded that the NHS required to adopt a more systematic approach to the collecting and monitoring of the performance of doctors. This could be achieved by a more accurate description of prescribing data to individual doctors and the routine monitoring of mortality rates by GPs. It also recommended the establishing of a central database containing this information to enable the better sharing of information between NHS organisations.

The Inquiry recommended improvements to encourage the raising of complaints and concerns from both patients and fellow professionals, and to ensure that primary care organisations took effective action on them. It was proposed that arrangements for making complaints about professional performance required simplifying, and patients should have the right to express complaints directly to the Primary Care Trust (PCT). Following this, PCTs should investigate systematically those complaints which related to issues of professional performance or patient safety. In addition, healthcare organisations (including GP practices) should clarify the arrangements for raising concerns about fellow professionals. Finally, statutory protection for 'whistleblowers' should be strengthened.

Shortly before the Shipman Inquiry began, the General Medical Council (GMC) published proposals for a five-yearly 'revalidation' of doctors. An effective revalidation cycle would provide the opportunity for concerns about a doctor's performance to be discussed, and for remedial action to be taken. This would provide the means by which doctors could assure their patients that they had maintained their skills and remained fit to continue in practice. The Inquiry concluded that the original concept of 'revalidation' had been 'watered down' to the point at which it no longer provided and 'independent' assurance of fitness to practice. Consequently, it recommended a complete review of both the appraisal and revalidation process. As early as 2007, the Government took action to strengthen the powers available to primary care trusts to safeguard patients. These included introducing checks on qualifications, professional history and police records of candidates for GP positions. In addition, they secured undertakings that GPs would participate in appraisal and co-operate with assessment by the National Clinical Assessment Service. New powers were introduced to enable Primary Care Trusts (PCTs) to suspend GPs or remove them from their local lists.

The Fourth Report examined in detail, the controlled drugs audit trail, in particular Shipman's ability to evade controls and to stock-pile lethal quantities of Diamorphine. He did this in two ways; by offering to collect prescriptions on behalf of his patients and collecting unused drugs from the homes of deceased patients but retaining them for his own use. The Inquiry proposed a number of changes to strengthen the audit trail, by restricting the number of prescribers authorised to prescribe controlled drugs, and to provide oversight of the whole system. The key proposals were the creation of a new 'controlled drugs inspectorate' to detect unusual prescribing patterns, the creation of a special register of prescribers authorised to prescribed controlled drugs, the collection and collation of information on the 'private' prescribing of controlled drugs, and of 'bulk orders' by GP practices for personal administration to patients. This also extended to the creation of an audit trail when health professionals collected controlled drugs on behalf of patients and special safeguards on the most dangerous controlled drugs dispensed for use in the community. It will never be

known what motivated an apparently caring family doctor who was popular with his patients, to commit atrocious crimes. Lessons need to be learned from the Shipman case, and to put into practice, safeguards needed to protect patients and the public from any recurrence.
Source: *"Learning from tragedy, keeping patients safe: The Government's Response to the Recommendations of the Shipman Inquiry"* February 2007, pp.8-12 (Crown Copyright)

The Inquiry Conclusions

At Shipman's trial, the jury found that he had given large injections of opiate to each of the victims. Since the giving of the injection was not for therapeutic purposes, this constituted an unlawful act. Since the dose administered killed the patient, the jury inferred that Shipman had intended to kill the patient. Murder is defined as 'the unlawful killing of a person carried out with the intention to kill or cause serious harm'. It was decided that in 9 of the 15 conviction cases, the bodies of the deceased had been exhumed, and morphine had been found in each of the remain. Therefore, in respect of each of those cases, there was compelling medical evidence that the actual cause of death was morphine poisoning. In the case of Mrs Kathleen Grundy, it had been suggested by Shipman that she might have been a 'drug addict', but the jury rejected this suggestion. For each of the other cases, Shipman offered no explanation for the presence of morphine in the bodies. The fact that Shipman was actually present with his patients in eight of the nine cases, either at the time of their deaths or shortly before the discovery of the body, provided convincing evidence that he had the opportunity for administrating the lethal injection. In respect of those eight cases, the jury reached only one conclusion, that Shipman had murdered them by injecting morphine or diamorphine to them.

In respect of the ninth case of Mrs Joan Melia, whose body also contained morphine, the prosecution was unable to demonstrate or prove that Shipman at been present at her death or been in attendance at her home before the death was discovered. However, the jury inferred that he had. In the other six cases, the bodies of the victims had been cremated so there was no physical evidence to establish morphine poisoning, and subsequently, less evidence to suggest Shipman's guilt. However, the circumstances of each case together with Shipman's conduct in respect of both cremation and burial cases, were considered to be so similar, that when considered together, the evidence in the cremation cases became compelling. As a result, the jury drew the inference that Shipman had indeed, injected all 15 victims with morphine or diamorphine. This is borne out by the highly relevant fact that the prosecution selected all the 15 cases because the evidence was strong.

The most striking feature identified in 14 of the conviction cases was the association between Shipman's contact with the victim and the victim's subsequent death. There appeared to be a direct correlation between the two. Only in the case of Mrs Joan Melia was the Crown unable to prove this direct link. Of those victims with morphine in the body, Shipman admitted that he had been with two at the moment of death; they were Mrs Ivy Lomas who in fact, died in his surgery, and Mrs Marie Quinn. Mrs Irene Turner and Mrs Jean Lilly were both found dead literally minutes after Shipman had left their homes. Mrs Kathleen Grundy and Mrs Bianka Pomfret were found dead not long after Shipman left. Shipman was also seen outside Mrs Winifred Mellor's house shortly before her death was 'discovered', although Shipman later denied having even visited her on the day in question. Mrs Muriel Grimshaw's death was discovered at home the day after Shipman's last visit to her. In each of theses eight cases, Shipman had been alone with the patient. Of the six cremation cases, where there could be no physical evidence of the actual presence of morphine, Shipman admitted that he had, in effect, been present at the time of death in case of four; Mrs Kathleen Wagstaff, Mrs Lizzie Adams, Mrs Norah Nuttall and Mrs Maria West. Of the other two deaths, those of Mrs Pamela Hillier and Miss Maureen Ward, the body of Mrs Hillier was discovered only about half an hour after Shipman had visited her. In the case of Miss Ward, Shipman claimed he had found Miss Ward dead when he arrived at her flat. In all these cases, the jury was unconvinced.

A second prominent feature to many of the conviction cases, was the fact that the patient was found sitting peacefully in a chair or on a sofa, as if asleep. Mrs West, Mrs Adams, Mrs Lilley, Mrs Wagstaff, Mrs Pomfret, Mrs Nuttall, Mrs Mellor and Mrs Melia, were all found sitting in their chairs or sofas. Mrs Turner, Mrs Grimshaw and Miss Ward, were lying on their beds, and Mrs Grundy was lying on the sofa. A third feature of the conviction cases was the fact that none of the patients was terminally ill and in no case did it appear that Shipman had been sent for on account of a sudden and serious deterioration in the health of his patient. In addition, these deaths were sudden and not expected by the respective family or friends. The most striking features of the circumstances surrounding the conviction cases were Shipman's proximity to the death, the appearance at the death of the victim, and the sudden and unexpected nature of the respective deaths.

It is very rare for a patient to die during a doctor's visit unless the patient is terminally ill. None of the six victims in the conviction cases were terminally ill, and none of them had called Shipman out to attend them. For Shipman to have been present at no less than 6 sudden unexplained or natural deaths over a period of 3 years would have represented a remarkable series of coincidences. However, the jury were not convinced that they were coincidences, the explanation being that Shipman had killed them. Shipman's presence is highly suspicious at these deaths. Likewise, it is unusual for a patient to be found dead shortly after a doctor has visited them. Obviously, any doctor would be expected to make arrangements for the patient to be admitted to hospital if he or she was convinced that the patient's death might be imminent. With Shipman, this happened frequently, in seven of the conviction cases. The jury became convinced that was too much to be due to coincidence. It is unusual for a doctor to discover a patient dead at home, although this may happen occasionally. In one of the conviction cases, Shipman claimed to have found Miss Maureen Ward dead when he went to her flat. The prosecution case was that Shipman made an unsolicited visit and had killed her; this the jury accepted. With Shipman, such events happened too frequently to be explained by chance. Shipman became a plausible and accomplished liar; he lied about the circumstances both of his attendance at deaths and of visits that he made to patients shortly before their deaths.

Standard of Proof

In a criminal trial, the jury is directed that, before they can convict the defendant, the prosecution must make them sure of guilt, satisfied 'beyond reasonable doubt'. This is a high standard of proof. In a civil case, the accepted rule is that the claimant must prove the case 'on the balance of probabilities', that is, the judge decides what 'probably happened'. So, in theory, this balance of probabilities means that the judge is 51% satisfied in respect of the crucial facts of the case, even though 49% of the evidence may point to the opposite conclusion. However, in practice, evidence cannot be so finally assessed, and judges do not usually need to make such fine calculations.

Occasionally, in a civil case, the judge will find the evidence finally balanced, but still has to reach a conclusion. If the weight of the evidence tips in favour of the claimant, he or she will succeed in their claim. If, however, it favours the defendant, or is evenly balanced, the claimant will fail, as he or she has not 'discharged' the 'onus of proving the case'.

In an Inquiry, there is no required 'standard of proof' and no 'onus of proof'. The whole objective in reaching decisions in the individual cases has been to provide an answer for the people who fear or suspect that Shipman might have killed their friend or relative. Shipman has been convicted of 15 cases of murder and sentenced appropriately. He will not be tried or punished in respect of any other deaths.

Source: The Shipman Inquiry: First Report (2002). pp 109-122 (Crown Copyright)

Media Reactions To The Inquiry Recommendations

'All the signals that there was something wrong with the way Harold Shipman was practising were there, but they were not recognised for what they were because no one was looking, no one was prepared to look, and the complacency inherent in the system meant that no mechanism was available to draw all the evidence together. The Shipman murders clearly represent a massive failure to monitor the medical profession adequately both locally and nationally. If there are any more Shipmans out there, we need to be confident that we can spot them.'

Source: Oldham Evening Chronicle – Weekend Review, The Independent, 5 February 2000

'Although lessons can be learnt and procedures tightened up, no guarantees can be given that any doctor, nurse or other clinician could not if sufficiently determined and perverse repeat Shipman's crimes. In the investigation following the Allitt murders, the Clothier Committee concluded that a 'determined and secret criminal may defeat the best regulated organisation in the pursuit of his or her purpose'. It is difficult to envisage any set of laws or regulations that will guarantee that the acts of a criminal as experienced, knowledgeable, cool and determined as Shipman can be prevented in the future.'

Source: British Medical Journal – Weekend Review, The Independent, 5 February 2000

'The public now realise a cunning serious killer was on the loose, murdering at will, for ten or more years. He did his grim work under the perfect mask, that of the healer, the carer, the trusted physician. But that cannot excuse the failures of many kinds, which made the killing spree possible. Shipman's trail of death is littered with loopholes, narrow escapes and guarded, it seems, by over-trusting individuals. Yet surely there should be enough checks and balances, and official oversight to prevent a general practitioner, however cunning, from committing mass murder. It isn't asking a lot.'
Source: The Yorkshire Post – Weekend Review, The Independent, 5 February 2000

'The biggest fear post-Shipman is that the media will dissect the doctor-patient relationship and claim it has been irrevocably damaged. Losing this trust would be a fatal blow to the central aspect of British general practice. But GPs should take heart that the public has enough sense to recognise their doctors are not intent on murdering them.'
Source: The Doctor: Weekend Review – The Independent, 5 February 2000

'Harold Shipman's cunning would have tested any system of professional regulation. But even allowing for the singular nature of his crimes and their extravagant scale, his actions have exposed GP regulation as inadequate and attitudes towards it as lax and complacent. But in theory a multitude of safeguards already existed in the system that so failed Dr Shipman's patients. All new measures will eventually become pieces of professional furniture, taken for granted. The risk is ever present that monitoring will become ritualised, a matter of ticking boxes. Circumventing that end result will be the real test for clinical governance.'
Source: The Health Service Journal: Weekend Review, The Independent, 5 February, 2000

Despite Shipman, There is Demand For GPs Who Work Alone

'Sir, You made a slur on nearly 3,000 GPs when your editorial (20 July) confused single-handed GPs with Dr Shipman. Your suggestion that I and my colleagues would become a dying breed because of the need to prevent mass murder is a piece of prejudice. Single-handers look after five million patients who could easily go elsewhere if they did not think that we offered something special, continuity, accessibility and quality of care, bettered by very few larger practices. Patients like personal care and the feeling that they know the person who will look after them and the feeling is mutual. Unlike many of my colleagues, I enjoy going to work because I meet patients who are almost like old friends. Unlike other patients, those registered with sole practitioners complain less because they get what they want more often. Shipman is a unique mass murderer who committed many of his crimes before he became single handed. Several agencies had an opportunity to stop him and the on-going Inquiry will find out why they did not do so. Every GP is single handed when in their consulting room. When will the media and politicians stop voicing the inaccurate perception that solo practitioners are potential murderers? The constant attack on these small practices is demoralising and unfair. We will be here as long as patients want what we have to offer – a long time if current demand is anything to go by.' Dr Laurence Buckman, London NW11.

Source: The Independent – 22 July 2002

Concluding Statements

'The basic statement that Shipman killed over 200 patients does not fully reflect the enormity of his crimes. As a general practitioner, Shipman was trusted implicitly by his patients and their families. He betrayed their trust in a way and to an extent that I believe to be unparalleled in history. We are all accustomed to hearing of violent deaths, both in the media and in fiction. In some ways, Shipman's 'non-violent' killing seems almost more incredible that the violent deaths of which we hear. Although I have identified 215 victims of Shipman, the true number is far greater and cannot be counted.

Shipman has also damaged the good name of the medical profession and has caused many patients to doubt whether they can trust their own family doctor. This trust forms the basis of the relationship between doctor and patient. It was said during the Inquiry that 'there would never be another Shipman'. This is an invalid argument. We know that he killed more people than any other serial killer yet identified, but we do not know how many other doctors have killed one or more patients. Some such killers have come to light, others may remain hidden. Shipman was able to kill for almost 24 years, before he was discovered, who can say with confidence that there are not other doctors, still unknown, who have not killed in the past? Who can say that there will be none in the future? If there is a risk that a doctor might kill in the future and if, as is now clear, the present system would neither deter nor detect such conduct, then surely the system must be changed.'

No one reading this report can fail to be shocked by the enormity of the crimes, committed by Shipman and to feel, as I do, the deepest sympathy for his victims and their families. His activities have brought tragedy upon them and also upon the communities in which he practised, and which gave him their trust. There are also the hundreds of patients of Shipman who have been deeply disturbed by the realisation that Shipman was not the kind, caring and sympathetic man they took him for. They too must feel betrayed. Although I believe that the overwhelming majority of patients will, on reflection, realise that they can indeed trust their doctor as they always have done, there will be some who will remain uncertain.'

Dame (Lady) Janet Smith. DBE. Chairman of the Inquiry.
Source: The Shipman Inquiry: First Report (2002). (Crown Copyright)

Chapter Four

'Nature or Nurture'

In any investigation whether it be social, historical, scientific, medical, forensic or criminal, there are six vital questions that require answers, they are the why, what, how, where, when and who? During the course of this work, readers have been exposed to a wealth of material, evidence and opinion regarding the various aspects of this case. They have also received the benefit of information contained in the most comprehensive and definitive account of the activities of Harold Shipman ever published, the Shipman Inquiry. The accompanying six reports examined every aspect of this unparalleled and deeply tragic case. These provide sufficient information to allow answers to be found to five of those vital questions. In this final chapter, an attempt is made to answer that missing or elusive question of why? What was the motive which drove Shipman to become a serial killer? It is very likely that we will never discover a definitive answer to satisfy everyone. However, this does not mean that we cannot or should not at least, consider the possible pointers and clues contained in the information we have regarding Shipman's pattern of activities. These may at least provide some indication as to what transformed this caring, respected and devoted family doctor into the most prolific serial killer in the annals of British criminal history.

Why do some people commit crimes? What turns a human being into a killer? Both these questions have one thing in common, they are concerned with the 'human mind' – a subject that is fraught with difficulties. There are many people who have an almost blind belief in science and are unwilling to contradict its findings. However, in reality, science frequently fails, especially in that sensitive area of human behaviour. By its very nature, psychology is largely a descriptive rather than an explanatory or predictive field of human inquiry. The more recent field of psychological 'profiling' is that area of investigation concerned with describing the mental outlook and general background of a person who has committed crimes, with the aim of assisting police to apprehend the person. Subtle 'clues' left behind by the offender are used to construct a picture or 'profile' of the inner narrative that guides the mind of the offender.

There is general agreement that individual human beings do have distinctive personality traits, but it is not possible to say how they acquired them in the first place. Human beings are complex creatures and their behaviour is simply not amenable to study. Is criminality inherited in the genes or is it acquired from experience, or is it a mixture of both nature and nurture? To my mind, the truth must be that both nature and nurture play a part in the roots of criminality. It is not simply a matter of nature (genetics) contributing a certain percentage and nurture (environment and culture) another percentage. Both work on each other in very complex ways, so that the resulting behaviour cannot be dissected in ways that allocate some traits to nature and others to nurture. There is no evidence that criminality is genetically inherited, nor can any such evidence be found. Most people would agree that criminality is a form of behaviour that offends our moral beliefs or constitutes behaviour that is forbidden under the law. Consequently, it is a moral concept or a legal one, but it is not a scientific one.

At the other end of the spectrum, we have the cultural determinists, who maintain that everything a human does is the result of their environment and upbringing. They claim that all ideas and beliefs are culturally determined. Where right and wrong were in the genes with the sociobiologists, they are in the culture with the cultural determinists. Then Geneticists maintain that criminality is in the DNA, psychologists that it is in the upbringing, and sociologists that it is in the culture. There is an element of truth in all of them, but their answers, individually, fail to satisfy. Harold Shipman, the subject of this work is said to have committed his crimes because he had an unhappy childhood and because his mother died when he was still a teenager. Why then, are other people able to refrain from murder, even though they had similar experiences? The truth is that we just do not know why Shipman did what he did. The best we can do is to examine those features of Shipman's behaviour which may possibly reveal his inner personality and perhaps what motivated him in his criminal activities. The Shipman Inquiry was unable to provide a 'conclusive' motive for his crimes. How then can we begin to explain why a well-respected GP would strike down so many of his healthy patients? Why should a man devoted to the healing arts become the very opposite of all that his life focused on? We are left with one central fact that he was a Doctor.

The Doctor has always been the epitome of

respectability in our society. There are today, huge changes in the progress of medical training which emphasises the person, not just the body, but Shipman was not part of that training.' What then happens to an arrogant man who believes he has the right to decide whether people should be allowed to suffer or helped in their passing? Here was a family doctor who had himself a dependency on mind-altering drugs. How might such a man evolve from over-prescribing analgesics to deliberately injecting lethal doses? There are clues to his personality in his sense of almost complete social dislocation. Colleagues found him aloof, with a chip on his shoulder. Following an active community life should have yielded a large circle of friends, yet Shipman had none. Psychologists have told the Inquiry that Shipman's arrogance and over-confidence were almost certainly a mask for poor self-esteem. In addition, Shipman's addiction demonstrated that he had many underlying problems. Though personal traits are not enough to explain his actions, there was a possibility that he might have developed a fear of death and therefore, a need to control death. He may have had a morbid interest in death and experienced a 'buzz' of pleasure from it.

The following two extracts, appeared in *The Independent* on Wednesday 2 February 2000, both written by experts in their respective fields, which throw some light on the psychological make-up of Shipman, each offering an alternative assessment.

'Dr Richard Badcock, the consultant forensic psychiatrist who conducted a brief consultation with Shipman to determine whether he was fit for police interview, suggested yesterday that he was a 'classic' necrophiliac, a man obsessed with the dead, but with the act of inducing death and controlling and observing the moment when life leaves the body. Dr Badcock, based at Rampton high-security hospital in Nottinghamshire, said: 'He doesn't have a mental illness, but he does have a personality disorder. He has a very controlling, arrogant personality, he is an extreme example of an obsessional type of person. The other disorder he has, I believe, is necrophilia, but that comes from looking at the crimes themselves. Even though there was no overt sexual involvement, he would have got a 'huge intellectual buzz' from the murders that would have become a power-based replacement for sex.'

Source: The Independent: Wednesday 2 February 2000. Page 3

'The Evolution of a Serial-Killing Doctor'

'If Harold Shipman had been born into a self-destructive dysfunctional family, been physically or psychologically abused, indulged in bizarre sexual activities or lived in a deviant or criminal underworld, replete with vulnerable victims, then the explanations for his crimes would have been in easy reach. But the men who emerge out of this morass of destructive familial life are not able to maintain the commitment and intellectual dedication that is needed to get a medical qualification. They do not manage an apparently stable married family life as Shipman seems to have done.

Doctors do go off the rails of course. They suffer from greed, lust, jealousy and the other deadly sins, like the rest of us. They can harness the killing power of medicines to satisfy these sins. There are many examples of doctors who killed to get rid of inconvenient spouses, embarrassing lovers or for financial gain. But none of these explanations is convincing. Even the botched attempt to forge Kathleen Grundy's will seems to have been an afterthought. If we put aside unconvincing peccadilloes, or the seething anger that characterises many violent criminals, we are left with the central fact he was a doctor. His building an evolving narrative for himself seems to me to be the most feasible account of how he came to be a serial killer.

I do not believe that Shipman decided at some point that he would kill a selection of his patients. I do not think, as some have suggested, that he harboured some psychological conflict about the death of his 43-year-old mother when he was a teenager, and that somehow he converted that conflict into the killing of his patients. For a start, some of his probable victims were men and many of his female victims were a quarter of a century older than his mother. A developing view of himself as a decider of human fates, starting at levels he was not even aware of and emerging into a full-blown campaign seems to be the most likely process. For such a process to evolve it had to have fertile ground. In this regard serial killings are not unlike industrial disasters. There are early warnings that are ignored. Communication between agencies break down. Individuals believe they are charmed or fated to carry on.

Shipman was a danger zone that no one was protected from. He became aware of that and it probably added excitement to the story he was creating for himself. He shows us that human frailty has many sides. In the century of the individual, where power and celebrity are so all-embracing, it may be that the

quest to exert authority you have in life-threatening circumstances is all that is needed to pull an aeroplane out of the sky or turn a doctor into a serial killer.'
Professor David Canter, Director – Centre for Investigative Psychology, University of Liverpool.
Source: The Independent; Wednesday 2nd February 2000, page 3

Research carried out by psychologists and criminologists have arrived at a consensus as regards the most common traits associated with serial killers. The table below displays these common psychological traits. Alongside these, have been included those identified traits displayed by Shipman for comparison. It can be clearly seen that Shipman corresponded almost identically with virtually every common trait.

Common Serial Killer Traits

Trait	Shipman
The need to control others	Yes
Inability to feel remorse	Yes
Poor Impulse Control	Yes
False Presentation of Self	Yes
Manipulative	Yes
Sensation Feeling	Yes
Narcissistic	Yes
Voyeuristic	Yes
Solitary	Yes
Abusive to Animals	?
Outward appearance as normal	Yes

It can be clearly seen that Shipman displayed approximately 91% of the accepted psychological traits regarded as commonly displayed by serial killers. Consequently, it is not an over-exaggeration to classify him as a 'serial killer'.

Shipman's early victims were terminally ill people, who presented the least danger of detection and probably appeared to him to be the least morally culpable. He killed them because they may have threatened his own security and therefore, could perhaps be justified to him in some way. The gradual increase in the pace of killing after 1994 demonstrates an 'addiction' to the practice of killing. There are psychologists who suggest that his lifelong motivation was to free himself of the trauma of his mother's death by re-writing his personal history. His pointless killing of usually elderly female patients were all bids to make his mother die painlessly. On one thing most psychiatrists agree, Shipman was a 'narcissistic control freak'.

There are relevant references to Shipman's activities in the First Report of the Shipman Inquiry which do indicate possible motives for many of his activities. At paragraph 13.16: 'It seems to me that Shipman could not rationally have thought that he would get away with Mrs Grundy's estate. The whole venture was grossly incompetent, and discovery was inevitable. It does appear that Shipman planned the forgery of the will well in advance of the killing, which suggests that money was his motivation. However, I am not convinced that Shipman decided to kill Mrs Grundy because he wanted her money. I think his thought processes must have been much more complex than that'.

Again, at paragraph 13.18: 'In short, if one defines motive as a rational or conscious explanation for the decision to commit a crime, I think Shipman's crimes were without motive. There is no evidence of any features that I have observed, that commonly motivate murderers.'

The Inquiry found that Shipman had the reputation in Hyde of being a good and caring doctor. With the benefit of hindsight, one could see that his willingness to make home visits to his patients created the ideal opportunities for killing. The Inquiry also commented on the fact that Shipman's attitude towards his patients was unpredictable. At times he could be encouraging and sympathetic, but at other times, cold, brusque and off-hand, and he certainly lacked empathy. Other well-marked traits observed in Shipman's personality were aggression, conceit, arrogance and contempt for those he regarded as 'intellectual inferiors'. Another highly relevant trait in Shipman's personality was that he was 'profoundly dishonest'. This was first revealed in 1975 when it was found that he had dishonestly obtained large quantities of pethidine by deception. The Inquiry also described Shipman has being an 'accomplished inventive liar who could lie spontaneously to get himself out of a difficult situation and did so on countless occasions' [para 13.43]. Shipman's dishonesty is also displayed by the way in which he fabricated medical records to invent explanations for death he had caused. He also made countless false entries on Medical Certificates of Death and cremation certificates. He was, in short, 'a consummate and inveterate liar' [para 13.46].

The psychiatrists who gave evidence to the Shipman Inquiry presented a psychological profile of how they considered Shipman to be. They thought that he was a person who always felt that the system owed him deference. He was arrogant, conceited and with a belief that there was a huge distinction between his ability and that of those around him. He had the supreme arrogance to believe that if he said something, then it would be accepted without question. In investigating a crime, the most important and valuable factor is the crime scene; the remains of a victim, where it happened, how it happened, why it happened and how it was committed. For those investigating Shipman's activities there was NO CRIME SCENE.

At the time of their deaths, no one thought Shipman's victims had been murdered. No record was taken of how the body was found, no post-mortem examination, no forensic evidence gathered. The only medical evidence came from Shipman himself which is highly suspect. One of the things to look for in trying to understand the motivation of a killer is the precise details of what happened in the crime. There was no discernible motive to Shipman's crimes. He used his professional position as the perfect vehicle for finding an outlet for his needs. Shipman's crimes suggested psychopathy, yet he did not fit the profile of a standard psychopathic serial killer. About 3% of the population are psychopaths, whilst the vast majority of the population have a capacity for guilt, for conscience, for remorse, for empathy, Shipman displayed none of these. In his eyes, people were there to be manipulated by him for his own gains and for gratifying his thirst for power over life and death. Shipman did demonstrate some of those features that are recognised in the established psychopath; he was aloof, cold and calculated.

He was a 'complex psychopath' with the ability to 'switch on' the professional doctor persona in which he could appear warm, caring and charming, all the qualities looked for in a family doctor. When Shipman was confronted with reality, as opposed to his own version of reality, he could not cope. The whole basis of death and cremation procedures was based upon mutual trust between patient and doctor, and doctor and undertaker. Shipman counted on this trust to allow him to literally 'get away with murder'. Shipman's preference for cremation and his persuading victims' families was entirely a matter of self-preservation and nothing whatsoever to do with helping families to cope with their loss. While some psychiatrists believe that Shipman's mother's death helps explain why he killed in the manner he did, others believe that this was just one event in a long chain that led to his overwhelming desire to kill. It would be wrong to treat this one past event as a seminal 'trigger'. Emotional distancing is a major clue to Shipman's psychological make-up. He was a man who, from early days, learnt to deal with intense internal feelings, so that when he dealt with other people, he could be matter-of-fact, calm, controlled and detached. He almost certainly went into medicine as a career with a 'vocational' prompt not to be a serial killer. However, the path he had chosen meant that within five years Shipman's vocational prompt and his psychopathic desire to kill, coincided with tragic consequences.

Was Shipman in effect, carrying out mercy-killing or was he killing to satisfy his own growing needs? There was no mercy-killings because as a psychopath Shipman could not feel compassion and had lost completely his 'moral compass'. He could only hasten a death for his own gratification. His victims were people he didn't particularly value except as a means to an end. It was a misguided perception of Shipman as the caring and intellectual professional that allowed him to kill undetected for so long. There was, for Shipman, a great experience of power in the act of deciding whether someone was going to live or die. No one is in any doubt that the reasons why the murders went undetected was because Shipman was a doctor. He was in a position of trust that his patients simply could not conceive of him abusing, yet he did. Shipman was born with psychopathic tendencies, but that did not make him a killer. His mother's illness and death fed and expanded that psychopathy, but that did not make him a killer either. When all this is linked to his genuine desire to become a doctor, he was able to explore his fantasies about death to a level unreachable to those outside the medical profession. This made him a potential serial killer.

Some psychiatrists believe that Shipman was a

psychopathic narcissist. This minority are so morally ego-centric that they literally feel that they can get away with murder. Such a person would kill for the sole purpose of self-glorification and others, for the sheer enjoyment of the act itself. In this sense, Shipman came somewhere between these two extremes. A medical doctor who has ready access to various forms of drugs will utilise more sophisticated ways of killing rather than strangling or stabbing. They will use poisons administered by intravenous injections. Yet, his training would have made him aware that morphine can be detected in a body's tissues after death. He could have chosen a wide variety of drugs that would not have been so easily detected, so why didn't he? It has been suggested that he simply believed that the morphine would never be found because, in his mind, it would not be looked for, against evidence of his omnipotent view of himself. It is firmly believed that Shipman's eventual suicide can be viewed as a final act of control by the man who had been able to enact the power of life and death over so many of his innocent patients.

Shipman managed to have a relatively 'normal' life with a wife and children and made social contacts but always on his terms. Unlike the majority of serial killers, Shipman's murders were non-violent and with no indication of sadistic or sexual interference. He did not choose his victims at random; he did not need to do; he had the opportunities his profession allowed. One way in which Shipman did fit into the usual category of serial killer was his attitude towards his victims. He became distanced from them and no longer considered them as human being, they became simply a 'means to an end'. Psychiatrists who have studied the case believe that the defining moment in Shipman's life was the death of his mother resulting in him suffering from a personality disorder. His choice of medicine as a career appear to stem from his mother's protracted death and the contact he had with the medical profession. It is highly likely that this began his life-long attraction to morphine which became an intrinsic part of his urge to kill. For many years he showed considerable skill in covering up his crimes and avoiding detection yet there is evidence that he was less careful with the circumstantial evidence of his killings. If his overall aim had been to commit the perfect murder, he would never have used a drug such as morphine for disposing of his victims. He must have realised that such a drug could survive within the tissues of dead bodies for a considerable period of time and could be identified through toxicological tests.

The following extract provides an interesting assessment of Shipman's possible motives:

'In Shipman's mind there was an irreconcilable nexus between his attachment to his mother, his rage at being abandoned by her through death, his further anger at being trapped by his wife and his utter inability to have any control over his domestic situation. By the time he finished medical school, the externalisation, displacement and projection are complete. Patients, especially women, who need him, are first seduced by his devotion, then dispatched in the one manner he knows – the swift lulling relief of a heroin overdose. He did it again and again, addictively repeating the displaced rage towards his mother and making them all, every single one of them, pay for what she had done to him. Shipman did not kill his mother, but he could never forgive her for deserting him the way she did. He identified with the escape she obtained from narcotic injections when dying of cancer; he displaced his rage by killing his patient victims.
"Medical Murder: Disturbing Cases of Doctors Who Kill" – Dr Robert M. Kaplan, Summersdale Publishers Ltd (Chichester) 2010 pp 112-113

With serial killers, the first murder tends to be unplanned where the murderer is in the frame of mind to do it, the opportunity arises, and he does it. Once this has been achieved, he can do it again and plan further opportunities. He can then become addicted to the adrenaline rush, the excitement. The more he carries on, the more he wants to do it, to re-create the original 'buzz'. In Shipman's case, there is a very clear picture emerging of the frequency of his crimes increasing from the occasional to every month and eventually several in one month. There is no doubt that Shipman was 'addicted' to killing. According to psychiatrists' view, as the number of deaths increased, Shipman was running out of control, one definite trait of a more 'typical' serial killer. It is characteristic of serial killers that at some point they do become disorganised as a direct result of the frequency of crimes they are committing, which dominate their lives. Although Shipman appeared on the surface to have held everything together, yet he was drawing attention to himself. It was the last killing, the murder of Mrs Grundy that sealed his fate. If Shipman did not anticipate being stopped, it was an act of supreme arrogance, proving that he had completely lost touch with reality. Again, several psychiatrists believe that the final murder was indeed, a bid on Shipman's part to be stopped in his criminal activities. He was clearly very efficient and competent so why draw attention to his crimes unless it is part of his all-embracing arrogance.

Although compared to other methods, poisoning is a relatively unusual method of killing. The choice of morphine was an intrinsic part of Shipman's urge to kill. Shipman's early addiction to Pethidine confirms that he had an addictive personality which persisted throughout his medical career. Most people cope with stresses of medical practice without substance abuse, although doctors do have a high rate of alcoholism. The combination of the stress and the easy availability of drugs means that some doctors do become drug addicts. Working in the medical profession, it is possible to deceive a lot of people for a long time. Why someone moves from being a carer to a deliberate killer is extremely difficult to say. We can only assume that there is some deficiency in their conditioning. When you are put on a pedestal by the local community as Shipman certainly was, then you need to remember that you are still mortal and not omnipotent, but quite clearly, Shipman had lost sight of this fact, and his arrogance became his nemesis.

Conclusions

Since Shipman's conviction and subsequent death whilst in custody, there are still two questions that will be debated for many years to come; what made an apparently caring competent and well-respected doctor become a prolific serial killer and why did he succeed without detection for so long? Harold Shipman, the GP convicted of the murder of 15 of his patients was not unique as portrayed by the medical profession back in 2000, but only the latest in a long line of deadly doctors. The medical authorities tried to present Shipman's activities as a one-off. However, research of doctors who have murdered more than once, reveals that medicine has thrown up more serial killers than all other professions. Scores have doctors have committed their crimes with the help of their medical training. There are enough recorded instances of multiple murders by doctors to make a least a prima facie case that the profession attracts some people with a pathological interest in the power of life and death. What cannot be known is how many killings may have been committed by doctors whose crimes were never discovered. Medical practitioners are in the unique position of having the knowledge of how to kill patients, the means to do so and the professional alibi that allows to cover their tracks.

It is difficult to absorb or even comprehend the enormity of the crimes committed by Harold Shipman. The fact that the most prolific serial killer in British legal history, should have been a family GP represents a grotesque perversion of what should be a relationship of implicit trust. That bond of trust between a doctor and patient is fundamental to the medical relationship. Shipman killed as others cured, methodically, meticulously, attentively, making his crimes all the more outrageous. A trust is fundamental to the doctor-patient relationship so abuse of that trust is the risk that will always be there. All the signals that there was something wrong with the way Shipman was practising were there but not recognised for what they were because no one was looking. No one was prepared to look, and the complacency inherent in the prevailing system meant that no mechanisms were available to collate all the evidence.

The Shipman Inquiry was set up in 2001 with the express aim of investigating the extent of Shipman's unlawful activities, enquiring into the actions of the statutory authorities involved, and making recommendations on steps needed to protect patients in the future. One lasting legacy of the Inquiry was the meticulous analysis of the weaknesses in the existing systems at the time which Shipman was able to exploit for his own criminal purposes. The Shipman Inquiry also heard from psychiatrists that Shipman may have had a rigid and obsessive personality, be isolated and have difficulty expressing emotions. There was also the suggestion that his arrogance and over-confidence was a façade or smoke-screen to hide his poor self-esteem. He also had a deep-seated need to control people and events. However, these traits on their own are not sufficient to explain why Shipman developed into a serial killer. For a doctor to give an overdose of opiate to a patient whose death was expected, would give rise to very little risk of suspicion or detection. The apparent interludes between Shipman's killings do suggest that he was able to refrain himself, hence he had self-awareness of what he was doing. However, the figures demonstrate that after 1994, his acts of killing gradually increased, reaching a high peak between 1997-98. Was this increase related to the ease with which he was able to obtain diamorphine, or was it evidence that he had become totally addicted to killing and was out of control?

    This theory can be supported by the forgery of Mrs Grundy's will which was a hopelessly incompetent act and bound to arouse suspicion. Shipman must have been aware that Mrs Grundy's daughter was a practising solicitor. Did he really believe that he could 'get away with it'? This would suggest that he had lost his sense of normality and reality. However, psychologists have confirmed that this is not uncommon for serial killers to be detected by simply drawing attention to themselves in an obvious way. Could this be Shipman's need to escape from a situation over which he had completely lost control? There can be very few people in Britain who are unaware of Harold Shipman, a respected GP practising in Hyde, Greater Manchester, who over a period of some 30 years was responsible for the murder of some 250 of his patients. The Shipman Inquiry was established to investigate the extent of Shipman's criminal activities, examine the role of the statutory and other organisation involved, and make recommendations on reforms necessary to protect patients in the future. The Inquiry produced six reports, the first and last addressed the extent of Shipman's activities as a GP and his early career as a junior hospital doctor. The other reports considered the various processes and systems which failed to detect Shipman's activities at an earlier stage. These included the 1998 police investigation (Second Report), death certification and the coronal system (Third Report), the systems for ensuring the safe use of controlled drugs (Fourth Report) and arrangements for the monitoring and disciplining of GPs (Fifth Report).

The Inquiry provided an in-depth analysis of the weaknesses in the existing systems which Shipman was able to exploit. It concluded with recommendations to provide a balance between the need to safeguard the processes of patient care and the need to protect the public from professional abuse. The Inquiry's reports confirm that Shipman was a devious and unscrupulous individual who used his professional reputation and plausible manner to cover most traces of his criminal activities. The Inquiry concluded that, if strong safeguards had been in place, Shipman could have been deterred from his criminal course or been detected much earlier. We will never really know what motivated this caring, popular and respected GP to become the most prolific serial killer in British criminal history.

'Looking at the systems in operation during Shipman's time, it can be observed how relatively easy it was for him to use these to his obvious advantage. One of the system failures was death certification. By relying on information provided by a single doctor, and without routine verification of the information, Shipman was allowed to give almost any cause of death. Or at least on one occasion he certified the case of death as 'natural causes' without giving any further details. Cremation certification involves the report of the attending doctor (Form B) being checked and confirmed by a second doctor (Form C), and then checked again by the medical attendant at the crematorium (Form D). Clearly, this procedure was lax in its operation.

In respect of 'Controlled Drugs', Shipman did not maintain a controlled drugs register, by claiming that he did not carry opiates. The routine inspection of general practice drug registers and storage facilities had lapsed, and there was no system in place to track the use or disposal of drugs after dispensing. This resulted in Shipman having little difficulty in obtaining illicit diamorphine to kill over 200 people through prescription fraud and the appropriation of unused diamorphine from patients or their families. Some people did make complaints about Shipman but none of these lead to a detailed assessment of Shipman's clinical performance. The fragmented and largely unconnected systems for dealing with complaints worked to protect Shipman from detection, rather than protect his patients from harm. There was no system to monitor 'mortality rates', none for assessment of the standards of record keeping. Appraisal and revalidation were not in operation. There was also the prevailing medical 'culture' which was deficient, there being no opportunities for informal peer review. When Shipman moved to the single-handed practice, he was more protected from review by colleagues. This made it virtually impossible for his staff to challenge him when patients died unexpectedly. In essence, there was a failure of some systems and an absence of others which only served to 'inhibit' both suspicion as a response to 'unusual' events, and the expression of concern if suspicion did arise.

'There is also the question of Shipman's relationship with his patients, which can best be described as 'paternalism' on his part, and 'deference' on theirs. Within the healthcare community in which he practised, he was regarded as a caring doctor, dependable, direct and always available. In such a relationship, it is very easy for a doctor to 'dominate' and even deceive the patient., unless there are external arrangements in place for detecting such breaches of trust. There were no adequate external arrangements in place, therefore Shipman exploited the situation and his patients to his advantage. Patients require information about their doctor and local repute has traditionally been used by patients to fulfil this requirement. However, this local network is not always reliable. It certainly failed in the case of Shipman. The problem in Shipman's practice was not single-handed practice but the patient-doctor relationship and the lack of any adequate external monitoring system. For Shipman, killing became a routine, yet serial killing can only ever become routine, where obstacles to its accomplishment have been overcome, and where systems for monitoring a doctor's activities are so inadequate as to allow murder in the same way, by the same means, by the same man to become repeated and established over decades.'

Source: "Patient-Centred Care after Shipman": Richard Baker, Journal of the Royal Society of Medicine, 2004 97 (4), 161-165

'Serial killing by a doctor must be extremely rare. When it happens again, the perpetrator is bound to try to avoid detection by whatever monitoring systems are then in place, and since it is impossible to predict the pattern that will be followed by the next serial killer, the construction of a process to detect that killer is difficult. It may be thought, therefore, that only limited effort should be developed to the reform of death certification processes, and to the introduction of a monitoring system. But although it is true that the detection of a small number of killings by a doctor would be difficult, a case such as Shipman's can never be allowed to happen again. Doctors would not deserve trust if they remain unable to identify a doctor who murders hundreds of patients. While the difficulties have to be recognised, everything possible must be done to make sure Shipman remains unique. General practitioners cannot be held responsible for the actions of Harold Shipman. They are, however, responsible for learning from what happened and making changes where they are needed. They must provide an answer to the question: What was it about general practice that enabled a general practitioner to kill more than 200 patients before the alarm was raised? There are practical changes that can be made to monitoring systems such as death and cremation certification, and review of controlled drugs handling. But there are also important general issues general practitioners and all doctors need to face, such as whether we are serious about revalidation as a procedure to ensure that patients can have reasonable confidence in their doctors. Shipman's murders have placed a duty on today's generation of general practitioners to learn every relevant lesson from what happened, and to respond accordingly.'

Source: *"Implications of Harold Shipman for General Practice"*, Richard Baker, *Post-Graduate Medical Journal, (2004,) 80, 303-306*

Physician As Serial Killer – The Shipman Case

'Faced with the revelations about Shipman, many doctors in the United Kingdom argued that there is no need for systematic reform because there will never be another Shipman. A common refrain was that Shipman was a killer who just happened to be a doctor. I take the view that it was the very fact that Shipman was a doctor that enabled him to kill and remain undiscovered. His profession provided him with the opportunity to kill, and the lack of safeguards and controls allowed him to avoid suspicion. Society invests great trust in doctors, giving us immense power. Shipman abused that trust, thereby exposing the profession's power and patients' lack thereof. In considering the role of trust and accountability in doctor-patient relationships, regulators and professional organisations must aim to equalise the power imbalance. Some of the best safeguards against another Shipman include encouraging a more questioning attitude toward doctors and implementing better systems for monitoring their work, especially their care of the most vulnerable patients. If this means greater regulation of the medical profession, then that may well be something we have to take on board. That is the real lesson of the case of Harold Shipman.'

Source: Dr A. Esmail, Professor of General Practice in Primary Care, University of Manchester – N ENGL J MED 352: p 1844, 18 May 5, 2005

IN MEMORIAM

The Trial of Dr John Bodkin Adams

First published by
Scott Martin Productions, 2020
www.scottmartinproductions.com

John Bodkin Adams (1899-1983)
Commons Attribution Photograph

Trial by jury is the lamp that shows that freedom lives.

Lord Patrick Devlin (1905-1992)

Acknowledgements

I am most grateful for the encouragement and support I have received from numerous quarters in the preparation of this work. In particular, I wish to express my sincere thanks to members of the medical and legal professions for the generous benefit of their experience, expertise and opinions on the many, and often emotive issues raised by this work. My thanks also go to those largely anonymous but ever obliging staff in the various institutions and libraries that I have consulted in my preparation for this work. Lastly, but by no mean least, I express my sincere gratitude to my publisher, Lesley Atherton, for her unfailing support and always helpful suggestions, and for keeping my feet firmly on the ground. My gratitude loses no sincerity in its generality.

The primary sources for this work have been R v Adams (1957) Trial Transcripts – National Archives, Criminal Law Review (1957) and Sybille Bedford's definitive verbatim account of the trial: 'The Best We Can Do'. In addition, a selection of other sources including books, legal and medical articles, and media reports have been consulted and acknowledged. I would, however, hasten to add, that none of the above are responsible for the contents of this work, and any errors are entirely my own.

David Holding, 2020

Introduction

This book being the second of a trilogy, takes the reader into the private world of medical doctors and their practices. Each book has centred upon one individual doctor who was a general medical practitioner living and working in England during the period from the mid-1920s to 1999. Whilst each of these practitioners came from different backgrounds, there is one common thread running through their respective lives. They were all charged and stood trial for murder, yet their motives appear to have been different.

Motives ranged from the exercising of the ultimate power over life and death, the obsession with wealth, privilege and social acceptance, and finally revenge and jealousy.

Each case received widespread public attention at the time, and all have been the subjects of numerous books, articles and media attention. This book, together with its two companions, is innovative in that it approaches the subject of 'murder' in an entirely novel way.

Each work commences by describing the early background of the subject and their career development. I also look into the personal characteristics that may help to provide an insight into the possible motives for their later activities. The work then progresses to the criminal investigation and subsequent arrest, culminating in the trial. Each work concludes with a general overview of the case to draw together all the essential strands of the case. By adopting this approach, the author's intention has been to involve the reader in each case from the outset, rather than simply allow them to remain 'passive' observers to the events. As each case unfolds, the reader is taken on a chronological journey and presented with the relevant information relating to the case. When the trial itself is reached, all the evidence, both for the prosecution and defence is available for the reader to consider - as would be the case in the actual trial. To conclude, the reader is invited to consider their own verdict based on all the evidence available. In this way, the reader is able to exercise their own judgement in a practical, yet enjoyable, way. In so doing, it is hoped that these works will provide the reader with an insight into the often complex processes involved in criminal investigation and trials, and the workings of our Criminal Justice System.

This second book of the trilogy centres on the trial of Dr John Bodkin Adams. Of Irish ancestry, this GP was based in Eastbourne, Sussex from the early 1920s. He was tried on one count of the murder of one of his elderly patients, Mrs Edith Alice Morrell, though the police claimed that Adams had also murdered a number of other elderly patients. They suggested that his 'modus operandi' was to administer the drugs, heroin and morphine, with the intention of making his patients addicts and therefore dependent upon him.

He was then in a position to induce them to leave him legacies in cash and kind in their wills. This having been achieved, his final action was to give them large doses of opiate drugs which caused their deaths. It was later suggested by the trial judge, Devlin J. that the police became fixated on the idea that Adams had murdered many elderly patients for legacies, so much so that they regarded the evidence of these legacies as legitimate grounds for their suspicions. The police investigated the wills of 132 of Adams' former patients between 1946 and 1956, in which he had personally benefited from a legacy. A list of around twelve names was prepared and this was submitted to the Director of Public Prosecutions. Judge Devlin considered that Mrs Morrell's case, which was the one eventually chosen by the Attorney-General for prosecution, looked the strongest of the twelve submitted, although others involved in the investigation disagreed.

As outlined in the Attorney General's opening address to the jury, it was the case that Adams either administered or instructed others to administer drugs that killed Mrs Morrell with the 'intention' of killing her. Such drugs were unnecessary as she was not suffering pain because she had remained in a semi-comatose condition for some time prior to her death. The prosecution suggested as motive that Adams had decided it was time for Mrs Morrell to die because he feared that she may alter her will to his disadvantage. In strict law, the prosecution did not need to show a motive but, if no motive was provided, then the prosecution needed to prove the offence by determining precisely how the killing was carried out.

Throughout the trial, the prosecution maintained Adams' motive was essentially a mercenary one. However, the prosecution did not consider a possible alternative – that Adams intended 'euthanasia' – which could be implied from the comment he made on his arrest: 'I was easing the passing'.

The prosecution initially argued that the large quantities of morphia and heroin prescribed by Adams in the months leading up to Mrs Morrell's death, had all been injected into her. This amount, they insisted, was sufficient to kill her, and they also insisted that it could *only* have been intended to kill her.

Accordingly, Adams was accused of

murdering Mrs Morrell by one of two methods, singularly or in combination. The first alleged method was as a result of the accumulation of the amounts of opiates given in the ten months before her death. The second was the result of two large injections of an 'unknown' but prescribed lethal substance prepared by Adams and injected into Mrs Morrell shortly before her death.

However, on the second day of Adams' trial, the defence produced nurses' note-books, which clearly showed that much smaller quantities of drugs had been given to Mrs Morrell than those the prosecution had estimated, based on Adams' prescriptions. More significantly, these note-books also recorded that the two injections made the night before Mrs Morrell's death, were recorded as being of Paraldehyde, which was a very safe soporific.

In response to the defence's production of the nurses' note-books, one of the prosecution's expert medical witnesses changed his testimony from that he had given at Adams' pre-trial Committal Hearing. Dr Douthwaite had previously introduced a new theory on how he believed Mrs Morrell had been killed. This was not accepted by the prosecution's own second medical witness, nor indeed by the defence's medical expert witness. The prosecution's only reaction was to argue (unsuccessfully), that the nurses' note-books were incomplete.

However, this assertion led Judge Devlin to comment that by this point in the trial, a conviction seemed unlikely because the medical evidence was inconclusive.

In his summing-up, the Judge stated that a doctor 'had no special defence but he is entitled to do all that is proper and necessary to relieve pain even if the measures he takes may incidentally shorten life'.

This established the legal principle of 'Double Effect'.

The Judge also gave direction to the jury, that they should not conclude that any more drugs were administered to Mrs Morrell other than those shown in the nurses' note-books.

The Judge concluded by indicating to the jury that the main argument for the defence was that the whole case against Dr Adams rested on mere suspicion, and that the case for the defence 'seems to me to be a manifestly strong one'. On these grounds, the jury returned a Not Guilty verdict after deliberating for just forty-six minutes.

After his acquittal on the charge of murder, Bodkin Adams resigned from the National Health Service and in July 1957, he pleaded guilty to fourteen of the sixteen other charges against him for forging prescriptions, making false statements on Cremation Forms and being responsible for other offences under the Dangerous Drugs Act.

He was convicted of these offences and was consequently struck off the Medical Register but was reinstated in 1961.

He spent much of the rest of his life in pursuing his favourite hobby of clay pigeon shooting, together with undertaking limited research and consultancy work. He also continued to receive legacies from his former patients.

After complications following the breaking of his leg in 1983, he was admitted to Eastbourne General Hospital where he died of heart failure on 4th July 1983. He was cremated and his ashes interred in the grave of his parents back in Coleraine, Ireland.

John Bodkin Adams was undoubtedly an incompetent doctor with little understanding of the true nature of the drugs he supplied. However, he was not considered to have shown disregard for the accepted standards of medical practice of the time. In this respect, he was considered to be no better and no worse than his GP contemporaries.

He may well have been perceived as a greedy and acquisitive individual, but the 'evidence' supporting the numerous claims that he was a 'serial killer' really amounted to little more than unsubstantiated gossip and rumour.

Chapter One: Early Years

John Bodkin Adams was born 21st January 1899 in Randalstown, County Antrim, Northern Ireland and was given his mother's maiden name of Bodkin. His father, Samuel, was a local magistrate, watchmaker, jeweller and engineer by trade. Samuel and his wife Ellen had two sons, William and John, and they all later moved to Coleraine, where John attended the Academical Institution. His father died when he was 15 and his younger brother died in his teens in the 1918 influenza pandemic.

John Bodkin wasn't regarded as a particularly outstanding student but was described as 'hard-working'. He entered Queens University Belfast Medical School at the age of 17 and gained his MB, BCh and BAO degrees in 1921, qualifying as a medical doctor.

Following graduation, he met Professor Arthur Rendle Short, a surgeon, at a Belfast conference, and Short invited him to join his staff as a junior casualty officer at the Bristol Royal Infirmary in England.

During this time, he studied for a Diploma in Public Health (DPH). Wendell Short encouraged him to apply for a post as a junior general practitioner because a hospital career did not appeal. In 1922, Adams saw an advertisement for a Christian practice assistant GP in Eastbourne, Sussex, with the possibility of a partnership. Adams applied to the practice of Emerson, Gurney and Rainey, and was successful in being appointed.

Being a new GP, he had to buy into the practice for £2,000 which he raised by means of a secured bank loan. He was joined in Eastbourne by his mother and cousin, Sarah.

In a relatively small town like Eastbourne in

the 1920s, a doctor had a standing in the local community, because of his close and special relationship with his patients. Once established in the town, he immersed himself in the 'social' life of the town by joining the Eastbourne Medical Society. He also organised Young Crusader's Bible Classes and was a supporter of Holy Trinity Church in the town.

The start of a fruitful relationship began when he was called to the mansion of William Mawhood, a wealthy retired steel merchant. His wife Edith had injured her leg and Adams referred her to a London surgeon who operated on it. The Mawhoods had a large home and land, even a gamekeeper for their estate. Adams was invited to join the pheasant shoots because he was a champion shot and as such, was welcomed into the 'country set'. Over time, he added many of the Sussex gentry to his patient list.

Within two years of joining the practice, Adams bought his first car and soon became an enthusiastic motorist and keen photographer. For four years he undertook research for his doctorate in Public Health which then enabled him to become a full partner in the practice in 1926, improving his financial status.

In 1929, a Victorian villa named Kent Lodge, went on the market and Adams was very impressed with it, since it had been a doctor's surgery in the 1880s. To purchase it, he borrowed most of the £3,000 required from William Mawhood, and also spent £2,000 of his own savings to convert the property. Around the time of Christmas 1930, he moved in with his mother, cousin Sarah, a servant and a chauffeur. On the social scene, Adams became a founding member of the Bisley Rifle Club and a local camera club. He was introduced to Lt Colonel Roland

Gwynne, a man of great wealth and social influence in Sussex, who was chairman of the Eastbourne bench of magistrates. To be in with the Colonel was to be part of the 'jet set' of the county – a group of men of wealth and influence with many contacts.

However, whilst Adams was certainly attracted by the high life, he did not forget his patients. He prospered and was popular with both his 'panel' (NHS) and private patients and never refused to visit patients at home.

Having obtained his Diploma in Anaesthetics (DA), Adams was appointed as part-time anaesthetist at the Princess Alice Memorial Hospital, Eastbourne in 1941. By the mid-1930s, Adams had a practice of 2,000 patients, around 1,000 'panel-patients' and the rest private. Panel-patients were working men who contributed to a national fund at work which paid the GP – this was a scheme introduced in 1910 by the prime minister, Lloyd George. Like most doctors at the time, Adams tailored his charges to the patients' financial state, in fact often not charging the very poor families at all.

However, by 1935, rumours began to circulate around the town regarding Adams' practices. A wealthy widow, Mrs Matilda Whitton, had been one of Adam's patients, and a friendly relationship developed between patient and doctor. When Mrs Whitton became incapable of driving herself, Adams would loan her his car and chauffeur.

As with most of Adams' activities, the motives could be interpreted in different ways. It could be argued that his kindly activities were in his patients' best interests, or that they were done with the intention of being remembered in her will. However, he was legitimately entitled to be appointed as Mrs Whitton's executor since none of her immediate family lived in Eastbourne. When she died of high blood pressure on 11th May 1935 at the age of 75, she left him £7,000 and also left £500 to his cousin. She also provided a codicil which bequeathed £100 to his mother, and the estate's total was around £200,000 by today's standards.

Mrs Whitton's family contested the will, although the High Court upheld it, quashing only the codicil. The publicity caused much local gossip, and some believe this to be the first of many adverse criticisms concerning Adams' character.

As early as the late 1930s, rumours were rife in Eastbourne about Adams receiving bequests and, more significantly, about the manner in which certain of his patients had died. It also appears that, at this time, there was much jealousy and envy among competing general practitioners in the town, with Adams becoming the most unpopular doctor there.

Another of Adams' failings was that he rarely kept records of his patients' details or of the drugs he prescribed, which did indicate a certain laxity in his administrative skills.

Also, it has been estimated that Adams' practice income was in the range of £7,000 a year. His private patients included nobility such as the Duke of Devonshire, the Sheriff of the County, Sir Roland Gwynne, and Richard Walker, the Chief Constable of Eastbourne. As a result of these patients, Adams was rapidly becoming the talk of Eastbourne. However, unlike other professionals, Adams had an unhealthy tendency to boast about his practices and was certainly ostentatious about his wealth. His partners were also critical of his excessive use of dangerous drugs and expressed their concerns to him.

Adams stayed in Eastbourne throughout the war, and he was described as being 'furious' at not being deemed desirable by other local doctors to be selected for a 'pool system' in which general practitioners in the town would treat patients of the doctors who had been called up for military service.

In 1941, Adams gained his Diploma in Anaesthetics which enabled him to work on a part-time basis at the Princess Alice Memorial Hospital in Eastbourne. In 1943, his mother died, followed in 1952 by his cousin Sarah who developed cancer. It is believed that Adams gave her an injection half an hour before she died, this being the only case where it could be considered that the doctor was 'easing the passing'.

Adam's career was very successful and by 1956, he was possibly one of the wealthiest GPs in the area. Whilst there were criticisms regarding Adams' overall competence, most observers agreed that he did appear to have an excellent bedside manner, particularly with his mostly elderly patients.

Over the succeeding years he built up a lucrative private practice attending to the needs of the many wealthy patients who had retired to the south coast, and many of them seemed to be grateful for his kind attentions.

Including a legacy for their doctors was not unusual in patients' wills. Adams received fourteen legacies totalling £21,000 from his former patients. As a doctor in receipt of such amounts, he soon became the subject of the usual gossip in the town, with various 'unsubstantiated' rumours circulating. One rumour was that the doctor had been responsible for the deaths, and that he his motive was the receipt of legacies.

One of Adam's patients, Gertrude Joyce Hullett, suffered from depression following the death of her second husband, Alfred John Hullett, in 1956.

Adams prescribed her barbiturates or 'barbitones' as they were known at the time, in order to help her sleep.

On the 22nd July 1956, Mrs Hullett lapsed into unconsciousness and Adams thought that she had suffered a brain haemorrhage or stroke. He immediately contacted the Coroner to arrange the necessary post-mortem. However, when the Coroner discovered to his obvious amazement and annoyance, that Mrs Hullett was still alive, he accused Adams of 'extreme incompetence'.

Despite this 'false alarm', Gertrude Hullett died the following day, and' although Adams recorded the cause of death as having been the result of a brain haemorrhage, the post-mortem revealed that she had in fact died after taking an overdose of barbiturates.

The subsequent Inquest held on 21st August, concluded that she had committed suicide 'of her own free will' as evidence had been provided that she'd repeatedly confided in her solicitor and friends that she intended to take her own life. However, the East Sussex Coroner, Dr AC Somerville, did note that Gertrude had experienced 'an extraordinary amount of careless treatment', and that the doctors attending her had failed to realise they were dealing with a case of barbiturate poisoning until it was too late to administer the antidote.

It was also noted that Adams had been left a Rolls Royce car in Gertrude's will and had also received a cheque for £1,000 only days before her death, and that Adams had requested the bank process this cheque with special clearance. It was at this time that Eastbourne police received an anonymous call claiming that Adams was responsible for turning Gertrude Hullett into a 'drug addict'.

The first unusual feature of the Inquest Hearing was the appearance of a Detective Superintendent Herbert Hannam from Scotland Yard. He was asked by the Coroner if there were any reasons why the Inquest should be adjourned. The Coroner explained that the Chief Constable of Eastbourne had requested the aid of Scotland Yard to investigate certain 'suspicious' deaths that had occurred in the neighbourhood. It remained uncertain why the Chief Constable decided to take this step, or why he thought it appropriate for this decision to be announced during the course of the Inquest into what appeared to be a straightforward case of suicide.

The second unusual feature of the Hearing was the extraordinary amount of interest being shown by the national press in what otherwise would have been an unremarkable Inquest. It became obvious that the press had been 'tipped off' that there was a potential story worth following in Eastbourne.

On the 22nd of August 1956, *The Daily Mail* ran a report of the Hullett Inquest under the headline: 'Yard Probes Mass Poisonings: Twenty Five Deaths in the Great Mystery of Eastbourne'. Although this report did not mention Adams by name, it became quite obvious that the article was referring to him.

This was followed with further press headlines such as: 'Enquiry into Four Hundred Wills: Rich Women Believed to Have been the Victims' appearing in *The Daily Telegraph*.

This gave the general impression that there was a mass murderer on the loose on the south coast, which certainly warranted police attention. It also appears that there was a confidential meeting at the Princes Alice Hospital in 1954 concerning certain aspects of Dr Adams' practices.

It was believed that Dr Adams might be

forging doctors' signatures in order to procure NHS Services for his private patients. This resulted in a cloud of suspicion and gossip hanging over Adams throughout the 1950s. The gossip mainly concerned the number of patients who had left money to him, and, while it had to be admitted that Eastbourne with its significantly high population of elderly people could expect a correspondingly high death rate, the rumours questioned how often patients leaving him legacies had died.

Whilst it could be expected that some of these deaths would be sudden, the question did arise: Were these deaths, in fact, being hastened by Adams?

Readers were informed that the Scotland Yard murder squad was investigating the suspected poisoning of hundreds of wealthy women in Eastbourne over a period of 20 years. As a result, detectives embarked on an investigation of Dr Adams' professional life, their brief being to look for any evidence of fraud and murder.

Eventually, a picture emerged of Dr Adams as a greedy, avaricious physician of dubious morality: an insatiable legacy hunter.

This view was fuelled by statements from solicitors and bank managers testifying to Dr Adams' persistence in pressing patients to alter their wills in his favour.

A painstaking search found 132 wills containing £45,000 in bequests to the doctor (a very large sum for the time). Cases were discovered of cremation forms in which the doctor had failed to declare his interest as a beneficiary under the will – an intentional omission that avoided the need for a post-mortem examination.

A study of the doctor's death certificates also raised questions about his diagnostic capability or honesty, since an unnaturally high proportion had 'cerebral haemorrhage' or 'cerebral thrombosis' entered as the cause of death.

Instances of sudden decline and death following closely after a will change excited particular interest, especially from the police.

Relatives also drew the Yard's attention to the case of 82 year-old Julia Bradnum, who died with unexpected suddenness in 1952, leaving the doctor as sole executor of a new will. The Yard subsequently exhumed her body. They also exhumed the bodies of the Mss Hilda and Clara Neil Miller, spinster sisters who died in 1953 and 1954. Hilda left everything to Clara, and Clara left most of her estate to Adams.

In late October 1956, Hannam submitted his dossier on the investigation into Adams' activities to Sir Theobald Matthew, the Director of Public Prosecutions.

Chapter Two: The Police Investigation

The investigation had been taken over from Eastbourne police on the 17th August 1956 by two officers from the Metropolitan Police's Murder Squad. The senior officer was Detective Superintendent Herbert Hannam of Scotland Yard who was known for having solved the Teddington towpath murders in 1953. He was assisted by Detective Sergeant Charles Hewett, and Inspector Brynley Pugh as liaison officer from Eastbourne police.

Hannam was in an unusual position. Instead of having to find a suspect for a known case, he already had a suspect in Dr Adams. However, he needed to link him to more offences of a more serious nature than forging prescriptions, making false statements on cremation forms and mishandling dangerous drugs. In pursuance of this, Hannam launched a detailed investigation into Dr Adam's professional activities in Eastbourne. It has been suggested that Hannam became fixated with the belief that Adams had murdered many elderly patients for legacies. However, his main ground for suspicion was that Adams had received several legacies but in reality, these were only as a minor beneficiary.

It was arranged for the Home Office pathologist, Dr Francis Camps, to examine 310 death certificates certified by Adams over a ten year period from 1946 to 1956. Camps considered that a total of 143 (46%) of these were 'suspicious'. He also highlighted the fact that a high proportion of these certificates certified death as due to 'cerebral haemorrhage' or 'cerebral thrombosis'. The police took numerous statements from the nurses who had treated Adams' patients. Some of these were favourable to him, whilst others claimed that Adams had given patients 'special' injections of 'unknown substances' which Adams refused to describe to the nurses.

These statements also claimed that his habit was to ask the nurses to leave the room before the injections were given. He would also isolate patients from their relatives preventing contact between them, and this was a rather unusual practice.

On the 24th August 1956, the British Medical Association (BMA), sent a letter to all doctors in Eastbourne reminding them of 'patient confidentiality' if they were interviewed by the police. Hannam regarded this as 'obstructing' his investigation. He, together with the Attorney General, Sir Reginald Mannigham-Buller, wrote to the secretary of the BMA urging him to remove this ban on police interviewing. However, it was not until 8th November that the Attorney General met with the BMA secretary personally and convinced him of the importance of the case being investigated. It also appears that during this meeting, he passed Hannam's report on Adams to the secretary.

It is very likely that this report was copied and found its way into the hands of Adams' defence team, before being returned at day later, to the Attorney-General's office. This in itself, was a very unprecedented move for a prosecutor to make, given the confidentiality of the file. Now convinced of the seriousness of the accusations levelled at Adams, the BMA secretary dropped his opposition to doctors being interviewed by the police.

Hannam came to the conclusions that he was 'confident' that Adams was a 'mass-murderer' and that he had certainly killed at least fourteen people. Rather unprofessionally for an investigating detective, Hannam is believed to have also passed this information to the 'ever listening' members of the press who had now descended on Eastbourne in their droves. Hannam based his 'theory' on the fact that Dr Adams made his victims dependant on drugs, persuaded them to change their wills in his favour, and then killed them with an overdose.

How much this theory was based on reliable or 'circumstantial' evidence or entirely on rumour and gossip, is anyone's guess.

In pursuance of his theory, Hannam contrived a meeting with Adams on 1st October 1956 by deliberately walking past his home with the specific intention of engaging Adams in conversation. During this conversation, Hannam raised the matter of the legacy that Adams had received from Mrs Edith Morrell – one of his patients. In particular, Hannam wanted to know why Adams had not declared that he was a beneficiary under her will on her cremation form – a form which he had completed and signed.

Adams's response to this was that it was 'not done wickedly but simply to allow the cremation to go smoothly for the sake of the relatives and it was not deceitful'. Hannam also mentioned to Adams that he had forged a prescription for drugs, to which Adams admitted 'it was wrong of me to do that'.

As a result of this 'unofficial' conversation, Hannam now established that he had evidence that there were indeed irregularities in Adams' professional activities. As a result, the police obtained a warrant under the Dangerous Drugs Act 1951, and arrested Adams on the 24th November 1956, and executed a search of his home and surgery. This search was undertaken by Superintendent Hannam and Inspector Pugh, head of Eastbourne CID. They explained to Adams that they were looking for morphine, heroin and pethidine drugs.

Adams' reply was that they would not find any in the house because he seldom used them. Hannam then asked Adams for his Dangerous Drugs Register which records drugs ordered and used by the doctor. His reply was 'I keep no register and have not kept one since 1949'.

When Hannam showed Adams a list of dangerous drugs which he had prescribed for his patient Mrs Morrell, and asked who administered them, Adams replied, 'I did nearly all. Perhaps the nurses gave some but mostly me'.

Hannam then pointed out, 'Doctor, you prescribed for her 75-1/6 grains of heroin tablets the day before she died'.

Adams replied, 'Poor soul, she was in such agony. It was all used, I used them myself'.

As a result of the search on 24th November 1956, Adams was taken to Eastbourne Police station where he was charged with eight offences under the Forgery Act 1913, four under the Cremation Act 1902 and one under the Larceny Act 1956.

The majority of the charges related to the forging of National Health Service prescriptions, whilst the charges under the Cremation Act related to the fact that he had made false representations on death certificates stating that he had 'no pecuniary interest in the deceased's estate' – a statement which he knew to be false.

On the 26th of November, Adams appeared at Eastbourne Magistrates' Court where he was remanded on bail of £2,000 and required to surrender his passport. Whilst at the police station Superintendent Hannam informed Adams that they were looking into the death of a number of his patients and in particular, Mrs Morrell. Adams' reply was: 'Easing the passing of a dying person is not all that wicked. She wanted to die. That cannot be murder. It is impossible to accuse a doctor'.

On the 19th December 1956, Adams was arrested a second time, charged with the murder of Edith Alice Morrell on a day in November 1950. Adams' reply to the charge was: 'Murder? Can you prove it was murder? I did not think you could prove murder. She was dying in any event'.

The police also charged Adams with two further charges under the Dangerous Drugs Act 1951 relating to his attempt to conceal drugs and obstructing the police during the search of his home, together with failing to keep a register of drugs as required under the Dangerous Drugs Regulations 1953. Adams was remanded in Brixton Prison to await the Committal Hearing.

The original list of cases that Hannam regarded as warranting prosecution was narrowed down to those of Mrs Morrell, Mr & Mrs Hullett, Clara Neil Miller and Julia Bradnum.

However, in the cases of Mr Hullett, Clara Miller and Julia Bradnum, there was no certainty of an unnatural death as there was evidence that Mr Hullett died of a heart attack.

As a result of the exhumations of Miss Miller, the pathologist concluded that she died of pneumonia.

The condition of Bradnum's body did not allow a cause of death to be stated.

Mrs Hullett had died an unnatural death of barbiturate overdose, but there was no evidence or admission that Adams had persuaded to take the overdose.

The Committal Hearing opened in Lewes on the 14th January 1957.

Adams was charged on the single count of murdering Mrs Morrell, although the prosecution also alleged that he had killed Mr and Mrs Hullett in a similar fashion. They introduced evidence relating to them as 'similar fact' evidence. Despite the objections of the defence team that this type of evidence was inadmissible, the magistrates allowed it. However, in cross-examination, the defence did force an admission from the Crown's expert witness, that Mr Hullett had died of a coronary thrombosis.

The defence made an application for the Committal Hearing to be held in private, believing it would be prejudicial for the defence to have the prosecution evidence on the Hullet case made public, when Adams was only facing the charge of murdering Edith Morrell. However, this was refused.

The Hearing lasted nine days, concluding on the 24th January with Adams being committed for trial on the Morrell charge. The Chairman of the magistrates was Sir Roland Gwynne, but he stepped down because of his close relationship with Adams.

A vital piece of evidence (the cheque written out by Mrs Hullett for £1,000) went missing after the hearing. While the culprit was never found, Scotland Yard suspected the Deputy Chief Constable of Eastbourne of having misplaced in an attempt to help Adams. He was known to have taken holidays with Adams and Gwynne.

Mr Justice Devlin, the trial judge offered the opinion later that it would have been wiser if the Committal Hearing had been in private.

Adams was returned to Brixton Prison to await trial. Following the Committal Hearing, the Attorney General informed the trial judge, that he would not be using the evidence regarding Mr Hullett in the Morrell trial but would seek a second indictment relating to Mrs Hullett, which he did on the 5th March 1957. Had he proceeded with a second indictment, then a second committal hearing would have been required. Consequently, the indictment relating to Mrs Hullett would have been held back for a possible second trial.

Chapter Three: The Trial

R v ADAMS

CENTRAL CRIMINAL COURT, LONDON, BEFORE MR JUSTICE PATRICK DEVLIN.

CHARGED WITH THE MURDER OF EDITH ALICE MORRELL ON THE 13TH DAY OF NOVEMBER 1950.

PLEADED: NOT GUILTY.

PROSECUTING COUNSEL: DEFENCE COUNSEL:

Sir Reginald Manningham-Buller, QC, MP.
Mr Geoffrey Lawrence, QC.
Mr Melford Stevenson, QC.
Mr Edward Clarke QC.
Mr Malcolm Morris.
Mr John Heritage.

Dr Adams faced two charges, firstly that he murdered Mrs Morrell and secondly that he murdered Mr & Mrs Hullett.

Following legal precedent, he first faced the charge of murdering Mrs Morrell. The case was heard at the Old Bailey in London, and the Medical Defence Union (MDU) had chosen Geoffrey Lawrence QC – a very skilful and persuasive barrister – to defend him.

The essence of the prosecution case was that an eighty-one year-old woman, half paralysed by a stroke, had died. The prosecution maintained that her death was not the result of age or illness but of poisoning by drugs. These drugs, they maintained, were prescribed during the last five days of her life without a medical reason.

The weight of the prosecution case rested on three pertinent questions.

Firstly, was the quantity of drugs prescribed actually administered and by whom?

Secondly, was the dosage of the drugs actually fatal or merely excessively large?

Thirdly, was there in fact, no medical reason other than murder to account for their administration?

According to Sybille Bedford's astute observation:

'Yet in a way the motive has already drawn sustenance from an irregular but not secret source; it has waxed big by headlines, by printed innuendo, by items half remembered from the committal hearing. There have been published rumours of rich patients, mass poisonings, of legacy on legacy in solid sterling. Everybody knows a bit too much and no one knows quite enough; there is a most disturbing element in this case, extra-mural, half-knowledge that cannot be admitted and cannot be kept out.'
The Best We Can Do (1989) p 24.

Described by Rupert Furneux in his *Famous Criminal Cases*, the trial of Adams was considered to be 'one of the greatest murder trials of all time', and by *The Times* as 'the murder trial of the century'.

The trial was presided over by Mr Justice Patrick Devlin (later Lord), who noted that the case presented the 'most curious situation' which was 'perhaps unique in these courts, that the act of murder has to be proved by expert evidence'.

The trial lasted seventeen days which, at the time, made it the longest murder trial in English criminal history. What Judge Devlin meant by his remarks was that the first task of the prosecution was to convince the jury that Edith Alice Morrell had in fact been murdered. This was a far from straightforward task, since they had no body, and since the formal cause of death had already been recorded as cerebral thrombosis by the very same doctor now being accused of murdering her.

Essentially, the prosecution argument was that Mrs Morrell had in fact died as a result of the various drugs given to her by Adams. In order to demonstrate this, the prosecution relied firstly on the testimony of the nurses who attended Mrs Morrell during her last days. They were questioned on the drugs they actually administered to her on Adam's instructions, and secondly on the expert medical evidence that it was this course of drugs that killed Edith Morrell.

Prosecution: Opening Address to the Jury

Opening the case for the prosecution, the Attorney General, Sir Reginald Manningham-Buller described Dr Adams to the jury as a doctor in his fifties who was charged with the murder of one of his patients, the murder occurring six years ago. He was a Doctor of Medicine and Bachelor of Surgery, with a Diploma in Anaesthetics. The victim was described as an eighty-one year old widow who left an estate valued at £157,000. She died in November 1950 having suffered a stroke two years earlier, the result of which left her paralysed. Adams was the doctor in charge of her care.

In addition, Mrs Morrell was attended to by four nurses who would give evidence that they never saw Mrs Morrell suffering from severe pain. The prosecution would be calling a Harley Street consultant who would confirm that, in his opinion,

Mrs Morrell was suffering from cerebral arteriolesclerosis or 'hardening of the arteries'. The jury would also be told of large quantities of drugs prescribed and administered by Adams over the course of months.

One of the questions to be considered was why were they given? The total quantity of the drugs given over a period of ten and a half months amounted to: 1,629 grains of barbiturates; 1,928 grains of Sedormid; 164 grains of morphia and 130 grains of heroin. The jury was informed that if these drugs were administered over a significant period of time, they would result in a 'serious degree of addiction' and a dependence on them. Since Dr Adams was the source of this supply, it follows that Mrs Morrell must have become dependent upon him. Another question arose of why these drugs were prescribed to an old lady who was not suffering from pain.

The jury was then informed that Mrs Morrell made three wills in 1947 in which Dr Adams was not mentioned. Then in April 1949 when Mrs Morrell had been receiving both morphia and heroin for several months, Dr Adams contacted her solicitor, Mr Sogro, to express concerns that Mrs Morrell was very anxious about her will and that she required to see him urgently.

The solicitor attended Mrs Morrell which resulted in her making another will in which she bequeathed Dr Adams an oak chest containing silver.

After a period of almost twelve months, Adams again visited Mr Sogro to inform him that Mrs Morrell had promised him her Rolls Royce car in her will, but that she had forgotten to include this in her latest version, together with the contents of a box deposited with her bank. Adams stressed to the solicitor that despite Mrs Morrell's illness, her mind was perfectly clear and that she was in a fit state to execute a codicil to her will.

Having reservations about this, Mr Sogro insisted that they should wait until Mrs Morrell's son came to visit her. Despite this, Adams suggested that the solicitor should prepare a codicil which could be executed but destroyed if it did not meet with the approval of Mrs Morrell's son. This resulted in Mr Sogro visiting Mrs Morrell once again, when she made another will in which she left Adams the chest of silver but left him the Rolls Royce car only on the condition that her son pre-deceased her.

In September of 1949, Dr Adams was away on holiday and Mrs Morrell was attended by Adams' partner, Dr Harris. Mrs Morrell was so annoyed with this that she executed yet another codicil to her last will, this time revoking her entire bequests to Adams.

At this point, the Attorney General then produced a graph showing the alleged prescriptions issued by Dr Adams which indicated how the rates of morphia had increased three times during the final thirteen days of Mrs Morrell's life, far more than at any time during the previous months, with the rate of heroin increasing by seven and a half times.

The Attorney General then raised the question of what had happened to Mrs Morrell that made it necessary for these large increases. He suggested that if she had been in severe pain, these increases could have been justified, but said that she was not in pain.

The jury were then informed that the nurses who attended Mrs Morrell would confirm that during her final days, Mrs Morrell was in fact, in a semi-conscious state (a coma). The Attorney General continued: 'Why did the doctor prescribe such quantities for which there was no medical justification? The submission of the Crown is that he did so because he had decided that the time had come for Mrs Morrell to die'.

Describing the night of her death, the prosecution said that Mrs Morrell was lying unconscious in a coma. At 10 pm, Dr Adams filled a 5cc syringe with a 'preparation' and instructed the night nurse to inject it into the unconscious patient, which she did. The doctor then refilled the empty syringe with another large quantity, instructing the nurse to give this second injection if the patient did not become quieter. The nurse gave the second injection, and at 2 am, Mrs Morrell died.

The jury was then asked to consider the question of why such large injections were given to an unconscious woman? The prosecution did concede that Mrs Morrell may well have been a dying woman when the injections were given. That being the case, the prosecution submitted that she was, in effect, dying from overdoses of morphia and heroin, prescribed by Dr Adams, this constituting murder by the doctor.

Similarly, if the two injections did in fact accelerate death, this also constituted murder. The Attorney General then told the jury: 'The prosecution will submit that the only conclusion to which you can come is that the doctor killed her, deliberately and intentionally'.

The prosecution then told the jury that on the same day that Mrs Morrell died, the 13th November 1950, Adams filled in the form to secure Mrs Morrell's cremation. To the question on the form: 'Have you, as far as you are aware, any pecuniary interest in the death of the deceased?' Adams wrote 'Not as far as I am aware'. Consequently, authority was given for Mrs Morrell's cremation.

In 1956, when police from Scotland Yard were making inquiries, the detective superintendent in charge of the investigation questioned Adams about this cremation certificate. Adams' reply was: 'Oh, that was not done wickedly. God knows it wasn't. We always want cremations to go off smoothly for the dear relatives. If I had said I knew I was getting money under the will, they might get suspicious, and I like cremations and burials to go off smoothly. There was nothing suspicious really. It was not deceitful'.

In November 1956, Detective Superintendent Hannam together with two other detectives visited Dr Adams at his home to execute a search warrant for dangerous drugs. The Superintendent asked Adams to look at a list of prescriptions he had made out for Mrs Morrell, with the comment: 'There are a lot of dangerous drugs here. Who administered them?'

Adams' reply was 'I did, nearly all. Perhaps the nurses gave some, but mostly me'. The Superintendent then asked Adams a further question: 'Were there any of these drugs left over when she died?' to which Adams answered: 'No none, all was given to the patient. Poor soul was in terrible agony.'

The prosecution then reminded the jury that the maximum quantity of heroin which should be prescribed in any period of twenty-four hours is ¼ of a grain. No less than eight grains were prescribed by Adams on one single day alone. The maximum dose of morphia recommended is ½ grain. Yet, between the 8th and 11th of November, a total of 40 grains were prescribed. Expert medical witnesses would confirm that Mrs Morrell could not survive the administration of those drugs during her final days.

The Attorney General concluded his opening speech to the jury by relating the fact that Dr Adams visited Detective Superintendent Hannam to inquire on the progress of the police investigation. He was informed by the superintendent that he was still inquiring into the death of some of his patients.

The doctor asked which patients he was referring to, and the superintendent replied: 'Mrs Morrell is certainly one'. To this, Dr Adams replied: 'Easing the passing of a dying person is not all that wicked. She wanted to die, that cannot be murder. It is impossible to accuse a doctor'.

In December 1956, Dr Adams was arrested and informed that he was being charged with the murder of Mrs Morrell. To this, Adams replied: 'Murder, can you prove it was murder?'

The superintendent then informed Dr Adams 'You are now charged with murder' to which Adams replied: 'I do not think you could prove it was murder, she was dying in any event'.

The prosecution concluded: 'I submit to you that the evidence I and my learned friends will call before you, will prove conclusively that this old lady was murdered'.

To summarise the prosecution case, an eighty-one year old woman, paralysed after a stroke had died. It was the prosecution's submission that she did not die of illness or of natural causes, but as the result of drugs prescribed during the final five days of her life.

According to Sybille Bedford: 'Three pertinent questions arose in relation to the prosecution case. Was the quantity of drugs prescribed actually administered? Was the dosage of these drugs actually fatal or was it merely very large? And, was there in fact, no medical or other reason short of murder for their administration?

The Best We Can Do by Sybille Bedford, Penguin

Books, Harmondsworth (1989) p23

To support the first strand of their case, the prosecution produced four witnesses in the form of the nurses who had attended Mrs Morrell in her final days, Helen Stronach, Helen Mason-Ellis, Caroline Randall and Brenda Bartlett. Nurse Helen Stronach, the first to take the witness stand, stated that at 9 pm she gave Mrs Morrell ¼ grain of morphia, then at 11 pm the doctor would give another injection but that she did not know what it was. Defence counsel, Geoffrey Lawrence QC asked if she had written these occurrences in the nurses report book, to which she replied: 'Yes, every time we gave an injection, we wrote it down, what it was, the time it was administered and our names'. Lawrence then suggested that 'anything and everything that happened of significance in the patient's illness would have to go down in these books?'

Nurse Stronach replied: 'We reported everything'.

Lawrence continued with his cross-examination. 'So that if only we had those reports now, we could see the truth of exactly what happened, night by night and day by day when you were there?' Nurse Stronach confirmed 'Yes'.

To everyone's complete surprise, Lawrence produced the nurses' note-books and asked Nurse Stronach to identify them. It was widely believed that such note-books had been destroyed after the patient's death.

Lawrence then proceeded to read out the entries that Nurse Stronach had to admit she had made. He then concluded his cross-examination of this prosecution witness: 'We have now been through the whole of your records for that time. We have not found a single instance where you gave that injection of ¼ grain of morphia by itself that you have been talking about. You recorded only one or two visits by the Doctor, and then we find you knew exactly what the injection was that was administered'.

Nurse Stronach had no comment to make on these revelations, Lawrence having effectively demolished her credibility. She was followed onto the witness stand by Sister Mason-Ellis, who, by now, was acutely aware of the existence of the note-books.

In cross examination of this witness, Lawrence read out her report for the afternoon preceding Mrs Morrell's death. This stated: 'Awake but quiet. Half a glass of milk and brandy, 3 drachms taken'.

Mr Lawrence continued: 'This indicates quite clearly that she was not in a coma'. In response to this revelation, Sister Mason-Ellis replied: 'Not according to my report'. To this, Lawrence replied: 'Did you not agree that the reports were where the truth was to be found? You do not want to go back on that now, do you?' Her reply was: 'Not at all'. Lawrence further replied: 'So when you wrote "awake" she must have been awake?' to which Sister Mason-Ellis replied that 'She must have been'. Finally, Lawrence concluded his cross examination of this witness with the comment: 'Therefore she could not possibly have been in a coma'.

Nurse Randall followed onto the witness stand, having been regarded as the prosecution's 'star' witness, because she had been present with Mrs Morrell during the final hours prior to her death.

The Attorney General had highlighted in his opening address to the jury that she would describe this crucial period in detail to them: 'The night nurse will tell you Mrs Morrell was very weak, except for occasional spasms, she was in a coma. At 10 pm the Doctor came and himself filled a 5cc syringe with a preparation'.

Holding up an empty 5cc syringe to the jury, the Attorney General stated that the doctor gave this syringe to the night nurse and told her to inject the contents into the unconscious woman, which she did. The doctor took the empty syringe and refilled it with a similar quantity which was far too large a quantity on each occasion to be morphine or heroin, and he told the nurse to give the second injection to the patient if she did not become quieter.

The nurse did not like giving another large injection from this unusually large syringe – whatever it was – and later in the evening, she telephoned the doctor. She received instructions and it was her duty to obey them. So, she gave the second injection, Mrs Morrell gradually became quiet, and at 2 am she died. The prosecution cannot tell you what was in the syringes.

The Attorney General did not ask this witness to repeat the evidence she had given at Dr Adams' Committal Hearing, because her 'written' report told a very different story to her 'verbal' one. In cross examination of this witness, Lawrence read out the entries from the report-book: 'Patient very weak and restless. 9.30 pm 'Paraldehyde' 5cc given intravenously by the Doctor. 11.30 pm, very restless no sleep. 12.30 am, restless and talkative and very shaky. 12.45 am seems a little quieter, appears asleep, respiration 50. 2 am passed away quietly."

There were no references made to 'spasms', no injections given by the nurse, no phone calls, one injection given by the Doctor; when the patient was not unconscious but restless, not with a lethal dose of powerful morphine or heroin, but a reasonable dose of safe, paraldehyde. Nurse Randall, in her original evidence to the Committal Hearing said that she had telephoned the doctor and given a second injection. However, Lawrence now in cross examination asked: 'Why give the injection when the patient was not restless but quieter and seemed asleep? Your memory isn't very trustworthy?' to which Nurse Randall replied: 'It appears not to be'.

It is apparent that the prosecution had led Nurse Randall to describe Mrs Morrell's jerky spasms because these were a common sign of a withdrawal symptom from opiate poisoning, the main contention of the prosecution's case. Still under cross examination by the defence, Nurse Randall continued: 'They were so bad I could not leave her, and they almost jerked her out of bed. I have never seen jerks as bad'.

In response, Lawrence commented that they were not bad enough to be recorded in her report, to which Nurse Randall replied: 'I wrote that she was very shaky'. Lawrence responded: 'Shaky? Was that the word for the spasms that almost jerked the patient out of bed?' to which the nurse replied: 'I just don't know. I suppose I wrote it down quickly'.

Answering a question from the judge, Nurse Randall stated: 'I think 4cc or 5cc of paraldehyde is a very large dose'. Lawrence then informed her: 'Do you know that the British Pharmacopoeia full dose is 120 minims or 8cc?'

The fourth and final nurse to take the witness stand was Sister Brenda Bartlett, who had shared the last night duty with Nurse Randall. She began by repeating some of the evidence she too had given at Adams' Committal Hearing. She told that the patient had 'twitching spasms and was semi-comatose'.

Once again, Lawrence read out her written

report: 'Awake, restless, talkative', to which Lawrence commented: 'This was hardly semi-comatose, not a spasm, twitch or shake'. It soon became obvious that the prosecution had expected the nurses' evidence to be undisputed. However, with the report books, Lawrence had been able to challenge the prosecution evidence, point by point, and in effect, destroying it over a period of one week.

The next prosecution witness was Dr Arthur Henry Douthwaite, senior physician at Guy's Hospital, London, the first of their medical expert witnesses. Like the nurses, he too, had given evidence previously at Adams' Committal Hearing and expected to be asked to repeat this same evidence at the trial. To reiterate the Attorney General's intention in his opening speech to the jury: 'The prosecution will call a medical authority who will tell you that in their view Mrs Morrell could not possibly have survived the administration of the drugs prescribed for her in the last five days of her life'.

However, that evidence was now challenged because the nurses' note-books indicated that Mrs Morrell had, in effect, been given only a small proportion of the drugs prescribed for her at the end.

Douthwaite stated that he believed Bodkin Adams must have meant murder if he gave his patient 41 grains of morphia and 39 grains of heroin in her last five days. However, the evidence proved otherwise. According to the prosecution chemist's calculations, the discrepancy between prescription and administration during the period, was 30 grains of morphia and 22 grains of heroin. In view of these significantly revised figures, together with the nurses' note-books, could Dr Douthwaite still maintain that he believed Dr Adams was trying to kill his patient?

Was he, in effect, influenced by prosecution

lawyers to give evidence they so badly needed to keep the case going?

The Attorney General asked Dr Douthwaite: 'Is there, in your opinion, any justification for injecting morphia and heroin immediately after a stroke?' The doctor replied: 'No justification whatsoever'. The Attorney General continued: 'Is it right or wrong to do so?' and Dr Douthwaite answered: 'Wrong in all circumstances, wrong'. Finally, the Attorney General asked Dr Douthwaite: 'What conclusion do you draw from the dosage administered in the last days, and what conclusions do you draw as to the intentions with which that dosage must have been prescribed?' Dr Douthwaite replied: 'The only conclusion I can come to is that the intention on 8 November was to terminate her life'.

Dr Douthwaite had been incorrect in assuming, when he gave his evidence at the Committal Hearing that for the last three or four days of her life, Mrs Morrell had been in a continuous coma, as this was demonstrated not to be the case. He had not made any inquiries regarding the symptoms of her stroke and the treatment she had been given for it in the Cheshire hospital where she was first treated. In cross-examining Dr Douthwaite, Mr Lawrence began to exert pressure on this witness: 'It would be most important to know before condemning the doctor's treatment from the outset what actually happened back in Cheshire'. To this, Douthwaite replied: 'It would be interesting to know'.

Lawrence then produced the clinical record obtained from the hospital in Cheshire, which was another major blow for the prosecution. Lawrence read from the document which covered the ten days in which Mrs Morrell had been at the hospital. This indicated that for every night, there was a record of morphia being injected. Lawrence then asked Dr Douthwaite a pertinent question: 'Does the field of condemnation that you are spreading from this witness-box include Dr Turner of Cheshire for having given the patient morphia after a stroke?' Dr Douthwaite's only response to this was: 'If that was the treatment for the stroke, yes'.

By now, it was becoming very clear that the prosecution's case was collapsing. There had been four doctors who had seen Mrs Morrell, and every one of them had prescribed morphia. This raised the question of whether everyone was wrong, with the exception of Dr Douthwaite, who had never seen her. Quite clearly, he had overstated his case. As the cross examination continued, his absolute certainty became more doubtful when asked by Lawrence what was in the doctor's mind. His guarded reply was: 'I don't know what was in his mind', to which Lawrence retorted: 'Did you not before, when you saw murderous intent?' Douthwaite made no comment. Even the trial judge himself felt that Douthwaite had clearly overstated his case.

The trial lasted a total of sixteen days to become the longest for murder in English criminal history up to that date. By this stage, it had become clear that the case for the Crown was virtually lost. There was no doubt that Dr Douthwaite had been over-persuaded by the prosecution to stick to his original theory regarding the use of opiates. It also served as a reminder to witnesses, that the real strength of any evidence is its reasonableness; it has to be both sound and defensible, and to convince the jury of that fact.

Despite their obvious weak position, the prosecution continued with the Attorney General believing that he could still turn the case around by cross examining Adams himself. He found, to his dismay, that the defence had decided not to call Adams to the witness-stand because Lawrence's 'demolition job' on the prosecution's case had been completely successful.

Defence: Closing Address to the Jury

Geoffrey Lawrence QC began his address to the jury by describing the case before them as being 'one of the most extraordinary'. He then outlined what the Doctor was accused of: 'It is this; that he deliberately murdered an old woman who was his patient at a time when she was already dying and had no more than possibly a very few days or weeks to live'. He then asked the jury to consider: 'Is that not a most extraordinary case that a doctor should be accused of murdering one of his patients when she was dying already'.

With no intervention of the Doctor's part, the end was inevitable, and that was the case alleged against Dr Adams. He then reminded the jury that 'the burden of proof lies on the prosecution and that means that possibility of guilt is not enough, suspicion of guilt is not enough, probability is not enough. It is certainty beyond a reasonable doubt that is required'.

Lawrence then explained to the jury why the accused had not given evidence himself. He outlined the strain under which Dr Adams had laboured during the process of the trial, and that he would be required to recall incidents that happened six years ago. He was unable to refer to any notes and was totally reliant on his own memory-recall. Mr Lawrence then emphasised that any failure on the Doctor's part, however minor, would be interpreted as an indication of guilt, however innocent that failure of recollection or accuracy may be.

Defence counsel then outlined for the jury, the background to the case of Mrs Morrell. Whilst in Cheshire in June 1948, she suffered a stroke. She was described as paralysed, autocratic, difficult and a very wealthy woman. Lawrence then described her first morphine injections given in Cheshire as the most 'significant signpost' in the whole case. The medical prognosis was that she had between six to twelve months to live. The question then arose of what the Doctor could do for her? He could make her life as bearable as possible, give her sleep at night and make her cooperative with the nurses attending her. Dr Adams put her on a course of morphine and heroin, with tablets to ease her pain. What the prosecution was doing, through the evidence of their medical expert Dr Douthwaite, was attacking the Doctor's use of heroin and arousing suspicion regarding its use.

Mr Lawrence reminded the jury that they were not judging whether the Doctor was proficient or not: 'There are good doctors, better doctors, and there are not good doctors, but all are honest men doing their best according to their individual skills'.

He claimed that Dr Adams was doing his duty to the best of his ability by providing his patient with a regular regime of drugs. It had been argued that this was wrong because Mrs Morrell became addicted.

To this view, Mr Lawrence explained that, 'to an old lady with only six to twelve months to live, given to brain problems and outbursts, why should a little dependence on drug therapy matter?'

In September, Adams' partner, Dr Harris, increased morphia because he found the situation worsening, and by November, the patient was dying and the restlessness getting worse. Mr Lawrence asked the question: 'Is a doctor to say, well, you have got very severe pain, and I am therefore entitled to relieve your misery with drugs, or to do nothing?'

Lawrence then put the most crucial question to the jury for their consideration: 'What was in the Doctor's mind when he gave Mrs Morrell these drugs? Was it an intent to kill, or was it an intent to do the best he could with his perhaps rather limited knowledge as a general practitioner, to ease the misery of this dying woman?'

He explained to the jury that on the evening of 12th November, it was clear that the morphia and heroin were not allowing this woman any sleep or peace. Dr Adams' in response to this situation, chose the safest drug available – paraldehyde, a well-established hypnotic drug. He drew the jury's attention to the important point that Dr Douthwaite, the prosecution's medical expert, gave his evidence before the nurses' note-books had been produced.

When asked by the Attorney-General what was his conclusion, he replied: 'I am driven to the conclusion that the Doctor formed the intent to murder on November 8th'. Yet, only two days later, he told the Judge for the first time that he had a theory on the Doctor's withdrawal of morphia on the 1st November.

Lawrence continued: 'On my cross-examination, this theory of the accumulation of morphia in Mrs Morrell's body breaks down. It had been dissented from by two other medical experts, Dr Ashley and Dr Harman. When you have two eminent medical men disagreeing with the whole theory, and if Dr Douthwaite's theory of accumulation in the body is wrong as a scientific fact, then the whole theory of murder comes collapsing to the ground'.

Mr Lawrence then explained to the jury that they were not looking at a morphia death. The doses that were prescribed during the patient's last days were well within the average doses currently prescribed. As the defence expert medical witness, Dr Harman stated: 'People just die'.

Lawrence concluded by stating that, if Mrs Morrell died from natural causes, she did not die as a result of drugs. If she did not die from drugs, then Dr Adams did not kill her, therefore he was not a murderer.

Lawrence then drew the jury's attention to what he considered to be the most significant aspect of the case: 'What I submit is one of the most significant features here, the behaviour of the nurses, trained women. As the case was closed and the last entry made in the note-books, they did not have the slightest suspicion that it wasn't one of the usual unhappy endings to a case, just another case'.

Nearing the conclusion of his closing address to the jury, Lawrence went over the facts of the case for the benefit of the jury. He asked the question of whether it was a murder for gain, because there was no evidence that Dr Adams was, in fact, short of money. He particularly emphasised that the gross value of Mrs Morrell's estate was £175,000. Various people received legacies, but of greater importance was the fact that Dr Adams received just one bequest – some silver in a cupboard valued at £275. The other gift, the pre-war Rolls Royce car was totally dependent upon the son dying before his mother. His comment to the jury was: 'It is too ludicrous to suggest that this doctor embarked upon a course of murder under these circumstances. Yet it is suggested that he had a motive'.

Lawrence then drew the jury's attention to the cremation certificate and particularly to Dr Adams' comment to the police. The doctor could not remember whether or not bequests had come to him or not. Then there was the police evidence when the Doctor is supposed to have told them that he gave nearly all the drugs prescribed to Mrs Morrell. Even if he had in fact stated this, his recollection was certainly incorrect because the records showed that most of the injections were given by the nurses and not by the Doctor.

To emphasise this point, Lawrence stated: 'The point is not what the Doctor prescribed in circumstances which no one could forecast with accuracy, but what was administered, and the evidence for that is in the note-books with Dr Adams' remark: 'Easing the passing of a dying person is not all that wicked, she wanted to die, that can't be murder''.

He further explained that there was a wide difference between giving drugs which shorten life, and giving drugs to ease the passing, not hastening it. Adams' further comment to the police: 'Murder, murder, can you prove it was murder? She was dying anyway' could not be taken as the confession of a guilty man. Lawrence stressed that they were, in fact, the reactions of an innocent man stunned by the mere suggestion of the charge brought against him in his capacity as a doctor.

Lawrence then laid particular emphasis on the fact that 'Trying to ease the last hours of the dying is a doctor's duty, and it has been turned and twisted into an accusation of murder'.

Geoffrey Lawrence concluded: 'Members of the jury, I do not suppose you will ever forget that for three weeks out of your lives, you were called to sit in judgement. Let it not be a memory that will haunt your conscience. When I have finished, my voice will be silent for the rest of the case. If you think, as I submit, there should be no conviction, be steadfast in that belief to the end, but steadfast and so reach a 'true' verdict'.

Prosecution: Closing Address to the Jury: The Attorney General

The Attorney General opened his address by remarking that the jury would have come to their own conclusions based upon the evidence they had heard and from the documents they had seen proved. He particularly stressed that 'No one wants to see an innocent man convicted on a charge such as this', but that on the evidence he had submitted, they may find it proved that Mrs Morrell was killed by a deliberate act by the Doctor who had killed for profit. He then made a rather contradictory remark that what occurred in the hospital in Cheshire was irrelevant to what took place later. He did agree, however, that since Mrs Morrell had been prescribed morphia whilst in hospital, 'it was not unreasonable to continue for a little while'.

The prosecution's main question for the jury to consider was, why, from July 1948 Dr Adams prescribed morphia in combination with heroin, despite the fact that he had told Superintendent Hannam when he was questioned about the use of these two drugs that 'I very seldom use them'.

A further question was put to the jury: 'Why was she made a drug addict by the Doctor?' The Attorney General volunteered an explanation. In spite of her stroke, Mrs Morrell being given daily heroin injections would enable her to feel some gratitude towards the Doctor, 'a feeling of euphoria' being one of the main characteristics of heroin use. It was further suggested by the prosecution that the Doctor's objective might have been to make: 'This rich lady well-disposed towards him with a view to benefiting under her will'.

A further suggestion was put to the jury in respect to the 'special' injections administered by the Doctor, and the fact that the nurses had no knowledge of their content. It was suggested that this was suspicious. The Attorney-General did acknowledge the fact that there was 'a very significant and important difference between the doses recorded in the nurses' note-books and the prescriptions given by Dr Adams'.

This led to the question of the existence of the note-books themselves, and who had kept them from 1950 to 1957. The nurses had explained that such books were usually destroyed after the patient's death. It was suggested to the jury that there could be only one person who would benefit from their retention – namely Dr Adams. If, as the prosecution had maintained, the Doctor had indeed formed the intent to murder, he would be at pains to secure such vital evidence to avoid incriminating himself.

The Attorney General then turned the jury's attention to the comments made by Dr Adams when informed by the police that he was being charged with the murder of Mrs Morrell: 'Murder? Murder? Can you prove it was murder?'

The prosecuting counsel then offered an alternative explanation to that suggested by Mr Lawrence, the defence counsel: 'Is it, as my learned friend suggested, the incredulous reaction of a man falsely accused? Or is it the sort of statement a shaken man might have made, a man who had committed murder, which he thought could not be proved?'

The jury was then reminded that whilst Dr Adams was on holiday, his partner Dr Harris carried on the course of medication begun by Dr Adams. We are told that Mrs Morrell was very annoyed that Adams had gone on holiday and left her. Why was this? The prosecution suggests that this was, in fact, because Dr Adams had been supplying Mrs Morrell with additional quantities of drugs, unknown to both the nurses attending her, and to Dr Harris. We then hear from the defence how Dr Adams gave instructions for the morphia injections to be stopped.

The prosecution suggested that the stopping of the main sedative, under normal circumstances, indicated that the patient's health was improving rather than deteriorating rapidly. It was this fact that led Dr Douthwaite to conclude that the intention was to terminate the life of Mrs Morrell.

Even the defence's own expert medical witness, Dr Harman, agreed that the policy was to give the patient an injection whenever she woke up, 'to keep her under'. The raised the crucial question of why this was done. The Crown's submission was that there was only one conclusion – 'To hasten death'. Both of the prosecution's medical witnesses, Drs Douthwaite and Ashby agreed that the 'jerky spasms' seen the last night, were due to heroin use. The Attorney General concluded by pointing out to the jury that the defence suggestion that Mrs Morrell died of 'natural causes' was unsustainable. 'On the evidence of the spasms leading up to the day of her death, of the injections of paraldehyde just before her death, to ignore that evidence and to say that her death was due to 'natural causes' would be to ignore the obvious'.

The Attorney General concluded: 'It is my submission, it is proved beyond all reasonable doubt that the cause of the death of Mrs Morrell was the administration of these drugs, and that her death was due to the morphia and the heroin, accelerated by paraldehyde. Members of the jury, murder in this case has been proved. It is for those reasons that I submit to you that the proper verdict in this case is one of murder'.

The Judge's Summing-Up to the Jury: Mr Justice Patrick Devlin

The Judge commenced his summing-up by reminding the jury that they: 'are the sole judges of the fact', and that his task was to interpret the law for them. He told the jury that there were four matters which required explanation, the first of which was the legal definition of murder:

'Murder is an act or a series of acts which were intended to kill and did, in fact, kill.'

The Judge then reminded the jury that there had been a great deal of discussion surrounding the circumstances in which a doctor might be justified in giving drugs which would shorten life in cases of severe pain. Judge Devlin made it abundantly clear that, in law, no special defence was available which covered these circumstances. The Judge then informed the jury of specific instances in which the law made allowance for discretion: 'If the first purpose of medicine – the restoration of health cannot be achieved, there is still much for the doctor to do, and he is entitled to do all that is proper and necessary to relieve pain and suffering, even if the measures he takes, may incidentally shorten life'.

Despite these 'exceptional' circumstances existing, the Judge reinforced the fact that: 'It remains the law, that no doctor has the right to cut off life deliberately'.

The Judge then proceeded to remind the jury of the essence of the case for the defence, which was that the treatment given by Dr Adams was specifically designed to promote comfort and alleviate pain and suffering. If this was considered to be the right and proper treatment, even if it incidentally shortened life, it did not give any grounds for convicting the Doctor of murder. The Judge then drew the jury's attention to the second matter which he regarded as 'one of the most troubling questions in the case'.

Were there any injections administered to Mrs Morrell, over and above those that were recorded in the nurses' note-books? On this specific question, the Judge directed the jury that, as a matter of law, there was no evidence which would lead them to draw such a conclusion.

The jury's attention was then drawn to what the Judge considered to be the third matter of law. This centred on the unavoidable publicity attached to the case, and the fact that the jury must have heard and read a great deal about Dr Adams in the media. In particular, he referred to the press reports covering the preliminary Committal Hearing. The Judge, deviating from normal procedure, expressed his own personal view that the Committal Hearing before the examining magistrates should have been held in private because of prejudicial reporting. He also reminded the jury that those proceedings before the magistrates were significantly different in character to the actual trial procedure. The Judge further warned the jury against paying too much attention to what was in fact, mere suspicions and gossip with no value at all. Instead, they should concentrate on the evidence that really proved something.

The fourth and final matter of law was that the burden of proof was upon the prosecution: 'It is their duty to satisfy you beyond reasonable doubt before you arrive at a verdict of guilty'. The Judge followed this up by stressing to the jury that: 'anything outside the evidence is outside your responsibility. What is not evidence is what you might think the Doctor might have said or not, if he had gone into the witness-box'.

Following on from his last statement, the Judge drew the jury's attention to what he then described as 'an unusual feature, that the accused had not gone into the witness-box'. He then explained that it would be, as a matter of law, 'Utterly wrong if you were to regard the Doctor's silence as contributing in anyway towards proof of guilt'.

This was followed by the Judge drawing the jury's attention to what he considered to be the 'essentials' of the case.

There were three things that had to be proven, and the prosecution had to prove every one of them.

Firstly, it had to prove an act or acts of murder, secondly, to prove that those acts caused the death of Mrs Morrell, and thirdly, that at the time when those acts were committed by the Doctor, he intended to kill. These the Judge regarded as the 'essentials' of the case.

Referring specifically to the 'second' essential, whether the act caused death, the Judge commented on defence counsel's submission. If the act did not cause the death, then the case ends. In respect of this, the defence submitted that the immediate cause of death was not drugs at all. Essentially, it was down to some other 'intervening' cause, possibly another cerebral thrombosis or simply 'old age'.

The Judge then drew the jury's attention to the fact that they had to rely very heavily on the 'medical evidence' to arrive at a satisfactory conclusion, regarding the 'cause' of death.

Dr Douthwaite, the prosecution's expert medical witness's evidence was clear and uncompromising – he regarded the overdose of drugs as the cause of death. The other prosecution witness, Dr Ashby, also regarded this as the 'most likely' cause but, significantly, he could not exclude 'other possibilities'. Dr Harman, the defence's medical expert witness, in contrast, believed that an elderly patient over eighty-years of age, and suffering from cerebral thrombosis: 'may die of anything at any time, and no one can say beyond reasonable doubt, what she actually died of'.

The Judge now turned the jury's attention to what he considered to be the 'central part' of the three 'essential' things, namely the act or acts of murder. He expressed that: 'It is a most curious situation, perhaps unique in these courts, that the act of murder has to be proved by expert evidence'.

What the prosecution were maintaining was that the 'act' was recorded somewhere in the nurses' note-books, but without a doctor to interpret these books, they cannot identify what is thought to be the act of murder. The Judge accepted that: 'It may be that it is much more difficult for the Crown ever to prove that a doctor murders his patient, than it was to prove other acts of murder'.

The prosecution identified three acts which they submitted to the jury, and which the jury had to be satisfied amounted to murder. The first act was the discontinuance of morphia with the specific intent that it should be re-introduced with fatal consequences. This was Dr Douthwaite's theory, but is it too dangerous to adopt this theory? The second act occurred round about 8th November when there occurred a sudden change in the treatment regime for

Mrs Morrell for which there was no medical justification. Was this an act which was capable of being a murderous act? The third and final 'act' was Dr Ashby's evidence which did not consider that Mrs Morrell could have survived the sedatives recorded at the doses prescribed.

However, Dr Ashby did agree that there was no maximum dose for opiates, and that Mrs Morrell had not requested an injection at any time. This in effect, blunted the prosecution's insistence that she was 'addicted' to the drugs. He also agreed with defence counsel's suggestion that death could be due to such 'natural' causes as pneumonia or a further stroke.

In view of the 'conflicting' medical opinion, the Judge expressed the view that: 'If you come to the conclusion that Dr Ashby's evidence was 'border-line' evidence, and it does not leave you with a clear impression that this change to 'keeping her under' accelerated death, then you must leave it. In the matter of murder, you can not act upon 'border-line' evidence, therefore you would not be safe in convicting'.

The Judge then advised the jury that if they decide that Mrs Morrell was killed by a course of medically-unjustifiable treatment given her by the Doctor, that they would then have to deal with the question of intent – whether it was done with the intention to murder.

The Judge proceeded to explain to the jury the essentials of 'intention': 'Intention is something that exists in a man's mind. It can only be proved by references that are drawn from his own actions. In considering what was in the Doctor's mind, you must look at the circumstances of the case'.

As regards 'motive', it was assumed from the

Attorney General's opening address that the motive in this case was gain. in that the Doctor wished to acquire a legacy by the death of Mrs Morrell. The Judge drew the jury's attention to defence counsel's submission that the chest of silver was a 'pretty paltry reward for murder'.

However, it could not be ignored that the Doctor did display a considerable interest in acquiring some legacy under Mrs Morrell's will. Mr Lawrence for the defence had stated that: 'The suggestion that the Doctor had anticipated her death by a few days or weeks for the sake of a chest of silver worth £270 was ludicrous'. Mr Lawrence also stressed that it was not what the actual position was; whether or not the Doctor was legally entitled to anything, but whether 'he thought he was'.

The only evidence available was the answer the Doctor gave to Superintendent Hannam which makes it quite clear that he knew or thought he knew he was going to inherit the chest of silver and the vintage Rolls Royce car.

The Judge further remarked: 'It must be remembered that it is one thing to give a statement to a police officer, and a quite different thing to go into the witness-box and say it on oath, subject to cross-examination and testing'. It was pointed out that the Attorney General laid particular stress on the statement the Doctor gave to Superintendent Hannam, some of which was difficult to justify on the evidence that was then known. In particular, the phrase that Mrs Morrell was 'in terrible agony' was incorrect because it is now clear that she was not in this situation.

The Judge then commented that the jury might have wished to have heard the Doctor's own explanation of the phrase he used. 'Easing the passing' could have been said innocently but it was, nonetheless, capable of a more sinister connotation. The jury was warned not to take phrases in isolation, but as part of the trend of the Doctor's statements as a whole.

The Judge then expressed the view to the jury that: 'It seems to me that the statements as a whole do show from the beginning to the end, that it had never crossed his mind that he was faced or might be faced, with the charge of Murdering Mrs Morrell'. At this stage in the proceedings, the Judge indicated that he would sum-up the issues in the case.

There were three points the Crown had to satisfy the jury. Firstly, that Mrs Morrell did not die from natural causes. If it failed to satisfy them of that, they would have to acquit. If it satisfied them, then they go to the second point. The Crown must satisfy them that there emerged an act of killing, something that was capable of being murderous. If that failed, then they were to acquit. If it succeeded, then they would go to the third point. The Crown must satisfy them that if there was an act of that sort, it was done with intent to murder. If that did not satisfy them, they must acquit and if it did satisfy, they must convict.

The Judge speaking to the jury said: 'Mr Lawrence has submitted to you that the whole case against the Doctor from beginning to end is merely suspicion. You sit in judgement to answer one limited question. Has the prosecution satisfied you beyond reasonable doubt that the Doctor murdered Mrs Morrell? On that question, the Doctor stood on his rights and did not speak. I have made it quite clear that I am not criticising that, and I don't criticise it at all. I hope that the day will never come when that right is denied to any Englishman. It is not a refuge of technicality; the law of this matter reflects the national thought of England. So great is our horror at the idea that a man might be questioned, forced to speak and perhaps condemn himself out of his own mouth, that we afford to anyone suspected or accused of a crime at every stage and to the very end, the right to say: 'Ask me no question, I shall answer none. Prove your case'.'

Judge Devlin then gave his concluding comments to the jury: 'This long process ends with the question with which it began. 'Murder? Can you prove it?'' Not infrequently have I heard a case presented by the prosecution that seemed to me to be manifestly a strong one, and sometimes I have felt it my duty to tell the jury so. I do not think, therefore, that I ought to hesitate to tell you that here the case for the defence seems to me to be manifestly a strong one. But it is the same question in the end, always the same; is the case for the Crown strong enough to carry conviction to your mind? It is your question; you have to answer it. It lies always with you, the jury. You will now consider what that answer shall be'.

On the sixteenth day of the trial, the Jury retired to consider their verdict at 11.16 am and at precisely 12 noon they returned to court. The foreman of the jury stood up to answer the Clerk of the Court's question: 'Are you agreed upon your verdict?'

The foreman replied that they were and in response to the question: 'Do you find the prisoner guilty or not guilty?' the reply was 'Not Guilty'.

After the not guilty verdict on the count of murdering Mrs Morrell, the normal process would have been to bring the second indictment regarding Mrs Hullett to trial, either a full trial or, in view of the acquittal in Mrs Morrell's case, so that Adams would plead not guilty, the Attorney-General would offer no evidence, and the judge would direct the jury to bring in a 'not guilty' verdict, which was the course expected by Judge Devlin.

However, the Attorney General, as a minister of the Crown, had the power to suspend an indictment through the legal process of : 'Nolle prosequi' (do not prosecute), something which Judge Devlin said had never been used to prevent an accused from an acquittal, suggesting that this was done because Manningham-Buller did not want a second acquittal, and the loss of both cases that he had indicted. Judge Devlin, writing afterwards in his account of the trial referred to this unusual procedure: 'The use of nolle prosequi to conceal the deficiencies of the prosecution was an abuse of process, leaving an innocent man under the suspicion that there might have been something in the rumours of mass murder after all'.

Manningham-Buller later explained to Parliament after the trial, that the publicity surrounding the Morrell trial would make it difficult to secure a fair trial on the indictment relating to Mrs Hullett, and that this second case depended greatly on inference, which was not supported by admissions as in Mrs Morrell's case. This was a reference to Adam's admissions that he had himself administered most of Mrs Morrell's opiate injections, but in the case of Mrs Hullett he never admitted that he had given more than two barbiturate tablets to Mrs Hullett. The final procedure was that the bail fixed by Eastbourne Magistrates for the offences that Dr Adams faced under the Cremation and Dangerous Drugs Acts had expired during the period of his trial. Mr Lawrence succeeded in obtaining an extension to bail from Judge Devlin. Dr Adams was accordingly discharged, bringing to an end what was regarded as the longest murder trial in English criminal history up to that point in time.

The Post-Trial Period

On 30th June 1957, on his acquittal, John Bodkin Adams resigned from the National Health Service. On 26th July 1957, he appeared at Lewes Assizes before Mrs Justice Pilcher and pleaded guilty to fourteen of the sixteen charges against him. He was fined £150 in respect of eight counts of forging prescriptions, £500 on each of the three counts of making false statements on cremation forms, £250 for the two offences under the Dangerous Drugs Act 1951 and £500 for the one offence of failure to keep a register of drugs as required by the Dangerous Drugs Regulation 1953. The total fines together with additional costs came to £2,400.

Having been convicted of these offences, the judge was obliged to refer the matter to the General Medical Council (GMC). On the 27th November 1957, Adams appeared before the Disciplinary Committee and was struck off the Medical Register as from 30th December 1957. He re-applied to be reinstated to the Register on two occasions, in 1959 and 1960 but failed., before being successful at his third attempt in November 1961.

On this occasion, he informed the GMC that he did not intend to return to general practice but would instead carry out research and continue with consultancy work. Despite all this, Adams still received legacies from his former patients in recognition of his past care for them.

In view of the evidence at Adams' trial, the verdict came as no surprise to the general public, except to the 'sensationally hungry' British press who had been virtually unanimous in their belief of his guilt. One notable exception was *The Daily Express*, who had been convinced of his innocence and who later paid Adams £10,000 to publish his story. Adam's solicitor announced that he was contemplating proceedings against a number of newspapers. On 26th April 1957, writs were issued against *The Daily Mail*, *The Daily Mirror* and *The News Chronicle*. He later complained to the Press Council regarding a report in *The Daily Herald* on the 4th March 1959. Following this, he issued a libel writ against Associated Newspapers, the publishers of *The Daily Mail*. This case was settled in May 1961, with the defendants apologising and paying damages and costs. As a condition of his settlement, Adams agreed not to proceed against any other newspaper, although it is almost certain that the 'un-named' papers made some contribution towards the cost of the overall settlement.

Adams spent the remainder of his life following his favourite hobby of clay pigeon shooting, serving as President and Honorary Medical Officer of the Clay Pigeon Shooting Association. Whilst out shooting at Battle, Adams broke his leg in a fall on the 1st July 1983, which resulted in him being admitted to Eastbourne General Hospital where he died of heart failure on 4th July 1983. He was cremated and his ashes returned to Coleraine to be buried in the graves of his mother and father.

Chapter Four: An Overview of the Case

The Case in Retrospect

The defendant, John Bodkin Adams, was a doctor who was tried on one count of murdering an elderly patient, Mrs Edith Alice Morrell. The police claimed that Adams had murdered a number of other elderly patients, suggesting that Adams' modus operandi was to administer heroin and morphine with the intention of making his patients addicted and under his influence. By this means, they were induced to leave him legacies in cash and kind in their wills. Finally, he gave them large doses of drugs which caused their deaths. One patient's bequest included a vintage Rolls Royce car although this patient did not, in fact, leave Adams anything in her final will. The police investigated the wills of 132 of Adams' former patients dating from 1946 to 1956, where he had received legacies under those wills. They prepared a list of around 12 names for submission to the prosecuting authorities. On this list were the names of Mrs Morrell, Mrs Gertrude Hullett and two other cases in which evidence had been taken on oath. The Attorney-General chose Mrs Morrell's case, considering it to be the strongest.

This case was based entirely on the police investigation, that Adams either administered or instructed others to administer drugs that killed Mrs Morrell, with the intention of killing her, and that these drugs were unnecessary as she was not suffering pain having been in a semi-comatose state for some time before her death. The prosecution suggested that the motive for Adams deciding to kill Mrs Morrell was because he feared she might alter her will to his disadvantage. Throughout the trial, the prosecution maintained that the motive was a mercenary one.

Initially, the prosecution argued that all of the large quantities of morphine and heroin prescribed by Adams in the months prior to Mrs Morrell's death had been injected into her, and that this amount was sufficient to kill her, therefore his only intention was to kill her.

On the second day of the trial, the defence produced the nurses' note-books, which clearly showed that smaller quantities of drugs had been given to the patient than those estimated by the prosecution, these being based on Adams' prescriptions. Significant to the defence case, these note-books recorded that the two injections given the night prior to Mrs Morrell's death, were for paraldehyde, a safe hypnotic drug.

In response to the production of the note-books, one of the prosecution's main medical witnesses changed his testimony from that which he had given Adams' Committal Hearing. Dr Douthwaite had previously introduced a 'new theory' of how Mrs Morrell had been killed. However, this was not accepted by the prosecution's second medical expert, much to the surprise of the prosecution team. This left the prosecution with only one alternative, to argue that the nurses' records were incomplete.

Despite these obvious weaknesses in the prosecution's case, the Attorney General still believed he could turn the case around by cross-examining Adams himself. However, to his complete shock he found that the defence had decided not to call Adams to the witness stand. This in effect, sealed the fate of the prosecution's case against Adams.

The Conduct of the Case

The parties involved in the prosecution case blamed each other for its failure to secure a conviction on the strong belief that Adams should have been convicted. The 'fairness' of this trial has been frequently debated in respect to this supposed failure, particularly with regard to the prejudicial pre-trial press coverage, and the prosecution introducing probably inadmissible evidence at the Committal Hearing. Judge Devlin, the trial judge, thought that Lawrence's concerns that Adams would not receive a fair trial were overstated. However, several legal experts have questioned whether the legal system existing in 1957 would have been capable of giving Adams a fair trial, especially if the 'lost' nurses' notebooks had not come into the hands of the defence.

I believe that the responsibilities of those involved in the initial investigation and final prosecution of Adams' case require some consideration. At the time of the case, the police role was to investigate reports of crimes, determine if one had been committed and arrest a suspect. It was police practice to decide on whether there was a case to prosecute early in their inquiry, then to find evidence to support a prosecution. Then, as today, the role of the Director of Public Prosecutions (DPP) would be to review the case and decide whether a prosecution was appropriate, then appoint counsel to conduct the prosecution. It was also normal practice for the DPP to refer serious crimes to the Attorney General or the Solicitor General. However, for most of the 20th century, the DPP by legal convention, limited consideration of the guilt of the accused based on the evidence collected by the police, in applying what was commonly referred to as the 50% rule, to confirm that there was a 'reasonable chance of conviction', today replaced by 'a reasonable prospect of conviction'. It was not, and still remains, the function of prosecuting counsel to decide guilt or innocence, but to plead their brief.

A valid criticism of the prosecution was that its preparation was weak and poorly presented. The case relied too heavily on the police evidence and the testimony of 'expert' witnesses. Neither of these sources had been thoroughly tested during the pre-trial period. This resulted in the prosecution expressing great concern when the nurses' note-books were produced, literally destroying their case. Finally, the fact that Dr Douthwaite changed his firmly-held opinion, based on what was later considered to be a 'discredited theory. Adding to this, the Attorney General's other counsel, Melford Stevenson's conduct at Adams' Committal Hearing, led to public disclosure of inadmissible evidence that was widely circulated prior to the trial. There is no doubt that Stevenson's unprofessional action was responsible for the sensational and prejudicial media coverage. Finally, there was the Attorney General's failure to adapt his case to the evidence presented by the defence. Instead, he stubbornly proceeded in the hope of relying on Adams' own admissions in cross-examination, which proved fruitless.

The Police Investigation

At a very early stage in the investigation, Hannam firmly believed he had discovered Adams' modus operandi, and that this 'blinkered' his overview of the investigation – a classic example of 'confirmation bias'. As a result of the prosecution's failure to secure a conviction, and criticism of the way in which the police investigation was conducted, the Metropolitan Police conducted an internal investigation into Hannam's conduct during the investigation, in particular his 'close' relationship with the press. Unfortunately, the results of this inquiry were never made public. However, in 1958, Hannam's police career came to an end, and he was later employed in a private security agency.

Suggestions of External Intervention in the Case

In December 1956, the police acquired a memorandum believed to be from a *Daily Mail* journalist concerning rumours of homosexual activity between a police officer, a magistrate and a doctor in Eastbourne (the latter appeared to imply Dr Adams). This information according to the reporter, originated from Superintendent Hannam himself. The 'magistrate' was Sir Roland Gwynne, Mayor of Eastbourne (1929-1931) and brother of Rupert Gwynne, MP for Eastbourne (1910-1924).

Gwynne was Adams' patient and he visited him on a regular basis. They went on frequent holidays together, having spent three weeks in Scotland in the September of 1956. The 'police officer' referred to was Deputy Chief Constable of Eastbourne, Alexander Seekings. What is of special significance in regard to these 'revelations' is that

Superintendent Hannam appears to have ignored these rumours as a possible line of inquiry, despite the fact that homosexual activity was a criminal offence in 1956. This reinforced the belief in Hannam's 'obsession' with the case against Adams. The memorandum clearly revealed the level of Adams' connections with the 'Elite' of Eastbourne at the time. At the same time, there were numerous other rumours circulating that Adams had three 'mistresses', but these were more likely to be just 'cover' stories to avoid too much suspicion. It was true that in 1933, Adams did become engaged to Norah O'Hara, a local butcher's daughter. This was called off two years later because Adams' mother did not approve of him marrying 'below' his status. It has been suggested that Adams, apart for his homosexuality, did not want the fact that he was married to interfere with his well-established relationships with his elderly female patients. However, Adams did remain friends with Norah for the rest of his life, remembering her in his will.

    The only recorded instance of intervention in the case concerned the Lord Chief Justice, Lord Goddard. He had proposed to Judge Devlin that in the event that Adams was acquitted in the Morrell case, he should be granted bail before the second charge of murdering Mrs Hullett. This has been regarded by legal observers as a concession to the defence, and as a warning to the prosecution of strong judicial displeasure over the Attorney-General's intention to proceed with the second indictment. Apparently, this was discussed between Judge Devlin and Manningham-Buller after the jury retired to consider their verdict. At the time of the trial, it was believed that the police had overlooked the nurses' note-books which were later 'discovered' by the defence. This differed from the police's own records, in particular, the schedule of exhibits given to the DPP office. This raises the very significant fact that the Attorney-General must have been aware of their existence. This being the case, there must have been high-level 'external' effort to undermine the case against Adams. Not surprisingly, there is no documentary evidence to support this contention, but the usual conspiracy theories abound.

Although the Adams' trial generated a great deal of coverage in the press, it did not feature prominently as being of political significance, in particular due to the Suez crisis at the time. However, George Wigg, the Labour member for Dudley called for an independent inquiry into the conduct of the case on 10th April 1957, but this did not take place, however, the case was debated in Parliament. The major political consequence of the trial was the widespread concerns that the press coverage of the Committal Hearing had prejudiced the subsequent trial.

Ronald Bell, Conservative member for Buckingham South, announced his intention of introducing a private Members' Bill under the ten minute rule to prohibit the reporting of cases during the magistrates hearing. Though this proposal did not materialise, the then Home Secretary established the Tucker Committee to examine the whole question of proceedings before examining magistrates. A report was delivered on the 29th July 1958 with the recommendation that although committal proceedings should continue to be held in public, the reporting of these hearings should be restricted only to the publication of certain 'limited' information, such as the name of the accused and the charges they faced. However, it was nine years before the Home Office finally responded, this culminating in the Criminal Justice Act of 1967.

There were also various concerns expressed regarding the reporting of the case by the foreign press who felt free to print what they liked, whatever the accuracy. In particular the European edition of *Newsweek* published on 1st April 1957, contained certain paragraphs which were regarded as being in contempt of court. Despite the fact that the British were unable to prosecute the American publishers of the magazine, they did however prosecute Eldon Griffiths, *Newsweek*'s European correspondent, together with Rolls House Publishing Company Ltd and WH Smith and Son Ltd for distributing the offending magazine. As a result, Griffiths was acquitted, whilst the two corporate entities were each fined £50 for contempt of court.

Bibliographical Review on the Trial

The first authoritative book to be published on the Adams case was *The Best We Can Do* by Sybille Bedford, the first edition in 1958 being followed by a reprint in 1989. It was Bedford's belief that Adams was innocent of the charge of murder. This was in fact, the only definitive work available that provided a verbatim account of the whole trial. When Adams died in 1983, Rodney Halworth, crime journalist for *The Daily Mail* published *Where There's A Will: The Sensational Life of John Bodkin Adams*. No longer in fear of libel action, Halworth alleged that Adams was a compulsive legacy hunter, that he was guilty of a number of murders, and that the whole prosecution had been mishandled by the Attorney-General. It is clearly apparent that most of the information it contained was from police sources in general and from Herbert Hannam in particular.

The work has been described as 'a sloppy production, careless with detail, presented suspicion as fact, poorly written and unconcerned about its obvious bias'. Following on from this publication, Percy Hoskins published *Two Men Were Acquitted* in 1984. Hoskins was the former crime correspondent of *The Daily Express* and regarded himself as being one of the two men, since Adams's acquittal was also a vindication of his own held belief in Adam's innocence. However, he did take the view that Adams was a 'smug and acquisitive man' who manipulated his patients into re-writing their wills in his favour.

Whilst Adams was not guilty, he was 'naïve' and 'avaricious'. He did however reveal that much of the anti-Adams press coverage had been planted by Scotland Yard to bolster their own investigation and gain credit.

The trial Judge. Patrick Devlin. also wrote his own book on the case entitled, *Easing the Passing* in 1985. This was largely concerned with the various legal and technical issues involved in the trial. Public interest in the case diminished over time but ironically became resurrected in 1999 with the arrest and conviction of Dr Harold Shipman of the murder of fifteen of his patients. As one may expect, this re-awakening of public interest was accompanied by newspaper headlines like: Did Dr Bodkin Adams Murder 400 Patients? in *The Daily Mail* on 31st December 1999. Similarly, 'Copying the model medic who got away with murder' followed in *The Daily Express* on 1st February 2000.

These headlines were based on the notion that Adams had in some way provided the model for Harold Shipman's campaign of murder. These press releases were the inspiration for a new raft of books, the first of which was *The Strange Case of Dr Bodkin*

Adams by John Surtees which appeared in 2000.

Due credit should be given to Surtees in that his book appears to have been 'even-handed', in his treatment of Adam's life, and significantly, it noted that at the time he was practising, it was commonplace for a doctor to receive bequests from their private patients, particularly in situations exactly like those that Dr Adams found himself in. Surtees concluded by regarding Adams as the victim of a 'police vendetta'. What might be called the case for the prosecution came in the form of *A Stranger in Blood: The Story of Dr Bodkin Adams* by Pamela Cullen appearing in 2004. She was the first author to be granted 'official' access to the Scotland Yard case files in 2003 although they were to be closed until 2033. Cullen took the same lines as those by Halworth, the book being marred by the tendency to treat suspicion as fact. However, it was enlivened on this occasion by the introduction of certain conspiracy theories.

The existence of the note regarding the suggestion of a homosexual relationship between a doctor and Roland Gwynne, a previous Mayor of Eastbourne from 1929 to 1931, was taken as 'proof' that Adams was homosexual. Likewise, the fact that Adams attended the 10th Duke of Devonshire during his last days, and that Harold Macmillan was married to the Duke's sister, is also taken as 'evidence' of a strong connection between Adams and the then Conservative government. According to Cullen, Adams may have killed more victims than Shipman. In her view, Adams was acquitted more due to the way the case was presented than to Adams' lack of guilt. She also highlights the fact that Hannam's investigation was 'blinkered' from the perspective of motive.

Opinion of Adams appears to be divided, although in recent years the view has tended towards him being a killer. Sir Patrick Devlin, the trial judge, stated that Adams may have been a 'mercenary killer' but, though compassionate, he was at the same time greedy and prepared to sell death. He did not think of himself as a murderer but a dispenser of death. He could also be convinced that Dr Adams had helped to end Mrs Hullet's life.

All these writers, with the exception of Lord Devlin, based their opinions almost entirely on the evidence given in court regarding the Morrell case. These opinions of Adams portray him as an incompetent doctor lavishly using heroin and morphia, with a successful and lucrative medical practice. However, it should also be realised that between the 1930s and 1960s, the medical profession in general, regarded death as a failure and consequently, subjected dying patients to treatments aimed at prolonging life rather than relieving suffering. This attitude was reflected in the post-war National Health Service, which failed to make adequate provision for end-of-life care. As a result, published medical commentary on care of the dying was very rare before the late 1960s.

The Legal Position of the 'Double Effect' Principle

This principle states that 'an action which has a good objective may be performed despite the fact that the objective can only be achieved at the risk of a harmful effect'. However, this analysis does require some clarification. The action itself must be either good or morally indifferent, the good effect must not be produced by means of the ill-effect, and there must be a proportionate reason for allowing the expected ill effect to occur. It is implicit and vital in this principle that the good effect must outweigh the bad, and this may involve a value judgement. For example, it might well be ethically right to administer pain-killing drugs in such dosage as simultaneously shortens the life of a terminally-ill patient. However, it would not be justified to give the same dose to a young man with identical pain who stood a reasonable chance of recovery.

Judge Patrick Devlin's classic direction was followed in R v Cox (1992) 12. BMLR.38, where the charge to the jury in this case was cited with approval by the House of Lords in Bland, where Lord Goff remarked: 'It is the established rule that a doctor may when caring for a patient who is, for example, dying of cancer, lawfully administer painkilling drugs despite the fact that he knows that an incidental effect of that application, will be to abbreviate the patient's life. Such a decision may properly be made as part of the care of the living patient, in his best interests, and, on this basis, the treatment will be lawful'.
Airedale NHS Trust v Bland, (1993) 1 All ER 821 at 890

There can be no doubt that active euthanasia is unlawful, and this was the position when Dr Nigel Cox was charged in 1991 with the attempted murder of Mrs Lillian Boyes, his patient who was suffering from rheumatoid arthritis, causing her unbelievable pain and suffering. She had expressed a wish to die and was already categorised as 'DNR' (Do Not Resuscitate). Dr Cox injected her with Potassium Chloride, a drug that stops the heart, and has no therapeutic or painkilling properties. Before Dr Cox's action came to the attention of the police, Mrs Boyes was cremated, and it could not be proved 'beyond reasonable doubt' that the injection given by Dr Cox killed her.

Consequently, Dr Cox was convicted only of attempted murder, the judge imposing a suspended sentence, and the General Medical Council (GMC) allowed him to continue in practise, subject to certain conditions. Had the link between his actions and Mrs Boye's death been clearly established, no such course would have been open to the judge. In his summing up to the jury in the Cox case, Judge Ognall stated: 'If a doctor genuinely believes that a certain course is beneficial to his patient, either therapeutically or analgesically, then even though he recognises, that the course carries with it a risk to life, he is fully entitled, nonetheless, to pursue it. If in those circumstances the patient dies, nobody could possible suggest in that situation the doctor was guilty of murder or attempted murder'.

Essentially, the problem for the jury in this case was one of intention. Did Dr Cox intend to kill his patient, or did he hope to give her a short pain-free period during the phrases of dying?

Obviously, we can never know the precise reasons for a jury's verdict, but some factors in the case must have alerted their attention. Mrs Boyes was incurably but not terminally ill, and Dr Cox injected a non-therapeutic substance. It is reasonable to assume that while public opinion in the United Kingdom will give great latitude to the medical profession in its fight against suffering, it is not yet prepared to accept the use of a substance with no analgesic effect, and which is known to be lethal when injected in concentrated form. As a result of this, Dr Cox was unable to plead 'double effect' or even the defence of 'necessity'.

The law condemns active euthanasia on the ground of intent. The terminally ill are beyond curative therapy by definition, and, therefore, their management becomes a matter of the relief from pain and suffering. Achieving this may, inevitably, involve some risk to life but it is the patient's comfort not their premature death, which should be the intended outcome. However, it is the terminally ill patient who most significantly sets the scene for the application of the concept of 'double effect'.

In 1957, at a meeting of the British Medical Association, the use of heroin to induce euphoria and oblivion was advocated. Although doctors were aware that hastening a patient's death was illegal, it was suggested that it was something that 'the law forbids in theory but ignores in practice'. In Adams' case, the court did not ignore the suggestion that he had hastened death and , as Judge Devlin made clear, he needed to clarify for the jury, and incidentally for the medical profession, the extent to which the law allowed the orthodox doctor to go in 'easing the passing' of the dying. Mahar regards Adams' statements to Hannam on Mrs Morrell as less about his guilt or innocence than a disconnection between the medical and legal views on assisted dying. Adams never denied giving his patients large doses of opiates, but denied it was murder.

This was not simply Adams' idiosyncratic view, as appears from the evidence of Dr Douthwaite for the prosecution, who accepted that a physician might knowingly give fatal doses of pain relieving drugs to a terminally ill patient. Devlin's directions to the jury confirmed that it was a 'medical' issue not a legal one, whether Adams' treatment was designed to promote comfort for Mrs Morrell. Devlin's view was that Adams may have been guilty of mercy-killing, but he was one who cared for his patients to the best of his ability. Adams eased the passing of Mrs

Morrell, but his greed brought his motives into question. Mahar notes an editorial in a medical journal following the case, which suggested that the publicity it caused might hamper medical discretion but claimed the use of opiates in terminal cases was essential. Adams may be seen as an extreme case in their use, yet other doctors also used them.

Psychological Profile of Adams

Dr Richard Badcock, the consultant psychiatrist who interviewed Harold Shipman, compared the characteristics of Shipman with those of Adams. The main differences between the two was that Shipman injected morphine intravenously usually killing the patient within minutes. In contrast, Adams preferred to sedate his victims, sometimes over lengthy periods of weeks or even months before their eventual death. However, one common thread was that they both preferred to work alone, rather than in group practice. Also, they both appear to have worked extended hours, often turning up unannounced at their patients' homes. Both had reputations for being rude, egotistic and uncompromising. The most significant characteristic was that they both paid many visits to patients who were not, as far as their medical records showed, ill or in need of medical attention.

Shipman's most overt characteristic was his display of self-importance, attention-seeking and a super-inflated ego. In contrast, Adams' arrogance was more muted and masked by his ingratiating expressions and overt religiosity. According to Badcock, they were both 'straight-forward psychopaths'.

There is evidence in Adams' activities and life-style that clearly indicate a sense of entitlement, yet he felt empty, living his life on the fringes. He did appear obsessed with the lives of the affluent and desperately wanted their lifestyle for himself. The closest Adams came to sustaining a relationship was with his mother who was possessive, domineering and highly critical. Here we can identify parallels with Shipman and his mother who died whilst he was a teenager. As a remedy for all his missed opportunities, Adams in company with Shipman, liked the feeling of control he had over his patients. Many believe him to have been a serial killer on a large scale. However, unlike Shipman, there are no obvious patterns which, taken together, confirm this assertion, only lingering 'suspicious circumstances'.

It has been further suggested that Adam's over-pious religious behaviour replaced a morality in which he viewed himself as a 'saviour' killer. Adams experienced severe personal loss during his formative teenage years with the death of his father and brother. It is believed that he had an over-dependent relationship with his mother. His one attempt to escape the impasse, was his engagement to Norah O'Hara which his mother wrecked. By the time his mother died, it was too late to rekindle this relationship. As regards Adams' alleged homosexuality, this must have influenced his view of himself as being on the periphery of society and leading a 'double life'.

There were also social factors influencing Adams' personal behaviour, coming as he did from a humble, pious family background in Ireland.

This goes some way to explaining his craving for recognition within the upper echelons of Eastbourne's society. This also influenced his perception of class distinction and social divisions so prominent in Eastbourne, as in other towns, with the belief that there were 'double standards', with one set of rules for the 'establishment', and one for others.

John Bodkin Adams undoubtedly killed many of his patients, and he admitted so himself, although from his point of view, he was simply 'easing the passing' of his dying patients. As far as the medical profession was concerned at the time, there was nothing particularly unusual in this practice.

In 1936, George V was helped by his royal physician, Bertrand Edward Dawson, who injected the king with morphine and cocaine to 'help him on his way'. No prosecution was ever brought against Dr Dawson for this clear act of euthanasia. Scotland Yard's files on the Adams case and those of the Director of Public Prosecutions were to be closed to public scrutiny until 2033.

However, these files were opened to public scrutiny in 2003. The following extracts reveal those witness statements gathered by Superintendent Hannam during the investigation, which supported his suspicions as regards Adams' activities. These statements were never revealed during the trial.

'August 1939 – Adams was treating Mrs Agnes Pike when her solicitors became concerned about the amount of opiate drugs she was being prescribed by Adams and requested another doctor, Dr Matthew to take over from Adams. He examined the patient in the presence of Adams and could find no disease present. According to Dr Matthew, 'the patient was deeply under the influence of drugs incoherent and visibly confused'. Later during the examination, Adams administered an injection of morphia, the purpose according to Adams was because 'she might become violent'. Dr Matthew also discovered that Adams had banned all the patient's relatives from seeing her. Once Dr Matthew took over the care of this patient, he withdrew Adam's medication and within eight weeks under his care, Ms Pike regained her full faculties.'

'December 24 1946 – Emily Louise Mortimer died, aged 75. Following her death, Adams took a bottle of brandy and a clock from her room. He claimed to the police that the clock had been loaned to Ms Mortimer by him and that it was not 'right to leave spirits in a nursing home'. Adams received the residue from Mortimer's will and by 1957 had earned £1,950 in dividends from the shares he inherited.'

'23 February 1950 – Amy Ware died, aged 76. Adams had banned her from seeing her relatives prior to her death. She left Adams £1,000 of her total estate of £8,993, yet Adams stated on the cremation form that he was not a beneficiary of the will. He was charged and convicted of this in 1957.'

'December 1950 – Annabelle Kilgour died, aged 89. She had been attended by Adams since July when she had a stroke. She went into a coma on 23 December, immediately after Adams started giving her sedatives. The nurse involved in her care later told the police she was 'quite certain Adams either gave her the wrong injection or far too concentrated a type'. Kilgour left Adams £200 and a clock.'

'3 January 1952 – Adams purchased 5,000 phenobarbitone tablets and by the time his house was searched prior to his arrest four years later, none were found.'

'11 May 1952 – Julia Bradnum died, aged 85. The previous year Adams asked her if her will was in order and offered to accompany her to the bank to check it. On examining it, Adams pointed out that she had not given her beneficiaries 'addresses' and that it should be re-written. She had wanted to leave her house to her adopted daughter, but Adams suggested it would be best to sell the house and then give money to whoever she wished. This she did, Adams received £661. The day before Bradnum died, she had been doing housework and going for walks. The next morning she woke up feeling unwell. Adams was called and saw her. He gave her an injection and stated 'It will be over in three minutes'. It definitely was, and Adams confirmed 'I'm afraid she's gone' and left the room. Bradnum's body was exhumed on 21 December 1956. Adams had stated on the death certificate that her cause of death was 'cerebral haemorrhage'. The forensic pathologist Dr Francis Camps examined her brain and excluded this possibility. The rest of the body was not in a state to deduce the real cause of death. It was also noticed that Adams her executor, had put a plate on Bradnum's coffin stating she died on 27 May 1952, yet this was the date her body was interred.'

22 November 1952 – Julia Thomas aged 72, was being treated by Adams for depression after her cat died in early November. On the 19th, Adams gave sedatives so she would feel 'better for it in the morning'. The next day, after more tablets, she went into a coma. On the 21st Adams told Thomas's cook that 'Mrs Thomas promised him her typewriter, I'll take it now'. She died at 3 am the next morning.

15 January 1953 - Hilda Neil Miller, aged 86, died in a guest house where she lived with her sister Clara. One of Hilda's friends asked Adams if he would visit

Hilda which he did. Adams was seen by Hilda's nurse to pick up articles in her room and then slip them into his pocket. Adams arranged Hilda's funeral and burial.

22 February 1954 - Clara Neil Miller died aged 87. Adams often locked the door of her room when he saw her for up to twenty minutes at a time. When one of her friends asked about this curious practice, Clara said he was assisting her in 'personal matters' such as pinning on brooches, adjusting her dress. She also appeared to be under the influence of drugs. Clara left Adams £1,275, and he charged her estate a further £700 after her death. He was the sole executor of her will. Her funeral was arranged by Adams and only he and Anne Sharp, the guest house owner were present. She received £200 in Clara's will. Clara's was one of the two bodies exhumed during the police investigation on 21 December 1956. Francis Camps concluded that she had broncho-pneumonia possibly brought about by high drug doses, but not a heart problem as Adams had stated on her death certificate. According to prescription records, Adams had not prescribed anything to treat the broncho-pneumonia.

30 May 1955 – James Downs, brother-in-law to Amy Ware, died, aged 88. He had become a resident at a nursing home as a result of a broken ankle. Adams treated him with a sedative containing morphia, which made him very forgetful. On 7 April Adams gave his nurse a tablet to make him more alert. Two hours later, a solicitor arrived for him to amend his will. Adams informed the solicitor that he was to be made a legatee to inherit £1,000. The solicitor amended the will and returned two hours later accompanied by another doctor, Dr Barkworth, who

declared the patient to be alert. The doctor was paid 3 guineas for his time. Down's nurse, Miller informed the police later that she had overheard Adams in April telling Downs that he hadn't mentioned Adams in his will. Downs died after suffering a coma which lasted 36 hours, only 12 hours after Adams' last visit. Adams charged his estate £216 for his services to Downs and also signed his cremation form, stating he had 'no pecuniary interest in the death of the deceased.'

14 March 1956 - Alfred John Hullett died, aged 71, the husband of Gertrude Hullett. Shortly after his death, Adams collected a prescription from a chemist in Eastbourne for a 10cc hypodermic solution containing 5 grains of morphine, made out in the name of Mr Hullett, the prescription to be back-dated to the previous day. The police presumed this was to cover morphine Adams had given him from his own personal supply. Mr Hullett left Adams £500 in his will.

15 November 1956 – Annie Sharpe, owner of the guest house where the Millers died and considered to be a major witness, died suddenly of cancer. Adams had diagnosed this five days earlier and made a prescription for her to receive injections of morphine and tablets of pethidine. She was cremated hastily. During his investigations, Superintendent Hannam had discovered that four members of Adams' own household had been prescribed either morphine, heroin or pethidine by Adams, all obtained on the NHS. This led Hannam to conclude that he was using their names and keeping the drugs for his own private supply, a certain act of fraud.
Source: John Bodkin Adams Wikipedia page.

Following Adams' death, there were comments circulating both locally and nationally, which, on the whole, were supportive of Adams. There were firmly-held views that Superintendent Hannam had encouraged press and local gossip by his suggestion that Adams was a 'mass murderer'. This could only have been for his own personal gratification.

Lord Devlin, in his detailed account of the trial, expressed that: 'The public is swept by waves of emotion which it doesn't reason about. No one wanted to hear about the possible innocence of Dr Adams, long before he was tried. He may well have blurred the distinction between helping symptoms and helping to die'.

The fact was that having Scotland Yard investigating the rumours surrounding Adams' activities lent support to innuendo and rumours. Professor Keith Simpson, the distinguished forensic pathologist remarked in his account of the trial that 'It is lawful to ease the process of dying. That is not euthanasia but a humane service. Drugs which can help can also kill, and there is no sharp definition between painless sleep and death'.

The Legal Issue of 'Causation'

The criminal law does not seek to punish people for their evil thoughts, but for their conduct. Where charged with a crime, the prosecution must prove the accused's acts or omissions caused the outcome. There are two strands to causation; factual and legal. Factual causation is where it must be proved that the outcome would have occurred but for the conduct of the accused. Legal causation is related to ideas of responsibility and culpability. On questions of legal causation, the jury will be directed to consider whether the accused's act was more than minimal in contributing towards the victim's death.

Here in Adams' case. a doctor faced a murder charge for providing his patient with pain-relieving drugs which led to an acceleration of the patient's death. The jury were directed by Devlin J, to consider that no act constituted murder unless it caused death. By 'cause' Devlin J, explained that it was not a scientific, technical or philosophical definition but what the jury would consider to be 'common sense'. Presumably, a jury's moral reaction would be that the doctor's sole aim was to relieve pain and that it was 'incidental' that the patient's death was accelerated. However, had it been a sole beneficiary who injected the patient with the aim of accelerating the patient's death so that they could benefit from their inheritance, then the jury's moral reaction was likely to be that the beneficiary caused the death. It does appear in R v Adams that the issue of causality became mixed up with the issue of motive because there was a strong moral imperative to clear the doctor of liability.

This led to the causality of the doctor's actions being doubted rather than his mental state (mens rea) of the offence. It was thought that a special defence was created to distinguish the doctor from a murderer in cases of life-shortening palliative care. It has been argued by some that Dr Adams was no different to Dr Harold Shipman who was also acting outside the law. The moral judgement of the judiciary can and clearly has, affected the application of the legal rules in relation to criminal causation. In R v Adams, this is a classic example where the law is clear that the doctor should have been guilty, as his actions caused the patient's death. However, in this case, there was a divergence of views between the medical profession and certain members of the police.

The debate about whether or not Adams was a murderer comes down to an argument about medical ethics and the question of euthanasia. There were certainly those that believed Adams to be a killer. The barrister Melford Stevenson (who led the prosecution at Adam's Committal Hearing) was of the opinion that he was 'incredibly lucky to have literally got away with murder'. The Scotland Yard Detective, Sergeant Charles Hewitt, whose views appeared in *The Times* of 11th July 1983, claimed that Adams was 'without doubt a mass murderer who deserved to be hanged 20 times over'.

However, the trial judge, Patrick Devlin, wrote: 'I certainly don't believe that he was a mass murderer' but instead described him as 'a mercenary killer'. There are, however, those who claim that Adams was essentially 'the victim of a vicious whispering campaign of rumour and vilification' as to how many he might have or have not killed, and claims that he killed 400 people are entirely fanciful, relating back to 'unsubstantiated and sensational' newspaper headlines.

Though a defendant had never been required to give evidence in their own defence, Judge Devlin reinforced in his summing-up that no prejudice should be attached by the jury to the fact that Adams did not give evidence.

The forensic pathologist Francis Camps believed that there were 163 'suspicious' cases. However, much of the 'solid evidence' for these assertions turned out to be false. It is likely that the nurses who perjured themselves at the trial had no real intention of doing so. Having been asked to recall the details of the treatment of a patient who had died almost six years previously, no doubt the nurses tried to be as helpful as possible to the police, and unintentionally told them what they wanted to know.

There was no doubt within legal circles, that Mannigham-Buller did aspire to the office of Lord Chief Justice but his 'lack-lustre' performance in the Adams case counted against him. However, whether the prosecution would have been more successful with a charge of manslaughter, given the divergence of the crucial expert medical opinion, is anyone's guess.

There is also suspicion that the police themselves wanted their share of the 'kudos and glory' of prosecuting a doctor for murder. Ironically, they had to wait another forty years before Harold Shipman became the first to be successfully prosecuted for homicide.

Few names strike fear and disgust in equal measure to the hearts and minds of the British general public as does Dr Harold Shipman, the general practitioner who was convicted in 2000 of murdering 15 of his patients.

Going back 50 years and we have a similar case with the trial of Dr John Bodkin Adams, the only difference here being that he was acquitted. However, there are remarkable similarities in the psychological profile of both of these people.

Bodkin Adams had an empty life and a sense of entitlement leading to his desire for social acceptance. It is believed that he killed not out of greed for money but instead, to cope with his resentment and social exclusion. Similarly, Shipman wasn't motivated by money, but by death itself, gaining satisfaction and pleasure from killings his patients.

Prior to Dr Harold Shipman's conviction, and 25 years after the Adams case, another British doctor, Leonard Arthur, stood trial for murder arising from medical treatment. Arthur was tried in November 1981 at Leicester Crown Court for the attempted murder of John Pearson, a newborn child with Down's syndrome. Similar to Adam's case, on the advice of his legal team, Arthur did not give evidence in his defence, relying instead on expert medical witnesses. He was subsequently acquitted. In 2000, Harold Shipman became the only British doctor to be successfully prosecuted for the murder of his patients. He was found unanimously guilty on 15 counts and the Shipman Inquiry concluded in 2002 that he had murdered another 200.

In conclusion, the vital question still remains: was John Bodkin Adams the mass murderer many believed him to be, or was he in fact, the bringer of comfort and peace to the dying?

Dear Reader, the verdict is yours!

Appendices

Appendix A: The Current Law of Homicide
Memorandum from the Attorney General

Murder

'Murder is defined as 'unlawful killing with malice aforethought'. This is to be contrasted with those forms of manslaughter which consist of killing without 'malice aforethought'.

The principal distinguishing feature between murder and manslaughter is that murder requires an intention to kill or to cause grievous bodily harm.

The penalty for murder is life imprisonment.

In summary, deliberately taking the life of another person, whether the person is dying or not, constitutes the crime of murder. Accordingly, any doctor who practices mercy killing can be charged with murder if the facts are clearly established.

The only exception is where the doctor acts to do all that is proper and necessary to relieve pain with the incidental effect that this will shorten the patient's life.

This was explained by Devlin J. in R v Adams [1957] Crim L.R. 773. Doctor Adams was charged with the murder of a patient. It was alleged that he had prescribed and administered large quantities of drugs that he must have known that death would result. In his summing up to the jury, Devlin J. stated: 'If her life was cut short by weeks or months it was just as much murder as if it was cut short by years. There has been much discussion as to when doctors might be justified in administering drugs which would shorten life. Cases of severe pain were suggested and also cases of helpless misery. The law knows no special defence in this category.'

However, he went on to say: '...but that does not mean that a doctor who was aiding the sick and dying had to calculate in minutes, or even hours, perhaps, not in days or weeks, the effect on a patient's life of the medicines which he could administer. If the first purpose of medicine – the restoration of health – could no longer be achieved there was still much for the doctor to do and he was entitled to do all that was proper and necessary to relieve pain and suffering even if the measures he took might incidentally shorten life by hours or perhaps even longer'.

This introduced into English law the 'double-effect' principle, that is if an act has two consequences, one good and one bad, the bad consequence may nevertheless be acceptable depending on the circumstances.

Source: House of Lords – Assisted Dying for the Terminally Ill Bill - Minutes (Parliamentary Copyright 2005)

Appendix B: 'All I Tried To Do Was Relieve His Agony, His Distress And Suffering'

'Campaigners for the legalisation of euthanasia were jubilant last night after a jury unanimously found a family doctor who gave an elderly patient a massive overdose of diamorphine not guilty of murder after only 69 minutes' deliberation. The case has ignited a nationwide debate about the rights and wrongs of hastening the deaths of terminally ill patients. The Voluntary Euthanasia Society called the acquittal of GP David Moor at Newcastle-upon-Tyne Crown Court a 'huge relief' to doctors and patients throughout Britain, but said guidelines were urgently needed to tell doctors how they could help dying patients without risking a similar prosecution. Had Dr Moor of Stamfordham, Northumberland, been convicted of murdering 85-year-old George Liddell, a cancer sufferer, he would have faced a life sentence, which is mandatory for murder.

Peggy Norris, chairwoman of the anti-euthanasia group Alert, said: 'I think this is a sad day for medicine as it makes the law unclear as to what is allowed. We cannot have a half-law when it comes to this'. The government is firmly opposed to legalising euthanasia, but the case is likely to spark renewed calls for the abolition of the mandatory life sentence for murder, a move favoured by senior judges. Dr Moor, 52, a high-profile GP who retired early because of the stress of the case, thanked all those who supported him through his 'extraordinary ordeal'. He specifically thanked Mr Lidell's son-in-law, Tony Ryan, who told the court he was a 'wonderful doctor'. The GP added: 'In caring for a terminally ill patient, a doctor is entitled to give pain relieving medication which may have the effect of a patient's death. All I tried to do in treating Mr Liddell was to relieve his agony, distress and suffering. This has always been my approach in treating my patients with care and compassion. Doctors who treat dying patients to relieve their pain walk a tightrope to achieve it'.

Dr Moor, who practised in Newcastle upon Tyne, was the first British doctor to be tried for murder purely for the mercy killing of a patient. In the only other murder case that of John Bodkin Adams in 1957, the Crown alleged that the doctor profited from the death of an elderly widow. He was acquitted. Dr Moor, a popular GP who broadcast on regional radio and wrote for a local newspaper, was arrested after a press interview in which he claimed to have helped many patients to 'pain-free' deaths. He denied in court that he had ever murdered anybody. His defence rested on the principle of 'double effect', which lays down that doctors may legally administer drugs which hasten a patient's death, as long as the intention was to ease suffering. The prosecution alleged that the huge dose of diamorphine, three times higher than Dr Moor had admitted administering, must have been intended to kill Mr Liddell, a retired ambulance man.

The jury delivered its verdict after a summing up by Mr Justice Holland which nudged them towards an acquittal. He told them they might consider it ironic that Dr Moor found himself facing the charge because he was caring enough to come out on his day off to see Mr Liddell. The turning point in the case came when the judge excluded key toxicological evidence, leaving the prosecution with no proof that the injection had caused the death. The judge awarded the defence team only two-thirds of the costs, saying Dr Moor had partly brought the prosecution on himself by 'very silly remarks to the press' and lying

to the NHS and police'. The Crown Prosecution Service defended its decision to prosecute. A spokesman said: 'Advice was obtained from senior treasury counsel, a member of the independent bar, and it was decided that a prosecution was required'. Michael Wilks, chairman of the British Medical Association's medical ethics committee said, 'The trial should not be seen as breaking new ground on the issue of euthanasia'.
Source: *The Guardian*, 12th May 1999, by Clare Dyer, Legal Correspondent.

The Trial of
Dr Buck Ruxton

First published by
Scott Martin Productions, 2020
www.scottmartinproductions.com

Buck Ruxton (1899-1936)
Courtesy of Glasgow University

'Truth will come to light; murder cannot be hid long.'

William Shakespeare (1564-1616)
The Merchant of Venice Act 1 Scene iii.

Acknowledgements

I am very grateful for the support I have received from numerous quarters in the preparation of this final work of a trilogy. In particular, I wish to record my thanks to members of the medical and legal professions and the police service for the benefit of their expertise and opinions on the issues raised by this unusual work. My thanks also go to those largely anonymous yet ever obliging staff of the various institutions and archives I have consulted in my research and preparation of this work. My gratitude loses no sincerity in its generality.

The primary source for this work has been the definitive volume, *Medico-Legal Aspects of the Ruxton Case* produced in 1937 by Professors Glaister and Brash. In addition, I consulted the *Trial Transcripts of R v Ruxton (1936)* at the National Archives, Kew. Finally, *The Ruxton Trial* in the *Notable British Trials Series 3*, edited by James H Hodge (dated 1950) provided very valuable background information.

In addition, a selection of other sources including books, legal, medical and forensic articles and media reports, have been consulted and acknowledged. I would hasten to add, that none of the above are responsible for the contents of this work, and any errors are entirely my own.

David Holding 2020

Introduction

This book is the final volume in a trilogy which takes the reader into the private world of medical doctors who were in practice in England during a period from the 1920s until the turn of the 21st century. Each of these practitioners came from different backgrounds, but the one common thread linking each of them was that they all stood trial for murder. Each of these cases received widespread coverage at the time, and all have been the subject of numerous books, articles and documentaries.

This book, together with its companion works, employs an innovative approach to the subject of murder. Each work commences with background information about the subject before examining the development of the case against each of them. The work then progresses to the criminal and medical investigations, culminating in the trial itself. Each work concludes with an overview of the case which draws together all the essential strands necessary to fully appraise the case. By adopting this particular approach, the author's intention has been to take the reader on a sequential journey through each aspect of the case. In so doing, the reader becomes fully immersed from the very outset rather than remaining a 'passive observer'. By the time the trial is reached, the reader is presented with all the evidence and background information to enable them to draw their own conclusions and reach their own verdict.

This final work centres on the trial of Dr Buck Ruxton, an Indian-born general practitioner, who stood trial in 1936 for the murder of his common-law wife and his housemaid. He was subsequently found guilty, convicted and executed. This case differs from its companion works in two important respects. Firstly, unlike the cases of Harold Shipman and John

Bodkin Adams, Ruxton's victims were not his patients but members of his own household. Secondly, this case is unique in that it was the first in which innovative forensic techniques were employed to provide conclusive evidence on which to bring a prosecution against Ruxton.

Buck Ruxton was born in Bombay, India, on 21st March 1899, into a Parsee family of Indian-French descent. His original name was Bukhtyar Rustomji Ratanji Hakim, which he later abbreviated to Buck Hakim. Ruxton was a highly intelligent youth who had received a good standard of education and even as a teenager, he had set his sights on a career in medicine. He entered the University of Bombay School of Medicine graduating as a medical doctor in 1923. Following his basic training, Ruxton served with the Indian Medical Service and was deployed in Iraq. In 1925, Ruxton entered into an 'arranged' marriage with a Parsee woman but the relationship was short-lived.

In 1926, Ruxton emigrated to Britain and settled in London under the assumed name of Buck Hakim. He completed further studies in medicine at London University College Hospital till 1927 when he re-located to Edinburgh, Scotland, to prepare for the examination for Fellowship of the Royal College of Surgeons of Edinburgh. He failed the entrance examination, but the General Medical Council allowed him to practice medicine in the UK on the basis of his qualifications gained in Bombay and London. It was at this time that Ruxton once again changed his name, this time legally by deed poll to 'Buck Ruxton'. It was whilst he was studying in Edinburgh, that he formed a relationship with a 26-year old woman by the name of Isabella Van Ess, who at the time was married to a Dutchman.

However, that marriage did not last long as she soon obtained a divorce. The relationship between Ruxton and Isabella flourished and in 1928 Ruxton returned to London with Isabella and was employed as a locum GP. The following year, Isabella had her first child, a daughter named Elizabeth. The couple did not marry but lived together as Dr and Mrs Ruxton. By 1930, the family relocated to the north of England, to Lancaster, the county town of Lancashire. It was here that Ruxton set up his general practice at 2 Dalton Square.

It does appear that Ruxton made positive efforts at assimilating into the community of Lancaster and created a reputation for being a diligent and caring GP who was well-respected among his predominantly working-class patients. In 1931, the Ruxton family increased with the birth of a second daughter Diane, followed two years later in 1933 by a son William. It was at this time that the Ruxton family employed a live-in housemaid Mary Jane Rogerson, a 20-year old woman.

However, in direct contrast to his professional and public persona, Buck Ruxton was an excitable, jealous and suspicious individual, prone to outbursts of rage and paranoia. It has even been suggested that Ruxton slept with a revolver under his pillow. The couple's life together was tempestuous, with Buck frequently abusing and assaulting Isabella.

On several occasions, intervention from the police was required to calm things down. Also, on several occasions, Isabella and the children left Lancaster to stay with her sisters in Edinburgh. However, these absences were short-lived and ended with Ruxton pleading her to return to the family home.

On Saturday the 14th September 1935,

Isabella had arranged to meet her sisters in the seaside resort of Blackpool where they were on holiday, to view the annual illuminations. She drove the 25-mile journey from Lancaster in her husband's car, leaving Ruxton behind, and is believed to have left the resort on her return journey around 11:30 pm. She arrived back in Lancaster in the early hours of Sunday 15th September. It appears that Isabella's prolonged absence led Ruxton to have a jealous quarrel with her later in the day, and the quarrel escalated into violence.

On this occasion it also led to two killings. The housemaid Mary Rogerson is believed to have witnessed Ruxton's assault on his 'wife' and therefore she too had to be killed. It was later confirmed that both women had been strangled and stabbed before having their bodies dismembered. It was later established that Ruxton had placed the two bodies in the bathtub in order to cut them into manageable sections. He then wrapped them in newspapers, pillowcases and sheets.

He was observed loading several parcels into his car on the Sunday. On Tuesday 17th September Ruxton was returning from the Lake District and outside the town of Kendal, he knocked a cyclist off his bicycle at around 12:35 pm. The cyclist managed to get the car registration number and reported the incident to the local police. Kendal police then contacted their counterparts in the small village of Milnthorpe where Ruxton was stopped and questioned at around 1:00 am. He was ordered to produce his licence and insurance documents to his local police in Lancaster. When stopped, he had claimed to be returning from a business trip to Carlisle. However, some believe that it may have been a trial run or in fact, that it was the day he actually disposed of the remains of the two bodies.

On the 29th September, a tourist visiting the Dumfriesshire town of Moffat was crossing a stone bridge on the Edinburgh-Carlisle road two miles north of Moffat, at a place known as Gardenholme Linn. When looking over the bridge below she saw what seemed to be a human arm protruding from a parcel lying on the bank of a stream which ran into the River Annan. She returned to her hotel and informed her brother of the discovery and he visited the site to confirm what his sister had found.

They reported the find to the police who instigated a search of the area and ravine below the bridge. This search revealed a total of 30 parcels containing various body parts.

Once recovered, these parts were examined by John Glaister, Professor of Forensic Medicine at Glasgow University, and James Couper Brash, Professor of Anatomy at Edinburgh University. They painstakingly re-assembled the bodies and confirmed that they were of two women.

A new technique of photographic superimposition was used to match two life photographs of Isabella Ruxton and Mary Rogerson with photographs of the two skulls found with the remains, and they both matched perfectly. They also used a relatively new forensic procedure known as 'entomology' (the study of maggots) to identify the age of maggots found on the body parts and thus to provide an approximate date of death.

Once the bodies had been identified as those of the two missing women from Lancaster, Ruxton was brought in for questioning by the Lancaster police. Armed with the positive results from the 'forensic' investigation, together with their own intelligence gathered in Lancaster and Scotland,

Ruxton was formally charged with the murders of Mary Jane Rogerson on the 13th of October, and on the 5th of November, with that of his common-law wife Isabella Ruxton, and he was remanded in custody on both counts.

A key piece of evidence against Ruxton was one of the newspapers used to wrap up some of the body parts. This was a special edition of *The Sunday Graphic* dated 15th September 1935 which was only sold in the Lancaster and Morecambe areas. A thorough search of Ruxton's house revealed vast amounts of blood in various parts, including the stairs, floor carpets and bathroom.

Ruxton's trial took place at Manchester Assizes Court on the 2nd March 1936 and lasted until the 13th March. The prosecuting counsel told the jury that 'It is very probable that Mary Rogerson was a witness to the murder of Mrs Ruxton and that is why she met her death'.

He informed the jury that the bloodstains found inside the house confirmed that both murders had occurred on the landing at the top of the stairs, outside Mary Rogerson's bedroom. Down the staircase, right into the bathroom, there were trails and enormous quantities of blood.

The prosecution further suggested that when Mary went to bed, a violent quarrel took place, resulting in Ruxton strangling his wife. It was said that Mary Rogerson caught him in the act.

Over 100 witnesses were called, together with over 200 evidence exhibits. Professor Glaister presented compelling evidence that the remains were those of Isabella Ruxton and Mary.

The only witness for the defence was Ruxton himself who denied his guilt suggesting that it was purely circumstantial, and he further challenged the identification of the bodies. At the end of the trial, the jury took just over an hour to return a guilty verdict and he was sentenced to death. Ruxton appealed the sentence which was heard in London but dismissed on the 27th April 1936. Ruxton was confined to prison to await his execution which was carried out on Tuesday 12th May at Strangeways Prison, Manchester.

A few days following the execution, Ruxton's signed confession was published in *The News of the World* dated 14th October 1935. It stated: 'I killed Mrs Ruxton in a fit of temper because I thought she had been with a man. I was mad at the time. Mary Rogerson was present at the time. I had to kill her'.

The prosecution of Ruxton's murders proved to be one of the most publicised legal cases of the 1930s. It is primarily remembered for the innovative forensic techniques employed to identify the victims and link Ruxton's home to the murders. This case emphasised the crucial importance of teamwork, particularly in relation to the medical and forensic aspects of the case, together with close co-operation between the respective police forces involved in the investigation.

During the 20th century, there have been many serial crimes in which mutilation of the victims was a distinctive feature. However, the Ruxton case was unique in that it was distinguished from the other cases by the extent and character of the mutilation of the two victims involved. The removal of identifiable features led to a novel comparison of the skulls and photographic portraits of the victims which proved their identification beyond doubt.

Finally, and somewhat ironically, there is the important part played by the errors and omissions of Ruxton in building up the case against himself. In this case, we see a classic example of the failure of the perpetrator of the crimes to realise the evidential importance of the identifiable articles left with the remains. The newspapers, the blouse, the child's rompers and cotton sheets in which the remains were wrapped, all helped to trace the remains back to the scene of the crime, to 2 Dalton Square, Lancaster, and to Ruxton.

Chapter One: The Discovery of Human Remains

The case of R v Ruxton began with the macabre chance discovery of human remains in a ravine approximately two miles north of the town of Moffat in Dumfriesshire, Scotland. The Edinburgh-Carlisle road crosses an old stone bridge under which runs a stream which is a tributary of the River Annan. This location is known locally as Gardenholme Linn.

It was on the afternoon of Sunday 29th September 1935 when Miss Susan Haines Johnson, a visitor to the area from Edinburgh, crossed the bridge and gazed below into the ravine and stream. On the bank of the stream she noticed a bundle wrapped in newspaper revealing what she believed was a human arm. Shocked by what she had witnessed, she hurried back to the hotel where she was staying with her brother Alfred. On hearing Susan's report, Alfred went to the ravine himself to confirm what had occurred. Climbing down into the ravine he discovered other parcels containing human remains some wrapped in newspapers and others in a cotton sheet. Their discovery was quickly relayed to the local police at Moffat who instigated a full search of the locality.

The search revealed four bundles; together with two heads, a thigh bone (femur), two forearms with attached hands, and various pieces of human flesh and skin. The collected remains were removed to the small mortuary attached to Moffat Cemetery. On close examination, the first bundle contained two upper arms and four pieces of flesh wrapped in a blouse. The second bundle revealed two thigh-bones (femora), two legs with most of the tissue removed and pieces of flesh, enclosed in a pillowslip. The third bundle which was covered with a cotton sheet contained seventeen pieces of flesh. The fourth bundle contained the chest portion of a human trunk, together with two legs tied together with a piece of hem from a cotton sheet, and mixed inside was straw and cotton wool. Around some of the bundles and also lying on the ground were pieces of newspaper. One particular piece of newspaper was identified as part of *The Sunday Graphic and Sunday News* dated 15th September 1935, and this was found in the first bundle. Later in the investigation, this proved to be an important clue.

Each of the two heads was wrapped in cotton wool and a pair of child's rompers, held in position with a piece of cotton twine. The initial police search was resumed at Gardenholme Linn the following day, 30th September, when another forearm with hand and a piece of flesh, each wrapped in newspaper, an uncovered thigh (femur), together with another bundle containing a pelvis, were found just below the bridge on the bank of the stream.

The police continued their search around the Linn and on the 2nd October another five pieces of flesh were retrieved. It was not until the 28th October that a roadman discovered a newspaper bundle containing a left foot on the side of the Glasgow-Carlisle road nine miles south of Moffat. Finally, on 4th November 1935, a woman walking along the Moffat-Edinburgh road, half a mile south of Gardenholme Linn, discovered a forearm and hand, wrapped in newspaper, lying in the grass at the road.

In total, the police search revealed seventy pieces of human remains, including two heads and one trunk. On the morning of Monday 30th September, the day following the discovery of the remains, they were examined at the Moffat mortuary by two local general practitioners, Dr David Huskie and Dr F W Pringle.

On the following day, Tuesday 1st October, Dr W Gilbert Millar, Lecturer in Pathology at the University of Edinburgh and Professor John Glaister, Regius Professor of Forensic Medicine also at Edinburgh University first visited the scene of the discovery, followed by a preliminary examination of the remains at the Moffat mortuary.

It was soon realised that identification of the dismembered and mutilated bodies posed a difficult problem, and that reconstruction would be essential. In addition, the decomposing and maggot-ridden remains required urgent preservation. Since there were no facilities at the mortuary to accommodate this mammoth task, the remains were transported to the University at Edinburgh.

The preliminary examination of the remains at Moffat did confirm certain basic facts. They represented at least two bodies which were described as 'well-developed and well-nourished'. It was also apparent that both heads had been mutilated by the removal of the main features - ears, eyes, nose, lips and facial skin - together with teeth extracted, most probably after death.

The less-mutilated head was considered to be that of a young woman, whilst the other first appeared to be that of a man but was later acknowledged to be that of an older woman when the accompanying pelvis was attached to the remains. It was of medico-legal significance that many of the missing parts were those that could reveal marks of violence suggesting possible cause of death

The unanimous view of the experts involved in the examination of the remains, was that the person or persons responsible for the mutilation and dismemberment of the two bodies displayed both medical and anatomical knowledge. This was further reinforced by the fact that the bodies had been dismembered into neat portions convenient for their ultimate disposal. This had been carried out by cutting through the joints with a knife or possible surgical scalpel. There were no visible signs that a saw had been used in carrying out this task.

Those parts of the remains thought likely to belong to each of the bodies were stored in separate boxes labelled 'Body No 1' and 'Body No 2'. The first box contained the head and the other various component parts which initially appeared to belong to the body of a young woman. Since the investigation would involve a wide field of medico-legal expertise, the specialists involved, were assigned to specific areas of investigation.

Professor Glaister, his assistant Dr FW Martin, together with Dr Millar, were responsible for the pathological and medico-legal aspects of the case. The anatomical investigation which would include the reconstruction of the bodies, was the responsibility of Professor Brash, assisted by Dr E Llewellyn Godfrey, a specialist radiographer. The dental examination of the skulls was undertaken by Dr ACW Hutchinson, Dean of the Dental Hospital and School at Edinburgh University, assisted by A Johnstone Brown, a local dental surgeon. By combining the medico-legal investigations, various lines of inquiry could be carried out in parallel, and frequent daily discussions ensured that the work was closely co-ordinated. Photographic recordings were undertaken of all the relevant body parts in preparation for anticipated criminal proceedings. This work was undertaken by members of the City of Edinburgh Police Force. Whilst there were essentially two investigations being undertaken simultaneously, one by the medical team the other by the respective police forces, close contact between the two was maintained to provide a co-ordinated overview of the case.

*2, Dalton Square, Lancaster, Ruxton's House
Commons Attribution Photo*

Chapter Two: The Police, Medical and Forensic Investigations

The Police Investigation

Following the discovery of the human remains at Moffat on 29th September, 1935, the police launched their own investigation which involved pooling their resources between three separate Scottish forces - Dumfriesshire Constabulary, Glasgow Police Force and the City of Edinburgh Police Force - each contributing its own specialist officers. This was a good example of inter-force co-operation, in helping to gather as much evidence as possible to ultimately secure a conviction of the person or persons responsible for this horrific crime.

Detective Inspector John Sheed, an officer attached to Edinburgh Police, was appointed as liaison officer between the medical experts at Edinburgh University and the respective police forces. This ensured that there was co-ordination between the medical evidence and the police lines of enquiry. At this point, Dumfriesshire Constabulary (on whose territory the remains were found) was the lead force.

One of the first tasks undertaken by officers of the Dumfriesshire Police (and assisted by other officers drafted in from nearby Lanarkshire Constabulary) was to carry out further searches along the stream at Gardenholme Linn, the site of the original discovery. This included observing the positions in which the remains had been found, and it was concluded that the remains had been thrown over the bridge parapet, very likely at night, by someone who was familiar with the locality, but not with the course of the narrow stream flowing below. By observing the state of the stream banks, it was revealed that the stream had recently flooded.

Information gathered locally at Moffat confirmed that the stream had been in spate during the night of 17th/18th September, the water still being relatively high on the 19th September. From local knowledge it was confirmed that floods in the stream tended to subside relatively quickly. This information was of particular importance to the police investigation because some pieces of flesh had been located on the bank of the stream, and others on the bank of the River Annan some 600 yards further down than the bridge. It had also been noted that after 18th September, this had been followed by four or five dry fine days.

This provided a provisional time-line for when the remains had been deposited in the ravine. It was suggested that this possibly occurred about the time that the stream was flooded, on the 16th, 17th or 18th September 1935.

Local weather records showed that the heaviest rainfall at Moffat during September had been on the 18th, when nearly one and a half inches of rain had fallen. Particularly during the night between Sunday and Monday, 15th and 16th September, there had been a fairly heavy rainfall. The chief difficulty facing the police at this point in their investigation in tracing the remains was that the Moffat-Edinburgh road is a main route between England and the North.

The police issued a statement that they required information from garages and petrol stations regarding any suspicious cars or occupants having used them. The next line of enquiry was to search recent reports of missing persons. The investigators deduced that it would be very unlikely that two persons, associated in some way, could disappear within a short time-frame without at least one other person being aware of the fact. Consequently, the police concentrated their attention on reports of dual disappearances.

It also became evident to investigators that if performed by one person, even if that one person had anatomical knowledge, the extent of the mutilations and dismemberment of the bodies must have made it a considerable undertaking. Equally important was the fact that there must have been the opportunity for carrying out this work undisturbed for several hours. This suggested that the bodies of the victims had been dismembered in the same location in which they had been killed. This theory was reinforced by the fact that many of the body parts had been completely drained of blood. In addition, various 'domestic' articles had been found with the remains, for example, newspapers, cotton sheeting, child's rompers, a blouse and cotton wool.

On the 9th October, the Chief Constable of Dumfries contacted the Lancaster Borough Police because of an article he had seen in *The Glasgow Daily Record* regarding the disappearance three weeks previously of a young Lancaster woman named Mary Jane Rogerson. She had been employed as nursemaid by a local Dr Buck Ruxton who was practising in Lancaster. He was informed by Lancaster Police that the disappearance of this girl had been reported to them. It is also of significance that on 24th September, Dr Ruxton had visited the police station in Lancaster complaining that local rumours had begun to circulate regarding the discovery that the human remains discovered in Scotland were those of his wife and maid. He maintained that these rumours were proving detrimental to both his medical practice and his general reputation. On this occasion, he also told the police that his wife had left him two weeks before and gone to Scotland.

The Newspapers

As part of their continuing investigation, the police had carefully examined the wrappings in which the human remains had been found, in an attempt to discover links between them. It emerged from this examination that the latest date of any of them was the 15th September, 1935. This proved to be a vital clue because this date was when the missing women from Lancaster disappeared.

Three different newspapers were identified; *The Sunday Herald*, *The Sunday Chronicle* and *The Sunday Graphic and Sunday News*. Two pieces from *The Sunday Graphic and Sunday News*, proved to be of vital importance to the police investigation. One of the pieces bore the serial number 1,067, and further police enquiries revealed that the newspaper was one of 3,700 copies of a special 'slip' edition which covered the Morecambe Carnival held on Saturday 14th September. This had been issued to a few newsagents in Morecambe, Lancaster and the surrounding districts only.

Police confirmed that the copies of the issue had been supplied to a wholesale newsagent in Lancaster. He had received 728 copies on Sunday 15th September, and he, in turn, had supplied 24 copies to another retailer in Lancaster. This retailer was able to confirm that Dr Buck Ruxton was one of his customers and that every Sunday for the past twelve months, he had a copy of the paper delivered to him. On Sunday 15th September 1935, a copy of the paper was duly delivered to 2 Dalton Square by a local paper boy.

The Blouse and Child's Rompers

Following the newspaper evidence, Scottish police visited the Rogersons in Morecambe and asked Mary's parents if they could identify any of the clothing found with the human remains at Moffat. Mrs Rogerson, Mary's step-mother, immediately recognised the blouse because of the distinctive patchwork repair she had carried out under one of the arms, prior to giving it to Mary.

While Mrs Rogerson was unable to recognise the pair of child's rompers, she suggested that the police show the article to a friend of hers Mrs Edith Holme, living at Grange-over-Sands. It transpired that Isabella Ruxton, Mary and the children had stayed at Mrs Holme's earlier in 1935 while on a short holiday to Morecambe Bay.

When the rompers were shown to Mrs Holme, she immediately recognised them as a pair she had bought and given to one of the Ruxton children. She had replaced the worn elastic waist band and secured it with her own unique style of knot. With this new information, the direction of the police investigation became firmly focused on Lancaster, and on Ruxton in particular.

It was at this stage that the overall supervision of the investigation was taken over by Lancaster Borough Police, the responsibility being transferred to Captain Henry J Vann, the Chief Constable. In order to assist the reader in placing subsequent events in context, a brief background to the Ruxton household and in particular, Ruxton's personality was considered useful.

The Ruxton Household

In addition to Dr Buck Ruxton and his common-law wife Isabella, the household at 2 Dalton Square, Lancaster, comprised their three children; daughter Elizabeth aged six, daughter Diane aged four and son William aged two. The Ruxtons also employed a live-in nursemaid Mary Jane Rogerson, aged twenty. The domestic housework and cooking were shared by two charwomen. Mrs Agnes Oxley worked at the house every day of the week starting around 7:10 am, and Mrs Elizabeth Curwen also worked every day, starting at 8:30 am except Sundays when she started work at 10:00 am. Both these charwomen lived in Lancaster and were not resident at Dalton Square.

Ruxton's Personality

Since settling at Dalton Square in 1930, there was no doubt that the relationship between Ruxton and Isabella had become strained and tense. This was because of Ruxton's paranoid suspicions of Isabella's alleged infidelity, demonstrated by furious outbursts and threats made in the presence of witnesses. Previous maids employed at the house recalled his threatening attitude towards his wife, and of him having a revolver in his bedroom. They even witnessed occasions when knives had been held at Isabella's throat by Ruxton, and the police had been called on at least two occasions because of his threatening and erratic behaviour. They had described Ruxton as 'acting like a madman, becoming so excited as to be completely incoherent'.

In 1932, Mrs Nelson, one of Isabella's sisters living in Edinburgh, had travelled down to Lancaster in response to a telegram she had received from

Ruxton informing her that Isabella had attempted to commit suicide. Again in 1934, Mrs Ruxton had gone up to Edinburgh with the children to escape the increasing threats and violence. She was followed by Ruxton and persuaded to return with him to Lancaster. There was no doubt that Ruxton's jealousy and growing belief in Isabella's infidelity was that of an unbalanced person. It has been regarded by many as the overriding factor in Ruxton's final criminal act. His extreme personality disorder was clearly demonstrated in two final events which occurred within one week of each other in early September 1935.

On Saturday 7th September, Mrs Ruxton visited Edinburgh in the company of local friends, the Edmondson family, comprising Mr and Mrs Edmondson, their daughter and son Robert. The party travelled to Edinburgh in two cars, staying overnight at the Adelphi Hotel, all occupying separate rooms. Ruxton was convinced that this visit was really an illicit meeting arranged between Isabella and the young Robert Edmondson, so he hired a car and followed the party.

His suspicions were completely unfounded but this event clearly demonstrated how even an innocent trip to Scotland became completely distorted in Ruxton's mind. The following Saturday, 14th September, Mrs Ruxton arranged to meet her two sisters who had come down from Edinburgh for a break in Blackpool. Each year they met up to view the illuminations together. Isabella travelled in her husband's car alone, leaving Ruxton with Mary the housemaid at home.

It was established that Isabella left Blackpool for the twenty-five mile journey back to Lancaster at approximately 11:30 pm. She is believed to have arrived back at Dalton Square in the early hours of Sunday 15th September, because Ruxton's Hillman Minx car was seen parked outside the house on the Sunday morning. Leaving Blackpool on the Saturday night was the last time that anyone but Ruxton saw her alive. Mary Rogerson the maid was last seen at the house around 7 pm.

On Friday 13th September, one of Ruxton's charladies, Mrs Curwen, was working at the house when she was told by Ruxton that since there was nothing for her to do that day, she could go home, and only need to report for work on Monday 16th September. Then on Sunday 15th September at 6:30 am, Ruxton visited his other charlady, Mrs Oxley, who was due to start work that day at 7:10 am, and told her that she too did not need to come to work, but that she should come as normal on the Monday morning. These two incidents have been interpreted by observers of the case, as evidence that Ruxton was preparing to carry out his crime and therefore ensured that there would be no witnesses present. Various people called at Dalton Square on the Sunday and commented on the delay in opening the door by Ruxton himself, when usually this was done by either Mary Rogerson or one of the two charladies.

Those visitors who commented about Ruxton's bandaged right hand were given various explanations for the injury. Amongst the explanations were the declaration that he had 'jammed it', or that he had cut it opening a tin of fruit for his children's breakfast.

Later that Sunday morning, Ruxton had visited two garages to obtain petrol. At 11:00 am, a Mrs Whiteside called accompanied by her young son to keep an appointment for a minor operation to be performed. Ruxton opened the door and apologised that he was unable to carry out the operation that day. The reason he gave was that Mrs Ruxton was away in Scotland and there were only himself and Mary his maid present. They were busy removing carpets in preparation for decorators arriving on the Monday morning.

At about 11:30 am, Ruxton took his children over to the Andersons, family friends in Morecambe, where the children would stay for a few days. On his return from Morecambe, Ruxton was alone at his house until about 4:30 pm when he visited one of his patients, a Mrs Hampshire. He requested that she help him clean the house because he had cut his hand and was finding it difficult. He explained that his wife was in Blackpool and Mary Rogerson was away in Edinburgh.

When Mrs Hampshire arrived back at Dalton Square, she found the house in a very untidy state. Carpets had been removed from the stairs and replaced by straw, and some of these carpets lay with a blue suit in the waiting-room. In the rear yard, she found other carpets, clothing and towels all heavily blood-stained. There was evidence that an attempt had been made to burn these items.

Mrs Hampshire noted in particular that the doors to two bedrooms were locked, and that in the lounge there was a supper laid out for two. This was untouched. She was particularly surprised to find that the bath was in a very dirty state, being stained with a dirty yellow colour. Mrs Hampshire was later joined by her husband to help with the cleaning. Later that evening, Ruxton offered the carpets and suit in the waiting-room to the Hampshires even though they were stained, and they took them away when they left the house at around 9:30 pm. From that time until the morning of Monday 16th September, nothing was known of Ruxton's movements.

At about 7:00 am on the morning of Monday 16th September, Mrs Oxley had arrived at Ruxton's house as usual, but could receive no answer so she went back home before returning at about 9:15. At 9.00 Ruxton visited Mrs Hampshire again to enquire about the carpets and suit he had given her.

It is particularly significant that Mrs Hampshire recalled Ruxton looking very ill, unshaven and wearing an old raincoat, certainly not in keeping with his usual smart appearance. Picking up the suit, Ruxton asked for a pair of scissors to cut out his name from the jacket which was then thrown on the fire. He told Mrs Hampshire that if she could not clean the items, then they should be burned. When Ruxton had left, Mrs Hampshire swilled the carpet with numerous buckets of water which turned red like blood. While Mrs Oxley was standing at the front door, Ruxton arrived in his car having just left the Hampshires. In later interviews, she described Ruxton's appearance almost exactly as that described by Mrs Hampshire. When Mrs Oxley eventually entered the house, she too found the same bedroom doors locked and the uneaten supper still in the lounge. It transpired that later on the Monday, Ruxton had left his own car at his usual garage for servicing and had hired another car. Nothing is known of Ruxton's movements for the rest of the day. On Tuesday 17th September at about 1:00 pm, Ruxton was stopped in his hired car at Milnthorpe, between Kendal and Lancaster.

It appears that he had knocked down a cyclist at Kendal that afternoon and failed to stop. He told the police that he had been to Carlisle on business. On Thursday 19th September, Ruxton requested an early breakfast from his charlady, telling her that he was going to see a specialist about his injured hand. At around 7:30 am, he brought his car to the back door of his house and was heard to go up and down the stairs several times and go out to his car. At approximately 8:00 am, he left Dalton Square and did not return until about 3:30 pm saying that he had been to Blackburn.

Later that day, his three children returned from Morecambe. When Ruxton had left on the Thursday morning, the charladies noticed that the two bedroom doors were open, and that there was an offensive smell in his bedroom. On Friday 20th September, Ruxton asked one of the charladies to go and buy a spray of eau-de-cologne which he then used throughout the house.

From information received by the police from various sources, suspicion was now firmly centred on Dr Buck Ruxton. His conduct at various interviews with the police, together with their knowledge of his jealous, violent disposition and unhappy relationship with Isabella, was a sufficient basis for this suspicion. The date of *The Sunday Graphic and Sunday News* found with the remains at Moffat was the very same date on which the two women disappeared from Lancaster.

This connecting link was further strengthened by the fact that circulation of this particular edition of newspaper was restricted to the Morecambe and Lancaster areas. On the 10th, 11th and 12th October, blood-stained carpets and stair-pads from Ruxton's home, together with the blood-stained jacket and trousers were recovered from Mrs Hampshire. Also, by the 12th October, the child's rompers and blouse had been positively identified as belonging to Mary Rogerson. Later that day, Chief Constable HJ Vann of the Lancaster Borough Police Force requested Ruxton attend the police station for an interview regarding the two missing women.

The most crucial element of the evidence linking the remains at Moffat with No 2 Dalton Square, Lancaster, were the numerous imprints found on articles in the house which were identical with the fingerprints of Body No 1 (Mary Rogerson). Those prints were found all over the house including in Mary Rogerson's bedroom and on articles which the maid would handle in the course of her work.

It can be seen from Table 1 (later in the book) that in the case of Mary Rogerson, numerous imprints were positively identified, notably the fingerprints of both hands, and palmar impression of the left hand. These placed the identify of Body No 1 beyond doubt.

On 13th October 1935, Detective Lieutenant Hammond, Officer in charge of the Finger Print Department of the City of Glasgow Police, visited Ruxton's house. He spent 11 days photographing fingerprints and palm-imprints, comparing them with those of the left hand of Body No 1, together with the other impressions from the hands of nine other persons with legitimate access to the house, including those of Ruxton himself. Three palm impressions and thirty-one fingerprints were positively identified as having been made by the left hand of Body No 1.

At Ruxton's subsequent trial, Lieutenant Hammond explained to the jury the principles underlying identification by means of fingerprints and palmar impressions. He demonstrated these on enlarged photographs, the agreement between those from the house and those of the left hand of Body No 1. In order to confirm that those fingerprints from the house were made by the hand of Body No 1, he would be satisfied with 8 points of similarity, showing characteristics and agreement.

In comparing the prints from various articles with the prints taken from Body No 1, he had shown more than 8 points of agreement in each case. In the comparison of the palmar impressions on the leaf of a table with the palmar impressions of the left hand of Body No 1, he had marked 20 points of agreement on the enlargement photographs.

Some of the strongest evidence against Ruxton came from his charwomen whom the police had interviewed on several occasions. In particular, Mrs Agnes Oxley and Mrs Mary Hampshire helped the police to construct a time-line of Ruxton's movements subsequent to the disappearance of Mrs Ruxton and Mary Rogerson on Saturday 14th September, 1935. The following two extracts from statements made by both women, helped to strengthen the police case against Ruxton.

Statement of Mrs Agnes Oxley - Charwoman

Mrs Oxley was a Charwoman employed by Dr Ruxton at 2 Dalton Square, Lancaster, to undertake domestic cleaning and share cooking with another Charwoman, Mrs Elizabeth Curwen. Mrs Oxley attended the doctor's house every day, commencing work at 7:10 am and finishing her work at various times. On Sunday, 15th September, 1935, she was preparing to leave her home to arrive at Ruxton's house for her usual time. However, at 6:30 am, Ruxton made an unexpected visit and spoke to her husband. He told him to 'Tell Mrs Oxley not to trouble to come down this morning. Mrs Ruxton and Mary have gone on holiday to Edinburgh. I am taking the children to stay in Morecambe with friends. Tell her to come down as usual on Monday'.

On the morning of Monday 16th September, Mrs Oxley arrived at Ruxton's house at approximately 7:00 am. After ringing the door bell several times and getting no reply, she went back home and then returned at 9:15 am to find Ruxton arriving in his car. Mrs Oxley noted in particular the appearance of Ruxton on that occasion, being used to Ruxton being very smartly presented. On this occasion he looked ill, was unshaven, without a collar and tie, and wearing an old raincoat, completely out of character. Mrs Oxley accompanied Ruxton into the house, made him some coffee and then went into the surgery to assist him to bandage his cut hand. He explained to her that he had cut his hand trying to open a tin of fruit for the children's breakfast with a tin-opener that was bent. In the process, he had lost a lot of blood.

Mrs Oxley noticed an untouched meal laid out in the lounge. All the stair carpets had been removed and the stairs scattered with straw. Rolled-up carpets, stair pads and a man's suit were lying in the waiting-room. In the back yard, she saw other carpets, clothing and towels all heavily blood stained, and signs that attempts had been made to burn them. She particularly noticed that the doors to the doctor's bedroom, the drawing room and the dining room were all locked and no keys left in the locks. She also remarked that she had never seen a bath in such a dirty state, stained with a yellow colour. She distinctly remembered that it was not in that state on the Saturday 14th September, because Mary Rogerson had cleaned it. She cleared away the untouched meal in the lounge, then left the house at 12:30 pm, her work complete.

On the morning of Thursday 19th September, Ruxton asked Mrs Oxley to make breakfast quickly because he was going to see a specialist regarding his injured hand. She was working in the kitchen around

7:20 am when Ruxton brought his car to the backdoor of the house. Mrs Oxley remembered that Ruxton made several journeys between his car and the upstairs rooms. He finally left the house at 8:00 am, arriving back about 3:30 pm. When Ruxton had gone, Mrs Oxley found that the doors to the upstairs rooms which had been previously locked were now unlocked. She also noticed a foul smell coming from these rooms.

Statement of Mrs Mary Hampshire - Patient

On Sunday 15th September 1935, at approximately 4:30 pm in the afternoon, Ruxton visited the home of one of his patients, Mrs Mary Hampshire. He informed Mrs Hampshire that he was preparing the house for decorators who would be coming on Monday 16th September. He had cut his hand and required some help in preparing for them. He told Mrs Hampshire that Mrs Ruxton had gone to Blackpool and Mary Rogerson was in Edinburgh. Mrs Hampshire went back with Ruxton to the house which she found completely empty. She noticed a meal laid untouched in the lounge. Finding that there was a lot of cleaning to be done, she asked Ruxton if her husband might be asked to help and he agreed. The carpets had been removed from the stairs and landings. She saw straw scattered around and some protruding from beneath the doors of the two bedrooms occupied by Ruxton and his wife, they were both locked. Some rolled-up carpets, stair pads and a man's suit lay in the waiting-room. Ruxton asked her to clean the bath which was a dirty yellow colour which came to within six inches of the top. In the back yard Mrs Hampshire found two carpets from the landings, together with stair carpets, one badly stained with blood, together with a blood-stained shirt and partially burned blood-stained towels.

About 4:30 pm, Ruxton left to take his children to a dentist family friend in Morecambe, the Andersons. He returned later to collect the children's night clothes. He took Mr and Mrs Hampshire into the waiting-room and told them that they could take away the stair carpets and the blue suit with blood stains if they wished to have them. They finished the cleaning and dusting and left the house at 9:30 pm. On Monday 16th September at approximately 9:00 am Ruxton called again at Mrs Hampshire's home asking that she gave him back the suit so that he could get it cleaned himself. He pointed to a tab in the pocket of the suit coat which bore his name and told Mrs Hampshire to 'cut it off and burn it' which she did. She asked Ruxton where Mrs Ruxton was, and he said that she was on holiday in Edinburgh. The suit waistcoat was so blood-stained that she could do nothing with it and burned it. She then untied the bundle of carpets and found that one of them, a stair carpet, was damp with blood. She took this carpet out into her back yard and threw between 20 and 30 buckets of water over it without being able to get it clean. The water which ran off the carpet was like blood flowing away.

The Medical Investigation

Even the substantial amount of evidence already collected by the police during their investigation was insufficient to obtain a conviction against Dr Buck Ruxton. If the medical experts at Edinburgh University were unable to establish that the remains discovered at Moffat were those of Isabella Ruxton and Mary Rogerson, the case against Ruxton would collapse. The experts combined not only well-established forensic methods in their task, but also employed innovative techniques to ascribe the remains to each of the respective bodies. Initially, they were given the designation of Body No 1 and Body No 2.

Reconstructed Bodies

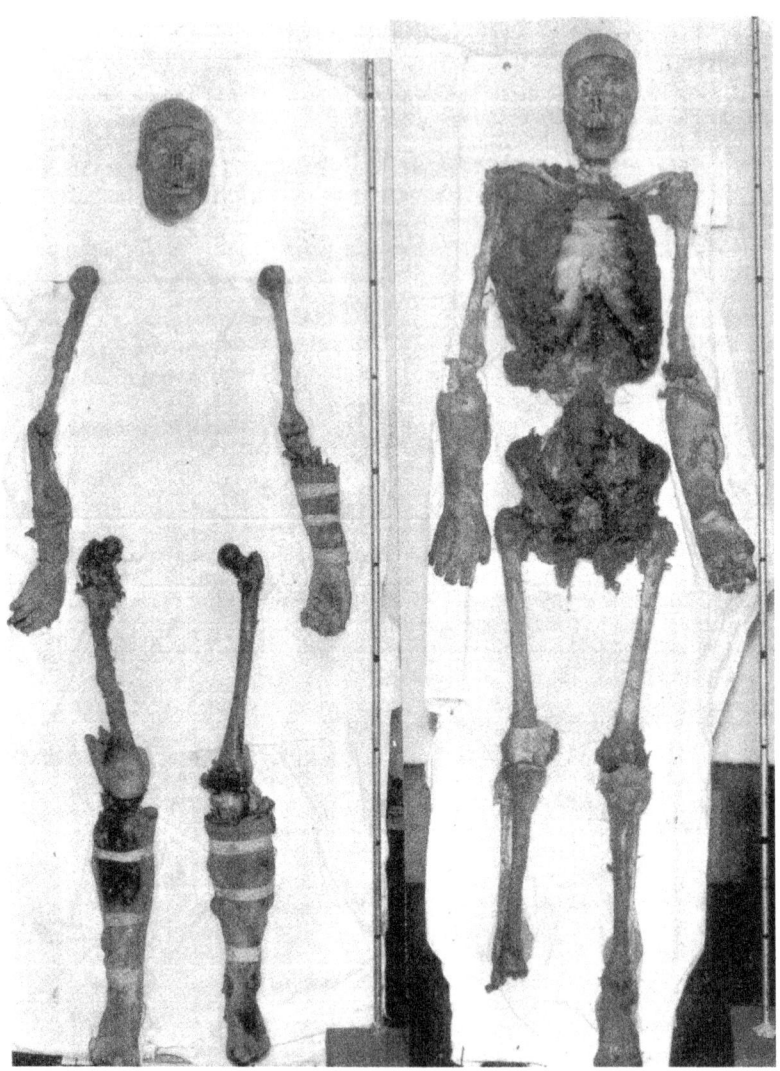

Body No 1 Body No 2
Source: Medico-Legal Aspects of the Ruxton Case, pg 61

As an integral part of the reconstruction process, it was crucial to establish the sex, age and stature of each of the two bodies.

Sex

The opinion as to the sex of Body No 1 was based on consideration of the soft parts attached to the skeleton, and of the general appearance of the skeleton itself. This was possible by examining the head and limbs only, since the trunk remained missing.

The features by which a skull is judged to be female are mainly negative. The skull retains the features of that of an adolescent person and does not display the heavier build and strong muscular attachments that develop in the male skull both at and after puberty.

The skull of Body No 1 was very lightly built and the same characteristics were displayed by all the main limb bones. They were short slender bones with ill-defined muscular markings.

All the results of the anatomical examination and measurements of the skeletal parts of Body No 1 consistently pointed to female sex. Therefore, there was no hesitation in drawing the conclusion that this body was female.

Body No 2 was also confirmed to be female because female sex organs were still present in the pelvis. Originally, it was believed that this body was that of a male, mainly because the skull and limb bones were of a heavier build than those of Body No 1. However, further detailed examination of the bones confirmed that the body was that of a female.

Body No 1

Observations of the parts available and especially the appearance of the face, despite mutilation, suggested that Body No 1 was that of a youngish woman. From a detailed examination of the epiphyseal ends of the limb-bones, of the sutures of the skull, and possibly the teeth, it was hoped to produce sufficient evidence to estimate the age within a narrow range.

Examination of the sutures (joints of the skull) revealed no sign of fusion or closure, which pointed to a strong probability that the age of the body was not over 30 years.

Taking the whole of the evidence, indications led to a probable age of between 20 and 22 years. A detailed examination of the teeth present in the jaws of Body No 1 centred on the eruption of the wisdom teeth. These do not usually appear before the 17th, but they are commonly erupted by the 21st to 24th years. It was estimated that the lower teeth indicated an age of 18 years and the upper teeth 20 years. Based on the calcification of the wisdom teeth, the approximate age of Skull No 1 was between 18 and 20 years.

Further examination of the epiphyseal ends of the limb bones of Body No 1 and their state of fusion, placed them within a range of between 18 and 25 years. All the available evidence led to the opinion that the most probable age lay between 20 and 21 years.

Body No 2

The estimate of the probable age of Body No 2 was based on observations similar to those made in respect of Body No 1. The complete union or fusion of the epiphysial end of the limb bones indicated a minimum age of 22 to 25 years.

Further examination of the skull of Body No 2 confirmed the general conclusion drawn from the examination of the limb bones but raised the minimum age to 30+ years.

The state of closure of the sutures of Skull No 2 was of particular value. Union of the bones was so advanced that there could be no doubt that the age was at least 30 years. Taken as a whole, the state of the sutures of the skull of No 2 Body justified the conclusion that the age lay between 30 and 55 years, whilst the balance of probability seemed to indicate that the ages lay more between 35 and 45 years.

Stature of the Bodies

When a body has been dismembered it may be possible to reconstruct it so that its whole length may be measured directly. Obviously, this depends to a large extent on whether all the parts of the body, including at least one of the lower limbs is available.

Body No 2 could be directly measured, but for Body No 1 the trunk was missing, so only indirect methods of measurement were possible. The formulae employed by the experts at Edinburgh were those devised by Karl Pearson, based on a mathematical study of measurements of limb bones and of statures of both male and female skeletons. The most reliable formulae were those that dealt with the measurements of four particular bones: the humerus, radius, femur and tibia.

Using Pearson's formulae, the living stature of

Mary Rogerson was estimated at between 4' 10" and 4' 11", whilst her actual known height was approximately 5' 0".

The probable living stature of Body No 2 of Isabella Ruxton lay between 4' 11" and 5' 1". The actual measurement of the reconstructed body was approximately 5' 3", while Mrs Ruxton's actual known height was 5'5".

In respect to the age and stature of Body No 1 and Body No 2, the conclusions of the medical experts corresponded closely to what was known of the missing women from Lancaster.

Mary Rogerson was 20 years of age whilst the estimated age of Body No 1 based on anatomical grounds was put at between 21 and 22 years. Dental analysis put the age at approximately 20 years and her stature was placed at approximately 5 feet in height. The estimated height from measurements of the limb-bones, was put at between 4'10" and 4' 11". Body No 2 Mrs Ruxton was 34 years of age whilst the estimated age was placed at between 35 and 45 years. Her living stature was approximately 5' 5" whilst the estimated height was placed at 5' 3".

Early in the examination, it had been observed that Head No 1 and Head Number 2 were very different in both size and shape. Known photographic portraits of the two missing Lancaster women indicated that Head No 1 could not be that of Mrs Ruxton and Head No 2 that of Mary Rogerson.

Professor James Brash did something that had never been attempted before in a criminal investigation in an attempt to achieve positive identification of the two victims. Two photographs of each of the women were used - a studio portrait of Mrs Ruxton and a photograph of Mary Rogerson. The two cleaned skulls were each photographed matching as closely as possible the positions of the heads in the photographs. The photographs were enlarged to the size of the skulls and shapes and features were traced in ink on transparent paper. Subsequent superimposition revealed that the portrait of Mrs Ruxton fitted the outline of Skull No 2 very well and similarly the picture of Mary Rogerson was found to fit over Skull No 1.

Portrait of Mrs Ruxton

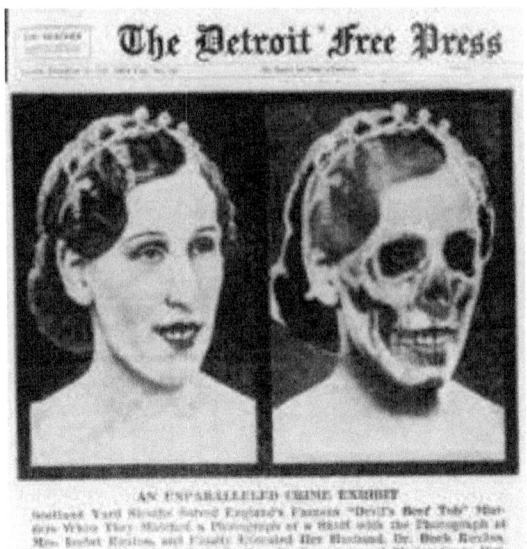

Skull of Mrs Ruxton. Skull Negative on Portrait of Mrs Ruxton
Source: Detroit Free Press

Cause and Time of Death

The final objective of the medical examinations carried out by the experts at Edinburgh University on the remains, was to establish the cause and probable time of death of each body.

In respect of Body No 1 (Mary Rogerson), in the absence of the trunk, with its organs and of the tissue of the neck, it was not possible to define the cause of death. However, the bruises on the face and arms showed that violence had been applied shortly before death. There was also evidence that the bruise of the tongue had been produced probably an hour or two before death. The swelling of the tongue might have resulted from asphyxia, by violence or from the process of decomposition.

The injuries found on Body No 1 consisted of a lacerated and incised wound of the scalp, two small fractures of the skull and bruising of the tongue and both upper arms. However, it was not possible to define the cause of death in respect of Body No 1.

In respect of Body No 2, the congested state of the brain and lungs, and the presence of petechial haemorrhages on the surface of the lungs, suggested that the probable cause of death was asphyxia. The condition of the hyoid bone suggested that the neck had been forcibly compressed, and that the cause of death was manual strangulation. The tongue was in the condition commonly found after strangulation, and the pressure marks on it corresponded to the empty sockets of the teeth removed after death.

Identification of the Maggots

Dr Alexander G Mearns of the Institute of Hygiene at the University of Glasgow undertook the investigation of the maggots that infested the remains. He concluded that the only larvae possible were those of the Musca domestica or Common Blue-bottle. Dr Mearns explained that the total life span of the largest larvae taken from the remains could not have exceeded 12 days and was probably less. It was considered very unlikely that the eggs had been laid more than a day or two after the remains had been deposited in the ravine. The stage of development of the larvae was compatible with the remains having been deposited in the ravine about 12 to 14 days before their examination on 1st October 1935.

The result of this line of investigation not only corroborated the opinions expressed on other grounds, but also fitted the hypothesis that the remains had probably been deposited in the ravine during the early hours of the morning of Monday 16th September 1935.

Final Medical Summary

The neat dismemberment of the bodies without the use of a saw, and with very little damage to the joints, clearly implied possession of some anatomical knowledge. The removal of identifying features and of parts that might have suggested the cause of death, combined with the evidence of anatomical knowledge and of some skill in the extraction of teeth, presented a picture that fully supported the hypothesis that the person concerned was able to bring more than lay knowledge to bear on the task of dismemberment.

The question of the time required for cutting up the bodies and reducing them to the state in which they were found was of significance. The police contention was that Ruxton had the opportunity and time enough to do the work unobserved in his own home before the latest hour by which he must have begun his journey to Moffat on the Sunday night, the 15th/16th September.

Professor Glaister gave the opinion that the disarticulation and mutilation of Body No 2, including the removal of the abdominal organs and of the flesh from the bones, would probably have taken about 5 hours to complete. This was assuming that the operator had proper light and sharp instruments and possessed some dexterity.

However, the time required to disarticulate and mutilate Body No 1 would be considerably less since there was much less mutilation involved, and so was more likely to have been completed in 3 hours. It was maintained by the police that the remains had been deposited during the night of 15th/16th September and that the last consignment had been removed from 2 Dalton Square, Lancaster on Thursday 19th September. It was later established that

Ruxton had been to Moffat in the past and he knew the road there very well.

Ruxton's Interview and Arrest

At approximately 9:30 pm on Saturday 12th October 1935, Buck Ruxton arrived at the Chief Constable's Office for an arranged interview regarding the missing women from Lancaster. A number of police officers were in attendance, including some from Scotland, and the interview lasted throughout the night.

When requested to account for his movements between the 14th and 19th September, Ruxton produced a document which he had entitled 'My Movements' which he handed to the investigators before making a 'voluntary' statement. During the interview Ruxton denied that he had ever been to Scotland, yet he was unable to explain why his car registration number had been logged by a young cyclist who he had knocked off his bicycle in Kendal on the 17th September.

The Lancaster Police suggested to him that this incident was circumstantial evidence of an offence that had occurred when he was driving back to Lancaster after visiting Moffat. He was unable to explain why a police search of his house had revealed extensive traces of blood stains on the stairs, railings, balustrade and various carpets. This was despite evidence that the house had been thoroughly cleaned, and that several walls around the staircase had been recently re-decorated. He was also unable to explain why traces of human flesh and body tissue had been discovered within the drains of the property, particularly in the section of drains leading directly from the bathroom.

Throughout the several hours of the interview

with Ruxton, Lancaster Police conversed with their Scottish colleagues who had previously visited Ruxton's home to remove objects such as sections of wallpaper, carpeting and silverware for detailed forensic examination.

In the early hours of Sunday 13th October 1935, news came through to Lancaster Police that the finger and palm prints on the second set of human hands discovered with the remains were found to be a complete match for impressions on items from Dalton Square which Mary Jane Rogerson had handled.

This latest news sealed Ruxton's fate and at precisely 7:20 am on Sunday 13th October 1935 he was formally charged with the murder of Mary Rogerson.

The Forensic Investigation

One of the many incriminating facts in the Ruxton Case was the presence of numerous blood stains in the house at 2 Dalton Square. Proving that these stains were made by human blood involved many separate tests. However, there were in Ruxton's home so many stains that appeared to be blood, that it was virtually impossible to test them all in situ.

Consequently, certain parts of the stairs and most of the fixtures and fittings in the bathroom were removed by Lancaster Borough Police and sent to the Department of Forensic Medicine at Glasgow University for analysis. Accompanying these were the pieces of carpet, the stair pads and the suit given by Ruxton to his patient, Mrs Mary Hampshire, that the police had recovered from her.

The question of the age of the blood stains on several of the exhibits were given particular attention. At trial, Professor Glaister, when questioned by the defence counsel, stated that it was likely that the blood of the stair carpets was not very old. However, at the time of the trial, there was no reliable method of estimating accurately the age of the blood stains, which provided the defence with an advantage, if only temporarily. The saturation of certain parts of the stair carpet was revealed by the presence of blood clots.

The finding of human protein inside several of the stair rod holders strongly suggested that blood had been present on those stairs at one time. These factors served as an indication that the amount of blood originally present on the top flight of stairs must have been very considerable.

The quantity of blood found in the bathroom was not large, but in view of the evidence that certain parts of that room, the floor, the top of the built-in seat and the bath itself, had been washed, and in view of the wide distribution of the stains, this suggested that the amount of blood originally present had been considerably greater.

The hypothesis of the prosecution was that both women met with violent deaths at Dalton Square, Mrs Ruxton first, and then Mary Rogerson because she was the only witness to the murder of her mistress.

It was further suggested that both bodies had been dismembered in the bathroom and drained of blood in the bath itself. Ruxton's injured right hand might have been responsible for the blood stains on the bannister provided that when coming downstairs he had held his hand above the level of the top rail. It is hardly to be expected that a doctor with such injury would have refrained from taking some steps to control the flow of blood. In any case, such injury could not account for the condition of the carpets or the bath. No stains on the carpets had been seen by the domestic workers employed at Dalton Square before the disappearance of Mrs Ruxton and Mary Rogerson. The conclusions reached were that the hypothesis of the prosecution was quite consistent with all the evidence concerning the blood stains. The blood stains on the top staircase were compatible with considerable haemorrhage from serious bodily injury to one or both of the women.

Following his appearance at Lancaster Magistrates Court, Ruxton was remanded in custody. These were weekly remands from that date until 5th November when he was further charged with the murder of his common-law wife, Isabella.

By this date, the medical team at Edinburgh University had positively identified the remains of Body No 2 as that of Isabella Ruxton.

Following this second charge, Ruxton was further remanded from week to week on the application of the Director of Public Prosecutions. On 26th November, Ruxton's Committal Hearing was held at Lancaster Magistrates Court when all the evidence, both from the police investigation and the medical enquiry was presented.

This hearing lasted from the 26th of November until 13th December, when Ruxton was committed for trial at the Manchester Assizes on both charges. Evidence concerning the death of Mary Rogerson was admitted at the trial, although Ruxton was not being tried on the count charging him with her murder. It was held that such evidence tended to prove the killing of Mrs Ruxton, and was particularly relevant to the question of identification of the remains.

The strength of the case for the Prosecution was largely dependent upon the identification of the bodies. In law it was not necessary that there should be a body in order that a charge of murder may be presented against some person or persons. However, Article 768 of Section 9 of Halsbury's Laws of England states: 'Where one body or part of a body has been found, which is proved to be that of the person alleged to have been killed, the accused person should not be convicted either of murder or manslaughter, unless there is evidence either of the killing or of the death of the person alleged to have been killed. In the absence of such evidence there is no onus upon the accused to account for the disappearance or non-production of the person alleged to be killed'.

It follows from this ruling that Ruxton would not be convicted unless it could be proved 'beyond reasonable doubt' that the bodies found at Moffat were indeed those of Mrs Ruxton and Mary Rogerson. When the news of the disappearance of Isabella Ruxton and Mary Rogerson was communicated to Edinburgh together with their descriptions, it was possible to build convincing comparisons with Body No 1 and Body No 2 (Tables 1 and 2 on the following pages).

TABLE 1 Mary Jane Rogerson Body No 1 - Female Source: Medico-Legal Aspects of the Ruxton Case, Glaister and Brash (1937) page 108

Age	Twenty years (8th October, 1935).	Certainly between 18 and 25. Probably between 20 and 21.
Stature	About 5 ft.	4 ft. 10 in. to 4 ft. 11½ in. (without shoes).
Hair	Light brown.	Hair from scalp and body light brown.
Eyes	Blue. " Glide " in one.	Removed.
Complexion	Light. Freckles on nose and cheeks.	Ears, nose, lips, and most of skin of face removed; complexion of remainder of skin consistent.
Teeth	Old extraction of six teeth, four of them named.	Old extraction or loss of eight teeth, including the four named (see Chapter VII).
Neck	Short neck.	Very small larynx very highly situated.
Tonsils	Subject to tonsillitis.	Microscopic evidence consistent with recurrent tonsillitis.
Vaccination Marks	Four on left upper arm.	Four on left upper arm.
Finger-nails	Maidservant.	Trimmed but not regularly manicured; scratches indicating some form of manual work.
Scars	1. Abdominal scar—appendix operation.	1. Trunk missing.
	2. Operation for septic thumb which had left a mark.	2. First segment of right thumb denuded of tissue; no scar on left thumb.
Identifying Peculiarity	Birth marks (red patches) on right forearm near elbow.	Skin and soft tissues removed from upper third of forearm, and lower two-thirds of front only.
Size and Shape of Feet	Left shoe as evidence.	Cast of left foot fitted shoe (see Chapter IX).
Form of Head and Face	Two photographs in different positions.	Outlines of photographs of skull in same positions fitted (see Chapter X).
Finger-prints	Numerous imprints from house at 2 Dalton Square (see Chapter VIII).	Positively identified as the finger-prints of both hands and palmar impressions of left hand.
Breasts	Age 20, unmarried.	Single breast, appearance and structure consistent.

TABLE 2
Source: Medico-Legal Aspects of the Ruxton Case – Glaister and Brash (1937), page 111

	Isabella Ruxton	Body No. 2—Female
Age	34 years 7 months (3rd October, 1935).	Certainly between 30 and 55. Probably between 35 and 45.
Stature	5 ft. 5 in. to 5 ft. 6 in.	5 ft. 3½ in. (without shoes).
Hair	Soft texture, mid-brown with patch of grey slightly to right of top of head.	Scalp completely removed; a few adherent hairs light to medium brown. Eyelashes dark brown. Available body hair mid-brown.
Eyes	Deep-set; grey-blue.	Removed.
Complexion	Fair.	Ears, nose, lips, and skin of face removed.
Teeth	Denture replacing three named teeth in gap which would show during life; old extraction of one other named tooth.	Old extraction or loss of fifteen teeth, including the four named (see Chapter VII).
Fingers and Nails	Long fingers. Recognisable nails — bevelled, brittle, growing tight at corners, rounded at ends, regularly manicured.	Terminal segments of all fingers removed.
Legs and Ankles	Thick ankles. Legs of same thickness from knees to ankles.	Soft tissues removed from legs.
Left Foot	Inflamed bunion of left big toe.	Hallux valgus of left foot; tissues removed over metatarso-phalangeal joint down to bone and joint opened. X-rays showed exostosis of head of metatarsal.
Size and Shape of Feet	Left shoe as evidence.	Cast of left foot fitted shoe (see Chapter IX).
Nose	Bridge uneven.	Removed, but bone and cartilage arched (see Chapter X).
Form of Head and Face	High forehead, high cheekbones, rather long jaw. Two photographs in different positions.	Corresponding features. Outlines of photographs of skull in same positions fitted (see Chapter X).
Breasts	Pendulous breasts: three children.	Appearance and structure of pair of breasts consistent.
Uterus	Three children.	Separate uterus. Could not be assigned but structure

Chapter Three: The Trial

Manchester Crown Court (Author Photograph)

R V RUXTON
MANCHESTER ASSIZE COURT.
BEFORE MR JUSTICE SINGLETON

CHARGED WITH THE MURDER OF ISABELLA RUXTON.

PLEADED: NOT GUILTY.

PROSECUTING COUNSEL:
DEFENCE COUNSEL:
Mr Joseph Jackson KC.
Mr Norman Birkett KC.
Mr David Maxwell Fyfe KC.
Mr Philip Kershaw, KC.
Mr Hartley Shawcross.

On Monday 2nd March 1936, the trial of Dr Buck Ruxton opened at Manchester Assizes and lasted a total of eleven days.

The trial began before Mr Justice Singleton and an all-male jury. Ruxton was charged with the murder of Isabella Ruxton his common-law wife, and a second charge of murdering Mary Jane Rogerson was added to the indictment, but he stood trial on the first charge only, to which he pleaded Not Guilty.

From the outset of the trial, the prosecution maintained that there was a witness to the murder of Mrs Ruxton, Mary Rogerson, and this is why she too met her death at the hands of Ruxton.

According to the prosecution, Ruxton who was inflamed by jealousy and paranoia, had murdered the two women in the family home at 2 Dalton Square, Lancaster on Sunday 15th September 1935. He had then disposed of the dismembered remains in the Gardenholme Linn stream near Moffat in Dumfriesshire, Scotland.

Mr Joseph Jackson KC stated: 'It does not need much imagination to suggest what probably happened in that house. It is very probable that Mary Jane Rogerson was a witness to the killing of Mrs Ruxton, and that is the reason that she too met her death. You will hear that Mrs Ruxton had received before her death, violent blows in the face then she was strangled.

The suggestion of the prosecution is that her death and that of Mary, took place outside the bedrooms on the landing at the top of the staircase. The reason for this is that from that point down the staircase right into the bathroom, there are traces of enormous quantities of blood. It is further suggested that when Mrs Ruxton went up to bed, a violent quarrel took place and Ruxton strangled his wife, and since Mary caught him in the act she too was killed. Mary's skull was fractured and she had several blows on the top of her head. She was then killed by some other means, probably a knife'.

Ruxton's defence counsel, Norman Birkett KC based the defence case on the contention that the bodies had been misidentified and that the two bodies recovered from the ravine were not those of Isabella Ruxton and Mary Jane Rogerson. He claimed that they belonged to two other unknown individuals and maintained that the prosecution evidence presented to the jury was flawed.

Birkett and his assistant counsel, Philip Kershaw KC, contended that the bloodstains found upon the suit and carpets that Ruxton had given to his patient Mrs Hampshire, had been innocently accrued over the years Ruxton had operated his medical practice in Lancaster. It was patently clear that the case for the prosecution had involved the most detailed preparation. There were over two hundred exhibits, together with eighteen complete sets of photographs of the various parts of the recovered bodies comprising 130 photographs to each set, and each member of the jury was given a set. There was also a long stream of witnesses, professors, pathologists, policemen, charwomen and dustmen each giving evidence.

On the 9th day of the trial, the sole witness for the defence, Dr Buck Ruxton himself, was called to the witness box. Birkett began his examination-in-chief by asking Ruxton some general questions about the years from 1930 to 1935. Birkett opened by asking Ruxton, 'What do you yourself say about your relationship with Mrs Ruxton during those years?'

Ruxton replied 'We could not live with each other, and we could not live without each other'.

Asked if there had been any quarrels between him and his wife, Ruxton replied that there had been, but that they lasted a very short time.

When the evidence of a police witness, Inspector Thompson of the Lancaster Police Force, was put to him that he had said his wife was unfaithful and he would kill her, Ruxton replied that he did not exactly say the word 'kill', although he did admit that he had 'unfortunately' accused his wife of being unfaithful.

Concentrating on the night of Saturday 14th September, Birkett asked Ruxton what happened when Mrs Ruxton came home from her visit to Blackpool earlier that the evening. He stated that Isabella came into the house and asked him for the key to the garage to put the car away. After she had done this, she came back inside and went up to her own bedroom.

Birkett then addressed Ruxton. 'It is suggested by the prosecution that on the morning of Sunday 15th September after your wife had come back home you killed her.'

In reply, Ruxton claimed that 'It is a deliberate fantastic story'.

Birkett continued by saying 'It is also suggested that on that Sunday morning you also killed Mary Rogerson,' to which Ruxton replied 'It is absolute bunkum with a capital B. Why should I kill my poor Mary?'

What happened on the Sunday according to Ruxton was that at about 6:30 am Mrs Ruxton came into his room and suggested they went out for the day, as they had done often before on the spur of the moment. When he got up, he went to get the car and on return found his wife and Mary in the living room. He went up to his bedroom and waited, and while he was in the bathroom, Isabella came in to make up and asked if he minded if she went to Edinburgh instead. Ruxton remarked: 'I got a little bit annoyed at Isabella for making me get up early and then changing her mind at the last minute'.

Ruxton then told her she could go but not in the car. As she was leaving, Mrs Ruxton said that Mary was going with her. He saw them leave the house together between 9:15 and 9:30 am. He could not say whether they had taken anything with them by way of clothing.

It was while he was looking for something for the children's breakfast that he found a tin of peaches. He tried to open the tin with a tin opener, but the blade was bent. He injured his right hand trying to knock the blade straight and the wound bled profusely as he went up the stairs to the bathroom.

Ruxton then offered various explanations for the blood stains in the house.

As for the bedroom doors, it was always his custom to keep them locked. He was also in the habit of buying petrol in cans because he used it to burn rubbish and waste in the rear yard. The extra supply of petrol he bought for the car on the Sunday morning was because his wife had used the car on the Saturday for her visit to Blackpool.

When further questioned by Birkett on the suit of clothes he gave to Mrs Hampshire, he denied that he had ever told her to burn them. As for the foul smell in the house, he attributed this to the charwoman stripping the walls and washing off the glue used to affix the wallpaper.

In concluding his examination-in-chief, Birkett asked Ruxton: 'So far as Mrs Ruxton is concerned, did you do any violence of any kind to her on the morning of Sunday 15th September 1935?'

Ruxton replied, 'Never, never, Sir' and Birkett continued.

'If she was strangled, had you any part or lot in it?'

Ruxton replied, 'Sir, I have never done it'.

'With regard to Mary Rogerson, so far as she is concerned, did you do any violence to her?' Birkett asked.

Ruxton replied, 'Never, let alone do it. I never thought of it. She has always been a dear child to my heart'.

Birkett continued, 'If Mary Rogerson is dead, had you any part in bringing about her death?'

Ruxton replied, 'Certainly not, a most ridiculous thing to suggest'.

Concluding his examination-in-chief, Norman Birkett asked Ruxton, 'Apart from what you have told us about their departure on the morning of Sunday 15th September, 1935, do you know anything else about their disappearance?'

Ruxton replied, 'No , I don't'.

On the tenth day of the trial, Mr Joseph Jackson KC, leading for the prosecution, rose to begin his cross-examination of Ruxton.

Jackson: I understand Mary was very dear to your heart?

Ruxton: Yes.

Jackson: You say she was a very loyal girl?

Ruxton: Yes, I would stake my reputation on that.

Jackson: One that would never allow any harm to come to her mistress?

Ruxton: She was not primarily meant for Isabella, she was loyal to everybody.

Jackson: She was a girl who would have stood by her mistress and defended her if attacked?

Ruxton: Yes, I am quite sure.

Jackson: Why is she not standing by you today if she is still alive?
Ruxton: That is not a question I can answer.
Jackson: Do you think your wife was unfaithful to you?
Ruxton: Yes, it has been going on since 1932.
Jackson: You have for a considerable time thought your wife unfaithful?
Ruxton: She has done some silly things that would not have been done by sensible women.
Jackson: Where do you say Mrs Ruxton is today if she is not dead?
Ruxton: Isabella has done the trick often of going to Holland without a passport. If one can do that, there is no knowing where she may be.
Jackson: If I understand your story, you were in the bathroom when she finally left the house, and she tapped on the door and said, Well, we are off, dear.
Ruxton: Yes, quite friendly.
Jackson: Have you ever been able to find a single person who ever saw your wife and Mary Rogerson leave your house on that morning?
Ruxton: I myself and my solicitor have made inquiries.

After a break in the proceedings, Mr Jackson resumed his cross-examination of Ruxton by asking him about Miss Winifred Roberts who called at his house about 9:00 am on the morning of Sunday September 15th.
Jackson: Miss Roberts delivered some newspapers and rang the doorbell three times and you opened the door a little way.
Ruxton: I don't recall that.
Jackson: She says you told her that Mary the maid is away in Scotland with your wife.
Ruxton: I don't recollect having told anything to

Miss Roberts. I don't think I saw her at all.
Jackson: She says you were agitated. What had you to be agitated about at nine o'clock in the morning?
Ruxton: Nine o'clock in the morning, it could not be because Isabella left after nine o'clock.
Jackson: She says you were very agitated. It could not be your wife leaving you that agitated you?
Ruxton: I am telling you that I have never seen Miss Roberts.
Jackson: May I suggest the reason why you took so long to answer the bell is that you were busy cutting up the bodies of your wife and Mary Rogerson.
Ruxton: May I respectfully suggest that three children were in the house with me at that time.

When Mr Jackson began to question Ruxton about the suit he had given to his patient, Mrs Hampshire, Ruxton replied that the blood on the clothes had accumulated over several years as the result of his work. However, Jackson pushed Ruxton on the point:

Jackson: But surely that suit was sent to the cleaners in August and returned on the 17th August perfectly clean?
Ruxton: Isabella does all the cleaning. I know nothing about it. I don't remember it.

At this point, Judge Singleton asked Ruxton; 'If you have a suit which goes away to be cleaned, don't you notice the difference when it comes back?'

Ruxton's reply was 'Yes, but I don't recollect this particular suit'.

Jackson said, 'If it was cleaned as I say, the whole of this blood had accumulated since August 17th'.

Mr Jackson then pointed to a portion of a sheet among the exhibits and asked Ruxton: 'If that is the sheet from your wife's bed, can you explain how it got round those bodies at Moffat?' The only answer Ruxton was able to give to this 'deadly' question was; 'How could it be, Sir?'

Jackson: Did you at any time purport to give away or deal with any clothes of Mary Rogerson?

Ruxton: Never.

Jackson: Did you at any time do any act of violence to Mrs Ruxton or Mary?

Ruxton: No, God is my judge.

Jackson: Or did you make any journeys to dispose of the remains?

Ruxton: No.

The rest of the tenth day of the trial was occupied with the closing speeches of counsel to the jury.

Prosecution: Closing Speech to the Jury – Mr Joseph Jackson KC

'Were these bodies found in the ravine those of Isabella Ruxton and Mary Rogerson? Once you are satisfied with that, I suggest you can have little doubt as to how they met their deaths. To be precise, Dr Ruxton, after having killed his wife by strangling her and when the maid came to the door, hearing a noise, the one witness to the crime, she too lost her life. She lost it simply because of the devotion and protection she had for her mistress.'

Outlining the inconsistencies in the accounts Ruxton had given to numerous individuals as to the whereabouts of his wife and maid, Jackson reminded the jury of the eyewitness testimony delivered by numerous individuals. He then turned to Ruxton's exhaustive efforts to destroy evidence, and to pacify Mary Rogerson's parents as to their daughter's whereabouts in the weeks between the murders and his final arrest. As regards the actual motive for the murders, Jackson concluded by suggesting that they lay in Ruxton's obsessive jealousy and violent temperament.

Defence: Closing Speech to the Jury – Mr Norman Birkett KC

In his closing speech delivered on Friday 13th March 1936, Birkett began:

'It is the duty of the Crown to prove beyond all reasonable doubt, the guilt of the person who stands at the bar as Dr Ruxton stands today. Suspicion is not enough, doubt is not enough, the accusing finger is not enough, the imaginative reconstructions of my learned friend are not enough. Even if the bodies found in the ravine were those of Mrs Ruxton and Mary Rogerson, it did not prove the Crown's case, particularly if Dr Ruxton's statement that they had left the house was true. Though their bodies were found in the ravine, though of a certainty these were the bodies, it has not been proved in the case against the defendant.

The Crown must prove the fact of Murder. Some other hand might have caused their death. The case for the Crown was that on the morning of Sunday 15th September 1935, the defendant's house was one of murder. Yet into that house came Mrs Oxley, Mrs Hampshire and two other women day after day seeing the stairs, the wallpaper, the carpets, the yard, the petrol and the fire, and none of them thought at the time that there was a single suspicious circumstance. There are many features of this case which are mysterious, dark and seemingly unfathomable.'

Birkett emphasised that the idea that the

motive for Mrs Ruxton's death (Ruxton's suspicions of his wife's infidelity) were merely conjecture. While some of the testimony delivered had alluded to the possibility that the bodies may have been those of Ruxton's wife and maid, these conclusions had been drawn from circumstantial evidence which did not prove that Ruxton had killed them. Closing his defence address, Birkett emphasised that in any British murder trial, the burden of proof was not on the defence, but the Crown.

The Judge's Summing-Up to the Jury: Mr Justice Singleton

The judge began by telling the jury that in order to prove the case for the prosecution, it must be proved that Mrs Ruxton had been murdered, and that the prisoner committed it.

Unless the Crown proved these two facts the case would fall. The prosecution sought to prove that Mrs Ruxton was murdered, by evidence that she had not been seen since Saturday 14th September, 1935, by evidence that her body or parts of it were discovered at Gardenholme Linn, and by evidence of blood-stains and marks found in the home at 2 Dalton Square, Lancaster.

The prosecution further sought to prove that the prisoner committed the murder by evidence that he was the only adult person in the house on the night or day of the disappearance, by evidence of the different accounts he had given, and by evidence of blood stains on his clothing and items in the house.

Allied to both questions were the body of Mary Rogerson and her clothing. The charge on which the prisoner was tried related to Mrs Ruxton but both she and Mary Rogerson were said to have been in the house on the night of 14th September, 1935. The prisoner was said to have told several persons that they were away together.

If Mary Rogerson's remains were firmly identified and if some portions of her body were found in the same bundle as those of Mrs Ruxton, that would help in determining the identity of Mrs Ruxton's body.

Dealing with the evidence of the witnesses who called at Dalton Square on the Sunday morning, 15th September, the judge asked the jury if it was not peculiar that if the prisoner had cut his hand with a knife or tin-opener, that he should be spending Sunday morning pulling up stair carpets. Similarly, if a doctor had cut his hand, it would be thought that he would have been very careful to have it well-bandaged.

The judge then drew the jury's attention to the state of the house on the afternoon of Sunday 15th September. He asked the jury if they could think from what they had seen in the case, that the cut hand would have accounted for the blood on the carpets, the shirt and the towels? Even if it could, then what about the bath? What inference could be drawn from the evidence of that bath which had normally been clean but was then a very dirty yellow to within six inches from the top. Down the front of the bath there were blood stains as well.

What inference could they draw when dealing with the evidence of one of the charwomen who said that Dr Ruxton had asked her to strip the paper from the stair walls, but not to bother with the top landing, which he would do in his spare time? Yet, he had an injury to his right hand.

Coming to the question of the bodies, the

judge said that the thing to be borne in mind was that there were two women missing from 2 Dalton Square at the time when the remains were found in Scotland. The bodies had been examined and the evidence undisputed. They were the bodies of two females. One was about 4ft 11ins or 4ft 11½ins, not much removed from the known height of Mary Rogerson. The other was about 5ft 4ins or 5ft 5ins, not much removed from the known height of Mrs Ruxton.

As to the age; one of the bodies was said to be between 18 and 25, the other between 35 and 45, Mary Rogerson's age was 20 and Mrs Ruxton's age was just over 34, meaning the figures were not far wrong.

The judge considered that whoever it was that dealt with those bodies had done it in a most extraordinary way. The bodies had not only been disarticulated completely, but also almost every sign which would enable the one or other to be recognised had been removed.

The jury's attention was then drawn to the time it would take to complete the disarticulation. Assuming that Mrs Ruxton had left Blackpool at 11:30 pm on the Saturday night, she would have arrived back in Lancaster at around 12:30 am on the Sunday morning. Was it possible for the prisoner to do that which it was said he had done by 9:30 am or 10 am on the Sunday morning?

Assuming that it was Mrs Ruxton who had been killed first, then between 12:30 am and 9:30 am on the Sunday morning, there was an available period of 9 hours.

The medical witnesses had stated that they had considered how long it would have taken to reduce Body No 2 into the state in which it was found. The consensus was a minimum of 5 hours.

Evidence was also given that in cases of asphyxia (strangulation) the blood remains fluid longer by up to possibly 12 hours. That meant there was time for the disarticulation of the bodies to take place late on Saturday night and Sunday morning. Everything, so far as one could gather, corresponded with the two missing women from Lancaster, and there was no evidence produced to the contrary.

Counsel for the defence had questioned Mr Jackson's assertion that if they were satisfied that those remains in the ravine at Moffat had been proved to be the remains of Mrs Ruxton and Miss Rogerson, their task was complete.

The judge then asked the jury to consider that if the two women went away on the Sunday morning as the prisoner had said, why should he be accused of the murder simply because they were dead? If the two women did go away, could they conceive who else might have murdered them? They could not have been cut up very well in that ravine, could they? They had been treated, according to the evidence, by a person of some anatomical skill - the disarticulations would appear to indicate that.

If these two women had been murdered by someone else, could they see the reason for the removal of signs of death or possible means of identification?

One by one, Judge Singleton called for the exhibits to be brought into court. Blood-stained stair-pads, the front panel of the bath, the child's rompers and the blouse which had wrapped one of the heads of the victims. All of these exhibits were shown once more to the jury.

The judge reminded the jury that the prisoner must be given the benefit of any reasonable doubt that there might be in the case. He also emphasised every point which could possibly be interpreted as being in the prisoner's favour. He particularly directed the jury's attention to the discrepancies between the statements of the prisoner and those of the witnesses, to the condition of the stair-pads and suit, to the attempts made by the prisoner to persuade witnesses to make statements which were untrue. He particularly emphasised the absence of any communication from the missing women in the long interval which had elapsed since their disappearance, and to the fact that no medical witnesses had been called to refute the evidence of those appearing for the Crown.

In his reference to the medical witnesses, he spoke in the highest terms of the 'distinguished body of evidence' which had been put before them. He had never 'seen expert witnesses more careful and more eager not to strain a point against an accused person'.

The judge continued by remarking that he found it difficult to imagine greater care and greater skill being used than was used by the distinguished professors of Edinburgh and Glasgow Universities in putting together the remains, in their examinations and arriving at their conclusion. He then referred to the 'coincidences' if the jury considered that is what they were - of a copy of the limited 'slip' edition of *The Sunday Graphic* which had been delivered to 2 Dalton Square, Ruxton's home, being found with the bodies, and the identical fault which existed in the portion of sheet found with the remains, and the single sheet left on Mrs Ruxton's bed. Mr Justice Singleton concluded his summing-up to the jury by saying that if there was any doubt in the case, the prisoner must have the benefit of that doubt, but if there was none, their verdict must be equally clear, and justice must be carried out.

Having retired to consider their verdict, the jury returned after deliberating for just one hour. They returned a verdict of GUILTY against Ruxton. Consequently, Mr Justice Singleton sentenced Ruxton to death. The judge was then informed by defence counsel Norman Birkett KC that the defendant intended to appeal the verdict.

Manchester Strangeways Prison
(Common Attribution Photograph)

The Appeal and Execution

Norman Birkett KC, Ruxton's counsel, lodged an appeal on the ground that the judge had misdirected the jury. He claimed the judge had omitted to direct them sufficiently as to the evidence of witnesses regarding the clean condition of Ruxton's car after the suggested journey to Moffat, and also about the state of the weather at Moffat at the material time.

The appeal was heard in the Court of Criminal Appeal in London on Monday 27th April 1936, before the Lord Chief Justice, Lord Hewart, Mr Justice de Parq and Mr Justice Goddard.

Birkett's argument centred around the fact that the doctor's car was clean on Monday 16th September although it had been raining at Moffat. His argument was that it was impossible that the car could have been driven more than 200 miles across wet moorland roads in Scotland. If the jury was satisfied that the car did not travel to Moffat on the night of Sunday, 15th September, then the whole case for the Crown would fall.

Birkett remarked: 'There was not a spot of blood on the car. Isn't that a most remarkable thing? Is it not of outstanding importance to the case that the car which was to connect the murder at Dalton Square with the ravine, had no spot of blood on it, and that having travelled all those miles on such a night, there was no mud and no staining?'

Without calling on Counsel for the Crown, the Appeal Court dismissed the appeal after consulting for only a few minutes. The Lord Chief Justice, Lord Hewart declared: 'The evidence that the dismembered bodies were those of Mrs Ruxton and Mary Rogerson were really overwhelming. There is nothing in the Summing-Up that can be said to faintly resemble misdirection. The application is of a kind which the Court cannot grant'. The appeal was therefore dismissed.

A petition from Lancaster residents urged clemency for Ruxton, and it collected over 10,000 signatures. Despite this, Buck Ruxton was hanged at Strangeways Prison, Manchester on the morning of Tuesday 12th May 1936.

Prior to the hanging, Ruxton was housed in the condemned cell situated at the end of 'B' wing in the central area of the prison and was guarded around the clock. On the appointed day, Ruxton was hanged by Thomas Pierrepoint, assisted by Robert Wilson.

According to Form LPC4, Ruxton was 5' 7½" tall and weighed 137 lbs, so he was given a drop of 7' 11" which was a textbook hanging.

The police had to deal with a very large crowd of people who had gathered outside the prison to see the execution notices posted on the main gates.

On the following Sunday 17th May 1936, *The News of the World* published a signed confession by Ruxton in his own handwriting admitting to the killing of his wife and maim. It read: 'I killed Mrs Ruxton in a fit of temper because I thought she had been with a man. I was mad at the time. Mary Rogerson was present at the time. I had to kill her'.

It does appear that while Ruxton was in custody in Manchester, he was visited by a representative of *The News of the World*. Ruxton handed the representative a sealed envelope telling him to take great care of it. He told him: 'They have charged me with murder, and I in turn charge you to place the envelope in safety and security. On no account must it be opened until my death, if I am to die. If I am acquitted, and I think I must be, you will hand it back to me'.

Ruxton saw the representative again during the trial and told him that in the event of his death, the envelope should be handed unopened to the editor. This request was duly carried out on the same day that Ruxton was executed. This sealed confession was unique in that as far as it is known, never before had such a document been entrusted to a reporter by someone facing execution.

It is believed that Ruxton's estate received £3,000 for the confession, his total estate being valued at £4,765. As for Ruxton's three children, Elizabeth, Diane and William, they were said to have been brought up in an orphanage in Cheshire. This ends one of the most gruesome yet fascinating crimes of the 20th century, particularly remembered for the innovative forensic techniques used to identify the victims and the location of their murder.

> Lancaster.
> 14.10.35.
>
> I killed Mrs Ruxton in a fit of temper because I thought she had been with a man. I was mad at the time. Mary Rogerson was present at the time. I had to kill her.
>
> B Ruxton

Buck Ruxton's Confession from The News of the World, Sunday 17th May 1936

Chapter Four: An Overview of the Case

'If doctors do take the law into their own hands, the facts are only likely to emerge by chance, through the whisperings of suspicion or rarely through carelessness in the disposal of the dead body.'

So wrote Professor Keith Simpson, the forensic pathologist in his autobiography, *Forty Years of Murder*, published in 1983. One of the blunders often made by those who attempt to dispose of the bodies of murdered victims is to leave identifiable articles with the remains. In this respect, the Ruxton Case is a classic example; the child's rompers, the newspapers, the blouse and the torn bed sheet all played a major role in tracing the remains back to 2 Dalton Square.

One of the first challenges facing a murderer is what to do about the victim's body. Disposal of a body requires method and resourcefulness, the main purpose being to conceal or at least, to delay the discovery of the crime. To overcome the difficulty of moving and transporting a body, murderers readily incline towards dismemberment. Reducing the body to small portions allows remains to be parcelled up for easier disposal. Once the body has been reduced to a number of basic components, the remaining parts may be individually wrapped for final disposal.

Unless carefully thought out in advance, this usually involves the perpetrator grabbing whatever clothing, bedsheets or blankets that come to hand to make a parcel or bundle. Newspapers have proved to be a popular material for this purpose, even though they may well offer valuable clues to the place and date of the crime. This is precisely what happened in the Ruxton case, where Ruxton wrapped parts of his victims in a special edition of a Sunday newspaper which provided police with vital co-ordinates to his crimes.

The date of *The Sunday Graphic and Sunday News* found with the remains coincided with the date on which the two women had disappeared from Lancaster. The circulation of this particular edition was restricted to the Morecambe and Lancaster areas of Lancashire. Evidence showed that a copy of this paper had been delivered to 2 Dalton Square, Lancaster on the morning of Sunday 15th September 1935.

The initial police investigation into the case began in Dumfries, Scotland, following the discovery of the human remains at Gardenholme Linn near Moffat on Sunday 29th September 1935. The enquiry centred on looking at recent reports of missing persons in the immediate area. It was considered very unlikely that two persons associated in some way, could disappear without at least one other person being aware of the fact. To this end, the police concentrated their attention to reports of dual disappearances.

At the beginning of October 1935, both Mrs Ruxton and Mary Rogerson had been reported missing to the Lancaster Police, and by the 11th October, it had been confirmed by anatomical examination that the remains found at Moffat represented two female bodies. Following press reports of the discovery of the remains, many of the inhabitants of Lancaster, including Ruxton's own charladies and some of his patients, harboured suspicions that there may very well have been a connection between these newspaper reports and the subsequent disappearances of Isabella Ruxton and Mary Rogerson.

Many of the mutilations found on the remains

did assist the pathologists in their search for evidence. The manner of dismemberment without the use of a saw, clearly demonstrated that the person or persons responsible was skilled in the use surgical knives and possessed anatomical and medical knowledge. Ruxton, in removing all those parts of the bodies that may have been of use in identification, he had undoubtedly tried to destroy evidence of sex. However, with that carelessness which so often leads to the undoing of criminals, he had left among the masses of flesh, fat and skin, three female breasts and parts of sex organs which proved that there were at least two female victims.

    Witnesses abounded in the Ruxton case, numerous people visited Dalton Square on the Sunday morning, the 15th September during which time Ruxton was busy dismembering the bodies. Several of the charladies recalled foul odours in the house and unexplained blood stains on the stairs and in the bathroom. Ruxton hired a car to dispose of the bodies and then collided with a cyclist outside Kendal on his way back from Moffat.

    Ever since the disappearance on the 14th September of Mrs Ruxton and Mary Jane Rogerson, Ruxton had been careering round Lancaster like a man possessed. He had fabricated all manner of stories to explain the women's disappearance, but none were convincing. He had hounded the Lancaster Police with demands that they search his house to quash vicious rumours he was responsible for the killing of his wife and maid.

    From information received from various sources, suspicion quickly fell on Ruxton. His conduct at various meetings with the police since the disappearance of his wife and maid, together with their own knowledge of his jealous and violent disposition, confirmed the police's suspicions.

It is quite possible that initially, the Lancaster Police viewed Ruxton as an unstable person. However, when the police finally took up Ruxton's offer to search his home, they found other incriminating evidence. Despite evidence of a lengthy and exhaustive clean-up, the police found numerous blood stains, and the drains revealed traces of human tissue.

During this search of Ruxton's house, the police retrieved personal diaries going back to the period from 1919 to 1934, but the diary for 1935 was (not unexpectedly) missing. One entry showed that on 4th February 1931, they had gone together by car to Edinburgh via Moffat. At the police interview before his arrest, Ruxton had asserted that he had never visited Scotland.

There are three cardinal requisites for murder; Why? How? and When? which can be translated into motive, method and opportunity.

The How? of murder is the method or means of carrying out the killing. The When? is choosing the right moment by creating the opportunity to carry out the murder. This can involve pre-meditation or planning or be the result of a sudden impulse. Therefore, some murders can be completely 'opportunistic'. Other murders committed in the 'heat of the moment' or provocation, may have little regard to 'opportunities' - they just happen.

In the Ruxton case there is evidence for pre-meditation in that on the Sunday morning 15th September, Ruxton's charlady Mrs Agnes Oxley was asked not to report for work on that day. This has been interpreted as ensuring that Ruxton would not be disturbed in his work of dismembering the bodies of Mrs Ruxton and Mary Rogerson.

One of the most important common denominators of murder is that the offender and the victim are known to each other. The legal test for murder is 'intention' defined in legal terms as the mens rea or 'guilty mind'. This is further defined as 'malice aforethought'.

Most murders are committed by people who would be regarded as 'normal and rational'. These are the sort of people who one would expect to make some risk assessment and plan when forming the intention to kill someone. Yet, how often do they? The murderer's aim is to fulfil the intention whilst at the same time to minimise the chance of getting caught.

However, at the crucial point when planning is called for, rational thinking is rapidly diminished, and events go into 'free-fall'. One particular group which would be expected to have some advantage over others are members of the medical profession. They have the knowledge and skills, and also have the means at their disposal, in theory at least. However, in practice, they turn out to be no better than others when it comes to committing murder. This is particularly so when they leave evidence of their 'professional' expertise as was the case with Ruxton.

As regards Ruxton's 'motive' in the killing of his common-law wife, it has been suggested that this was the result of his jealous and violent disposition. Ruxton's relationship with Isabella was both stormy and passionate; he was excessively jealous and suspicious. They quarrelled incessantly because he firmly believed that she was having relationships with other men. It was observed by one commentator of the case that the mere sight of her dancing or even speaking to another man threw Ruxton into incontrollable fury.

The episode shortly before her disappearance when Mrs Ruxton visited Edinburgh in the company of the Edmondson family displayed just how firmly the idea was embedded in Ruxton's mind, when he believed that Isabella and the young Edmondson had spent the night together.

Ruxton did admit that sometimes there was a sexual motive behind the arguments with both himself and Isabella. They experienced enhanced pleasure from intimacy as part of their 'making-up' routine.

From a psychological perspective, it has been argued by psychologists that jealousy plays a vital role in keeping a relationship healthy. The one fundamental and dramatic gender difference is that women are much more likely than men to try to invoke a bit of jealousy in their partner. Psychological research has shown that most men misinterpret what a woman's smile really means and make the mistaken assumption that it is a signal of sexual interest.

A significant majority of women use jealousy to test the depth of their relationship. It would appear that women who feel less desirable than their partners are prone to using jealousy as a way of correcting the imbalance.

The problem with this psychological reasoning is that if jealousy is encouraged in a person who is vulnerable to delusions and paranoia, and is of a violent personality, it can bring about very dangerous consequences. The unanswerable question remains; were Ruxton's suspicions of his wife's infidelity unfounded and nothing more than mere conjecture, or was it a ploy on the part of Isabella to re-kindle a flagging relationship? Unfortunately, we will never know the answer to this question.

In retrospect, Ruxton's invitation that Mrs Hampshire and her husband take away the stair carpets and suit was certainly a reckless oversight on his part. This particular evidence alone could have convicted him. Evidence of carpets soaked in blood, strange stains on the bath, and clothing stained with blood found in the back yard all contributed to Ruxton's eventual downfall.

All these items provided an observable trace of clues left at the scene of the crime. These were welded into a complete watertight case by the police and scientific experts. It was the unassailable scientific testimony that weighed so heavily against Ruxton, together with the testimony of his own

> MEDICO-LEGAL ASPECTS
> OF THE
> RUXTON CASE
>
> BY
>
> JOHN GLAISTER, M.D., D.Sc., Barrister-at-Law
> Regius Professor of Forensic Medicine, University of Glasgow
>
> AND
>
> JAMES COUPER BRASH, M.A., M.D., F.R.C.S.Ed.
> Professor of Anatomy, University of Edinburgh
>
> With one hundred and seventy-two illustrations
>
> EDINBURGH
> E. & S. LIVINGSTONE
> 16 AND 17 TEVIOT PLACE
> 1937

charladies. The most enlightening aspect of the

Ruxton case was the information derived from superimposing a photographs of the skulls of Mrs Ruxton and Mary Rogerson on to photographs of the heads of the missing women. The results of this innovative technique revealed how every detail of the skulls fitted with the photographs of the living victims. It could be argued that there was no certainty about the identification by this comparative technique, but Professor Brash never claimed there was.

In addition, Professor Brash had flexible casts made of the feet of the two reconstructed bodies. These casts fitted accurately into the shoes of both of the missing women. Although even this could not be accepted as incontrovertible proof of identity, it was nevertheless one more link in the chain of circumstantial evidence.

The Ruxton Case stands alone. It is notable primarily because the extent and character of the mutilation of the two victims provided a problem of reconstruction which demanded for its solution anatomical work in detail not hitherto required in such cases. It is also notable because the purposive removal of identifying features suggested a novel comparison of skulls and portraits which, with other circumstantial evidence, helped to place identification beyond doubt. In addition, much work in different branches of forensic medicine and in other specialised fields was found to be necessary. Attention is drawn to the important part played by the errors and omissions of the perpetrator of the crime in building up the case against him.

Even today, the Ruxton case is the single most quoted murder discussed in modern forensic science. The area around Gardenholme Linn in Dumfriesshire where Ruxton disposed of the dismembered body parts became known locally as 'Ruxton's Dump'.

Ruxton's house at 2 Dalton Square, Lancaster remained empty for decades following the trial. In the 1980s, it underwent internal renovation before being acquired by Lancaster City Council for offices. Since the crimes, the building has remained firmly 'non-residential'.

The bath which featured prominently in the investigation and trial was removed to Lancashire Constabulary Headquarters at Hutton, near Preston. It was adapted for use as a water-trough for the police mounted section. It is believed that Ruxton's three children Elizabeth, Diane and William were brought up in an orphanage in the Wirral area of Cheshire.

'In many respects the murderer's canvas is his crime scene on which he leaves his brush strokes, either by design or by default. We may be shocked, entertained or informed by what we read while knowing that in murder cases, the unbelievable is all too often true. To read about murder, is to open a door into the territory occupied by those who transgress the boundaries observed by civilised society.'

Bizarre Crimes: Incredible Real-Life Murders by Robin Odell (Constable and Robinson Ltd, London, 2010) pp xiv-xvi

Selected Bibliography

Harold Shipman

Baker R *Harold Shipman's Clinical Practice 1974-1998*, Department of Health, (London), 2001.

Hurwitz B "Murder most medical, disposal most discreet", *Lancet*, 364, 38-339 (2004).

Kaplan RM, *Medical Murder: Disturbing Cases of Doctors who Kill* Allen & Unwin, pp 59-601 (Chichester, 2009).

Kinnell, HG *Serial Homicide by Doctors: Shipman in Perspective* MBJ, 321, 154-7 (2000).

Peters C *Harold Shipman: Mind Set on Murder* Carlton Books, (London 2005).

Sitford M *Addicted to Murder* Virgin Publications (London 2000).

The Shipman Inquiry: Reports One to Six (2002-2005), Home Office/Department of Health London, (Crown Copyright).

Whittle B & RJ *Prescription for Murder: The True Story of Dr Harold Frederick Shipman* Little Brown (London 2005).

John Bodkin Adams

Bedford S *The Best We Can Do* Penguin, London (1989).

Cullen P *A Stranger in Blood: The Case Files on Dr John Bodkin Adams*, London, Elliott and Thompson (2006).

Devlin P *Easing the Passing: The Trial of Doctor John Bodkin Adams*, London, The Bodley Head, (1985).

Hallworth & Williams M *Where There's a Will: The Sensational Life of Dr John Bodkin Adams*, Jersey, Capstan Press, (1983).

Hoskins P *Two Men Were Acquitted: The Trial and Acquittal of Doctor John Bodkin Adams*, London, Secker and Warburg, (1984).

Mahar C *Easing the Passing: R v Adams and Terminal Care in Post-War Britain, Social History of Medicine, Vol 28, No 1* (2012).

Otlowski M *Voluntary Euthanasia and the Common Law*, Oxford UP (2004).

Robins J *The Curious Habits of Dr Adams: A 1950s Murder Mystery*, London, John Murray, (2013).

Simpson AWB 'The Trial of Dr John Bodkin Adams' in the *Michigan Law Review*, vol 84, No 4/5 (1986).

Surtees J *The Strange Case of Dr Bodkin Adams: The Life and Murder Trial of Eastbourne's Infamous Doctor, and the views of those who knew him*, Eastbourne, (2000).

Buck Ruxton

Blundell RH & Wilson GH 'The Trial of Buck Ruxton': *Famous Trials 3*, James H Hodge (ed) (Penguin Books, Harmondsworth, 1950).

Glaister J & Brash JC *Medico-Legal Aspects of the Ruxton Case* (Livingstone, Edinburgh, 1937).

Goodman J (ed) *Medical Murders: Classic True Crime Stories* (BCA, London, 1992).

Hardwick M *Doctors on Trial* (Jenkins, London, 1961).

Hyde HM *Norman Birkett: The Life of Lord Birkett of Ulverston* (Reprint Society, London, 1964).

Lane B *The Encyclopaedia of Forensic Science*, (Headline Book Publishing Plc, London, 1993).

Maples WR & Browning M *Dead Men Do Tell Tales: The Strange and Fascinating Cases of a Forensic Anthropologist* (Arrow Books, London, 2002).

Marriner B *Forensic Clues to Murder* (Arrow Books, London, 1991).

Odell R *Bizarre Crimes: Incredible Real-Life Murders* (Constable and Robinson Ltd, London, 2010).

Potter TF *The Deadly Dr Ruxton: How They Caught A Lancashire Double Killer* (Carnegie Publishing, Preston, 1984).

Simpson K *Forty Years of Murder* (Granada Publishing Ltd, St. Alban's, 1984).

Smith SA *Mostly Murder* (Guild Publishing, London, 1959).

Wilson C *Murder in the 1930s* (Carroll and Graff, London, 1992).

Wynn D *On Trial for Murder* (Pan Books, London, 1996).

Buck Ruxton Archive Sources

Forensic Medicine Archive Project: Royal College of Physicians of Edinburgh: Sydney A. Smith Collection: Buck Ruxton (1935-1936). Ref: 12 (111-25/185.

Edinburgh University Library: Special Collections and Archives: R v Ruxton (1936). Ref: GB/237 – E 91-13.

Forensic Medical Archive Project: University of Glasgow, Case File R v Ruxton (1936). Ref: GUAFM. 2A/25.

'Gruesome Evidence at Ruxton Trial' in *Aberdeen Journal*, December 12th, 1935, Page 10.

'Trial of Dr Ruxton' in *Dundee Courier*, March 10th, 1936.

Printed in Great Britain
by Amazon